Their only objective

CROSS

U.S. Marine Lance Corporal Tom "Moose" Ferran, Vietnam, 1967: One afternoon, Ed Pool and I were in a hide when we saw a squad of VC. I crosshaired the last man, intending to start there and work forward. I dropped the last man, then the man in front of him. A third. A fourth. . . . Then the rest went to ground, undoubtedly trembling with fear at the unseen bolts of deadly lightning out of nowhere. . . .

U.S. Marine Corporal Frank Roberts, Beirut, 1983: One afternoon a guy loosed some random shots, then hid. . . . I spotted him peering out an opening in his bunker. . . . All I saw were his eyes. That was enough. I placed a bullet through the slit. A moment later, a woman dressed in black ran out flailing her arms and crying. I must have shot her boyfriend or husband. He should have stayed home. . . .

U.S. Marine Sergeant Joshua Hamblin, Iraq, 2003: The adrenaline rush was indescribable. However, training and discipline took over. . . . We paced ourselves: Spot a target, sight in, squeeze, watch the shot, work the bolt. Pick another target and keep the pace going. Over and over. . . . Not many of the fighters who jumped out of the pickup got back in it under their own power. Not a body was left behind. Nothing but smears and puddles of blood and shreds of flesh on the street. Quiet once more settled over the kill zone.

Other books by Craig Roberts:

Combat Medic—Vietnam, Pocket Books, 1991
Police Sniper, Pocket Books, 1993
Kill Zone: A Sniper Looks at Dealey Plaza, Consolidated Press
    Int'l, 1993
Hellhound, Avon, with Allen Appel, 1994
JFK: The Dead Witnesses, Consolidated Press Int'l, 1995
The Medusa File: Crimes and Coverups of the US Government,
    Consolidated Press Int'l, 1997

Other books by Charles W. Sasser

Hill 488 (coauthored with Ray Hildreth)*
Detachment Delta: Deep Steel
Detachment Delta: Iron Weed
Detachment Delta: Punitive Strike
Encyclopedia of The Navy SEALs
Raider
Taking Fire (coauthored with Ron Alexander)
The Return
Arctic Homestead
Operation No Man's Land (writing as Mike Martell)
Liberty City
At Large
First Seal (coauthored with Roy Boehm)*
Smoke Jumpers
Always a Warrior
Homicide!
Last American Heroes (coauthored with Michael Sasser)
The 100th Kill
One Shot—One Kill (coauthored with Craig Roberts)*
Shoot to Kill*
The Walking Dead (coauthored with Craig Roberts)*
Magic Steps to Writing Success
Fire Cops (coauthored with Michael Sasser)*
Doc: Platoon Medic (coauthored with Daniel E. Evans Jr.)*
Arctic Homestead (coauthored with Norma Cubb)
No Gentle Streets

*Available from Pocket Books

CROSSHAIRS ON THE KILL ZONE

**American Combat Snipers, Vietnam through
Operation Iraqi Freedom**

CRAIG ROBERTS
CHARLES W. SASSER

POCKET STAR BOOK

New York   London   Toronto   Sydney

An *Original* Publication of POCKET BOOKS

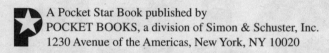 A Pocket Star Book published by
POCKET BOOKS, a division of Simon & Schuster, Inc.
1230 Avenue of the Americas, New York, NY 10020

Copyright © 2004 by Charles W. Sasser and Craig Roberts

ISBN 13: 978-0-7434-8295-0
ISBN 10:   0-7434-8295-6

First Pocket Books printing July 2004

10   9   8   7   6

POCKET STAR BOOKS and colophon are registered
trademarks of Simon & Schuster, Inc.

Cover design by Rod Hernandez
Cover art by Dennis Lyall

Manufactured in the United States of America

For information regarding special discounts for bulk purchases,
please contact Simon & Schuster Special Sales at 1-800-456-6798
or business@simonandschuster.com.

To all the brave warriors
with whom the authors have served

AUTHORS' NOTE

The information in this book is based primarily on interviews with American snipers from the various wars and conflicts in which the United States has been involved from Vietnam to the present time. However, a variety of other sources contributed: official U.S. military documents and After Action Reports; diaries; newspapers; books and other published accounts; and interviews with participants, witnesses, and other authorities. The authors wish to thank all these people and sources for helping make this book possible, and especially we would like to thank all the fine men who participated in reliving experiences, filling in the gaps of history, and sharing with us the stories that appear in these pages. Their help in the monumental task of researching and writing this book made a difficult project an enjoyable experience.

We would also like to express our gratitude to the following authors and published works, in no particular order, from which we drew in writing this book: *Sniper* by Adrian Gilbert (New York: St. Martin's, 1994); *Inside the Crosshairs* by Michael Lee Lanning (New York: Ivy Books, 1998); *Marine Sniper* by Charles Henderson (New York: Berkley, 1986); *13 Cent Killers* by John J. Culbertson (New York: Ballantine, 2003); *In the Company of Heroes* by Michael J. Durant with Steven Hartov (New York: Putnam, 2003); *Black Hawk Down* by Mark Bowden (New York: Atlantic Monthly Press, 1999); *Inside Delta Force* by Eric L. Haney (New York: Delacorte, 2002); *The Road to Kosovo* by Greg Campbell (Boulder, CO: Westview, 1999); U.S. Naval Institute *Proceedings,* 1984; "Bolt Actions Speak Louder Than Words" by Rob Krott, *Soldier of Fortune,* June 2003; Dave Francis, *Canadian Snipers* e-article, 22 May 2002; Nancy Walbeck, Anacortes *American,* July 2003; Master Sergeant Bob Haskell, National Guard Bureau press release, 25 April 2001; *Sniper Country Duty Roster* "Women in Combat," 13 August 2003; *Vietnam* magazine, October 1991; Second Lieutenant H. J. Halterman, "Snipers in Bosnia," press release, 11 April 2003; "Stealth Warriors," *Washington Post,* 9 March 1997; "Sniper" by Colonel Low Wye Mun, *Specialoperations.com,* 11 April 2003; "True Bravery" by Sergeant Thomas Blahnik, *Snipercountry.com,* 11 April 2003; "The Concept of the Modern Battlefield" by David R. Reed, *Snipercountry.com,* 11 April 2003; "Sounding Out Snipers" by Gary Stix, *ScientificAmerica.com,* July 2001.

Finally, we would like to thank the dozens of other people—military contacts; librarians, career NCOs, professional marksmen, and others too numerous to list but whose assistance is gratefully acknowledged. Special thanks go to Major James Land, USMC (Ret.), Major Dick Culver, USMC (Ret.), Sergeant Major Richard P.

Lamilin, Staff Sergeant Darrell French, Major Matt McLaughlin, and Captain Mamiecolee Ward, all of the U.S. Marine Corps, who helped guide the authors in writing this book. Also, thanks to stenos Connie Butcher, Laura Griffin, and Janice Hensley, who worked through hours of taped interviews to provide workable copy.

Actual names are used throughout except in those rare instances where names were lost due to either memory loss or lack of documentation, where privacy was requested, or where public identification would serve no useful purpose and might cause embarrassment.

In various instances dialog and scenes have necessarily been re-created. Time has a tendency to erode memories in some areas and selectively enhance it in others. Where re-creation occurs, we strived to match personalities with the situation and the action while maintaining factual content. The recounting of some events may not correspond precisely with the memories of all involved. In addition, all data has been filtered through the authors. We must therefore apologize to anyone omitted, neglected, or somehow slighted in the preparation of this book. We take responsibility for such errors and ask to be forgiven for them.

While we are certain to have made interpretational mistakes, we are just as certain that the content of this book is accurate to the spirit and reality of all the brave men who participated in the events described in this book.

"Go, bid the soldiers shoot."

Shakespeare, *Hamlet*

FOREWORD

The U.S. Marine Sniper Instructor School in Quantico tested a sensor in 1996 that was designed to detect body heat from afar, thereby unmasking enemy soldiers advancing through the bush. Observers declared the device "unbeatable." Even the undersecretary of defense, Walter Slocombe, asserted it would make snipers virtually obsolete since they could be "seen" from distances outside effective firing range.

"I beg to differ," objected Master Sergeant Neil Kennedy Morris, senior instructor at the school.

For the next hour or so, lookouts kept their eyes peeled on the surrounding terrain as Morris maneuvered to prove his point. The sensor remained mute. The crusty gunny remained at large and "unseen."

Suddenly, not fifteen yards away, the sergeant erupted from a mound of dirt and weeds, rifle pointed. "You're dead!"

He had camouflaged an old umbrella obtained from a flea market and used it to deflect the beams from the sensor, once again proving that a rifle and a man with ingenuity, courage, and an unerring eye still have a place on a battlefield otherwise dominated by computer-directed "smart bombs" and billion-dollar stealth jets and satellites.

The rise of the sniper as a respected professional with special mission capabilities has not been easy. Although each war of this century produced a need for snipers, they somehow offend the American notion of fair play. The standard reaction by both the military and the American public is to use them if need be, don't tell anybody about it, and then cork them back into their bottles after the need ends. Such old prejudices that view the sniper as a "bushwhacker," as somehow unethical and perhaps even unlawful, have to be overcome before he attains his proper respect.

As recently as 1992, the Pentagon felt compelled to issue a memorandum defending the use of snipers. "Soldiers lawfully may be attacked behind their lines," it said. Any suggestion that "a sniper is less than legal . . . is the unenlightened view of sniping; it is also incorrect."

America's most celebrated sniper is, without question, U.S. Marine Gunnery Sergeant Carlos Hathcock, who died recently partly as a result of war wounds suffered in Vietnam. His legendary exploits have been chronicled in numerous magazine articles, in at least four books, and in one movie. Records indicate 93 *confirmed* kills; the actual number is nearer 300.

In 1989, Gunny Hathcock spent time in Tulsa, Oklahoma, with the authors of this book during preparation of our first sniper book, *One Shot—One Kill*. He was a polite, soft-spoken, and deeply spiritual man.

"The question," he said, "shouldn't be how many

2

men I killed. The question should more properly be: How many lives did I save? That was the way I looked at it. Every hamburger I killed out in Indian Country meant one more Marine or GI would be going back to the world alive."

American snipers save lives by killing the enemy before the enemy can kill. Hundreds of American soldiers and Marines survived World War I, wrote U.S. Marine Corps General George O. Van Orden in 1940, "because [the sniper's] rifle crack, joining with others of his kind, becomes a menace more to be feared than the shrieking shells from cannon. . . ." It is an observation as true today as it was back then.

The sniper's rifle is a weapon of discrimination. Weapons such as artillery and aircraft—even computer-guided "smart" munitions—are relatively indiscriminate, frequently making mistakes that cost unintended lives. The sniper is a professional soldier who uses his skills to select only key enemy personnel and deny them access to a battle area. Valid targets include officers, machine gun and artillery gunners, communication specialists, and key leaders. In the process of carrying out his mission, the sniper adds to the security of his outfit.

Technology is not apt to replace the sniper on the battlefield within the foreseeable future. Musketry, the ability of a rifleman to hit his target, remains a very important skill even in the technological age. In fact, the demands and mission requirements of a rapidly changing and increasingly dangerous world have led to the widespread deployment and employment of snipers.

The highest military award given for valor during the past decade, the Medal of Honor, was won by two Special Operations snipers from Fort Bragg, Master Sergeant Gary Gordon and Sergeant First Class Randy Shughart. It is through the courage and resourcefulness of men like them—of Chuck Mawhinney, Carlos Hathcock, Thomas "Moose" Ferran and others highlighted in this book—that the lone wolf of the battlefield has become a formidable and respected weapon.

Master of woodcraft and concealment, armed with unerring eyes and infinite patience, the sniper proves repeatedly that the most deadly weapon on any battlefield is the single well-aimed shot. Nowhere on the field of battle is the enemy safe from the sniper's crosshairs on the kill zone.

CHAPTER ONE

U.S. Marine Corporal Greg Kraljev
Vietnam, 1969

Some days I killed someone, some days I didn't. I worked a lot with Bravo Company out of the 5th Marine base at An Hoa. Captain Castagneti was the CO. A great commander, a great Marine. His outfit did very little sitting around on their butts killing time while the gooks killed them. Bravo, unlike many other companies, moved around a lot at night. Charlie rarely expected to see a Marine before daylight. The captain put us into positions and situations where we inflicted some real hurt on the enemy.

In late September, Jolly Green Giant CH-53 helicopters jinked Bravo up into the mountains on a battalion search-and-destroy. It was getting toward winter in the tropics, the air was clear and not too hot at night, and there was little rain. Not bad weather for fighting a war.

The operation to flush the VC out of their hiding places—find him, fix him, and frag him over—continued for about thirty days. Toward the end of the period,

Bravo was humping to the top of a mountain ridge, driving up out of one forested valley and over the mountain into the next valley, when the battalion point element ran into a real shitstorm. Captain Castagneti called for "snipers up."

My spotter Jim Seely and I chugged up to the head of the column. We sprawled out on the ridge summit among some boulders and scabby trees and peered down into a low spot in the valley choked with jungle growth. The foliage screened from sight what was going on down there, but from the sound of things there was a badass fight, a real slugfest. Mixed AK-47 and M16 fire raged at a feverish pitch, rolling together like a thunderstorm.

If events followed the normal script, it wouldn't be long before the guerrillas broke and ran. A ravine gouging its way out of the valley and up the side of the opposite mountain appeared to offer a perfect escape route. The range was about 700 yards, but I would be shooting across a valley from one high point to the next, which made the shooting a bit tricky. I pointed the ravine out to Jim. He nodded.

The gooks lasted longer in the fight than I expected. Sounds of the battle below surged and ebbed for nearly a half hour. Then, sure enough, Jim spotted movement flashes as two figures in black pj's pulled out of the scrap and hauled ass up the ravine, climbing it like a pair of cockroaches caught in a sink when the light comes on. Did I know Charlie or what?

Seely's binoculars afforded him a much wider range of view than my rifle scope. He called the action. "Okay, Greg. . . . There's five or six more directly below those two. Range, what? About six? They'll be busting out in the open in that patch of weeds. . . ."

"I'm on 'em, Jim. . . . Call my shot. I'm going for number one in the larger group."

It was challenging all right. Not only was I shooting across the valley, but these guys were carrying the mail, letting no grass grow beneath their feet, darting and dodging through the underbrush like ol' Satan was on their butts with a fiery pitchfork. I trailed the lead man with my scope, holding the crosshairs at about the nape of his neck. The angle of shot was down from my high point and across the lowlands.

I squeezed off and came back out of recoil.

"About a foot to the right . . . a little low . . . ," Jim intoned.

I bolted in a fresh round, caught the target in my scope a second time and adjusted my aim. This time I didn't miss.

"He's down," Seely calmly reported, although the adrenaline must have been pumping as hard in his veins as in mine.

I managed to drop two before the rest escaped. It wasn't a bad morning's work, considering the conditions. Even under Captain Castagneti, a turkey shoot like that occurred only now and then. Most of the time, Jim and I had to bust our asses for a good kill.

The way it generally worked, I went out on a patrol and dropped off somewhere to hide and wait in ambush. There was me, a spotter—usually Jim Seely—and a third Marine to work the radio. Radiomen were volunteers from the company. A few of them were always wanting to go out with snipers for the experience. Few ever went out a second time. It was simply too scary, what with only three of us out in Indian Country with our asses hanging out.

The best place to set up a hide was on terrain that afforded a three-sixty field of fire so you could get a shot off in any direction. I tried to choose a shallow rise with good cover in the middle of an open field. First of all, the gooks seldom expected a sniper to be hiding in grasslands. Secondly, tree lines spooked me because of the potential for booby traps.

We camouflaged ourselves with face paint and foliage before going out. I was always cautious about the enemy watching when I dropped out of a patrol. It was hard to overlook when a guy six feet five suddenly disappeared.

As soon as the patrol moved on, I radioed in map coordinates of our location so the mortar section knew exactly where we were in the event shit hit the proverbial fan and we required fire cover. I then checked out possible avenues of enemy approach, pinpointing ranges and angles where targets were most likely to show up. Lastly, I laid out an escape plan if things got too hot and we needed to bug out. I was methodical about such things, careful about the details. After all, we were gambling our skins. I wanted all the trumps we could get.

Some days I killed someone, some days I didn't.

Captain Castagneti received intelligence about an enemy base camp deep in no-man's-land. I was ready. Sounded like another rare possible turkey shoot. Bravo Company saddled up at oh-dark-thirty—the birds weren't even up—and moved into position for an assault before the sun rose.

Seely and I along with a radioman selected a rise with a good field of fire into a thick forest of large trees with relatively little underbrush. The base camp supposedly lay just inside the woods. The company stripped itself of any gear that might rattle, bang, or catch on brush and cautiously moved out in the darkness of the predawn, leaving behind a depth of silence that made even loneliness seem cacophonous.

Daylight slowly seeped into the landscape, replacing darkness with the mist and soft shadows of morning. Gradually, I picked out well-camouflaged bunkers, tunnel openings, cooking fire rings, and a few low-to-the-ground hooches and shelters. Seeing them at all was like one of those novelty pictures where you had to stare deep into a maze of colors before you actually saw what was there.

It was a camp for the North Vietnamese Army, not a VC guerrilla hangout. My little sniper party lay silently waiting for the attack. It was like opening day of hunting season before any shots had been fired and you could still anticipate the coming action. We had the best stand location in the woods.

It was bright and clear with only a smear of haze through our opticals, about a half hour after sunrise, when Bravo's Marines struck with such surprise that the NVA soldiers were literally caught with their pants down. Many fled in their skivvies as rifles banged in long, fierce fusillades and grenades popped. Through my scope I watched Marines blazing into the base camp, picking off any rabbits that jumped up, dumping grenades into the openings of bunkers and tunnels, and laying fire down on fleeing survivors. A fog of smoke eddied in and out among the trees.

My eyes scanned the outskirts of the action as I waited for bad guys to start coming out the back door. I didn't want to chance shooting among the Marines. Soon NVA were running out in numbers through an area about one hundred yards across. Ranges varied from about 600 yards to 800, depending upon where the targets emerged as they fled the chaos.

I started shooting, but I could only shoot so fast with a bolt-action rifle. A constant chatter of conversation passed between Jim and me as we spotted and selected targets.

"I'm going for this one. . . ."

"One to the left, Greg. . . ."

Seely watched the impact of rounds through his binoculars. Little explosions of foliage. Geysers erupting on the ground.

"Up and to the right, Greg. . . ."

"Okay. This one's coming out. . . ."

"You got him. He's down. He's not moving. Check the bunker, three bunkers up. . . . He's sticking his head out. He's going to make a move. . . ."

"Here he comes. I'm on him. . . ."

"Good shot. There's another bunch. See 'em?"

It was a major adrenaline rush. Both of us vibrated from the excitement. I tapped off forty or fifty rounds in about thirty minutes, putting down at least four targets to stay. I might have nailed several more. Who was counting? Jim merely told me whenever I hit one, whereupon we skipped to the next target.

It was a huge day for Bravo Company. The body count was about 350. Dead gooks littered the base camp and out the back door. Blood was spilled everywhere, the smell of it so sickeningly fresh and strong mixed with gunpowder and exploding grenades that it carried to us on the rise above. I was exhausted when the killing ended—mentally, emotionally, and physically.

Like I always said, some days I killed someone, some days I didn't.

CHAPTER TWO

August 1965 in I Corps. The sun rose out of the South China Sea, casting hard rays against the peaks of the Hai Van Mountains. Marines waiting with their armored amtracs on the opposite banks of the Song Cau Do River began to sweat. Within an hour, the heat would become so intense that breathing the air was like sucking on flames.

Word came. Marines mounted their green metal monsters, crossed the muddy river into VC country, and headed toward a village marked on the map simply as "Cam Ne." Actually, Cam Ne was a complex of six hamlets within a checkerboard of rice paddies. Located only five miles southwest of the new American air base at Da Nang, Cam Ne was a nest of Vietcong activity with communist connections stretching back to the French Indochina War.

In July, sappers from Cam Ne attacked the Da Nang air base and blew up two airplanes and damaged three others. Long a thorn in the Marines' side, Cam Ne had to go down. Operation Blastout I tasked 1st Battalion, 9th Marines, and 1st Battalion, 3rd Marines, with rooting out the estimated company-size element of VC in the hamlets and destroying it. Delta Company 1/9 would attack on-line across the rice paddies, acting as a hammer to drive the enemy into the anvil provided by 1/3.

At approximately 1015 hours, Delta Company came under well-aimed sniper fire as it advanced across a maze of rice paddies toward the villages. One Marine cried out in pain and shock as he dropped in the echo of a single distant rifle shot.

The Marines pressed on, reaching the tree line at the edge of the first village. Amtracs following the infantry crashed through hedgerows and bamboo fences, setting off several mines and booby traps. The sweeping force shattered into small fighting groups as it worked its way into the settlement. The VC pulled back ahead of the advance with only minor resistance.

A fighting trench ringed the hamlet. Nearly every grass hootch sat near or over a bunker, tunnel, or spider trap. Booby traps, punji pits, and foot traps of every imaginable devious design were set up to snare unsuspecting intruders. Interconnecting tunnels and camouflaged firing positions favored VC hit-and-run tactics. Enemy snipers used them to their best advantage. As squads of Marines reached huts and moved on, snipers suddenly popped up behind them, took an accurate shot, then just as suddenly disappeared. Other assailants vanished into the tunnels after firing bursts from assault rifles and light machine guns.

The combination of harassing fire, heat, and slow movement frustrated the Marines. By late afternoon Delta had progressed only a quarter of the way through the complex. As night approached, company commander Captain Herman B. West Jr. accepted that he had neither the assets nor the strength to occupy Cam Ne after dark. He ordered a withdrawal.

Vietcong snipers surfaced from the tunnel complex and reoccupied the tree lines. Harassing fire continued against the exhausted and frustrated Marines. It became apparent to Marine commanders that the VC possessed a weapon the Marines did not: well-trained snipers effectively employed to pin down and kill Americans with tactics that were both effective and efficient. A few dedicated soldiers could slow or halt the movement of a superior force while utilizing a minimum of resources.

Eight days later, a squad of Hotel Company 2/6 Marines patrolling a trail on the west side of the complex took fire from a VC sniper lying in a rice field. The first shot thumped into the skull of the Weapons Platoon leader, Lieutenant Richard Regan. As he dropped to the ground, dead, a second shot drilled the machine gun ammo bearer, PFC Gonzales, through both calves and sent him splashing into the muddy rice water, where he writhed agony.

The Marine squad dropped to their bellies and, after frantically scanning the surrounding terrain, opened fire on a distant structure that seemed the most likely hide for the gunman. As M14 rifles blazed away, the sniper made the mistake of attempting to shift positions. Lance Corporal Craig Roberts, an automatic rifleman, spotted movement about 150 meters into the rice field. He triggered a long burst on full auto at a glimpse of head and shoulders. The first rounds erupted into the water below the shooter, then walked up and stitched the sniper's chest with a line of exploding blood and flesh. The body slammed backward, splashing in the water.

At almost the same instant, Lance Corporal Albert Ekstein burst a white phosphorous rifle grenade over the body, engulfing the corpse in flames and quickly charring it almost beyond recognition. While Delta Company on its previous assault claimed to have killed seven VC snipers, a fact hard to corroborate because the enemy habitually dragged off their dead, this one was a definite confirmed. He would shoot no more Marines.

Two weeks after the launching of the Blastout operation, the commander of 2nd Battalion, 9th Marines, Lieutenant Colonel George R. Scharnberg, received orders to clear out Cam Ne and put an end to the constant sniping at Marine patrols. Two of his companies set up as the blocking force during the night of 17 August—the "anvil"—while two others moved up as the "hammer."

At daybreak, loudspeaker-equipped helicopters flew over the hamlets warning villagers to leave. They also dropped leaflets urging the local VC to surrender. A trickle of villagers exited. No VC surrendered. Marines entered the complex.

Cam Ne was deserted. Smoke from charcoal cooking fires added to the eerie stillness. Pigs, chickens, and water buffalo wandered about. Two Marines were wounded when a booby-trapped mine exploded next to a fence gate.

The heat was unbearable and movement slow through gauntlets and mazes of trip wires and booby traps. Exhausted leathernecks, once more frustrated by Cam Ne, collapsed into a perimeter on the eastern outskirts of the first hamlet late in the afternoon.

A shot rang out from a tree line across the paddies. A young Marine eating from a can of C rations while perched on the edge of a VC trench jerked backward and fell, shot through the chest.

Immediately afterward, the tree line sparkled with muzzle flame, rattling furiously as a reinforced company of hard-core Vietcong initiated its ambush. Impacting bullets kicked up small geysers of dirt and water, almost like a hailstorm. AK-47s and SKS carbines rolled in thundering cadences, while here and there the unmistakable crack of a Moison-Nagant sniper rifle punctuated the thunder.

Hotel Company chewed up a small temple about 400 meters away, from which hostile fire originated, and lay a belt of steel and lead into the tree line. At the same time a sniper drilled a Marine machine gunner through the lungs, killing him instantly. PFC George Renninger spotted the shooter hiding behind a bush 200 meters away. His shot flipped the VC into a fatal somersault.

Hotel's skipper, Captain Joe Gugino, ordered his FO to call in artillery support. The artillery forward observer studied his map, then sprinted forward with his radioman to a jut of land from which he apparently decided he could more accurately direct fire on the enemy. Then occurred one of those freak incidents of "friendly fire" caused by someone in the chain making a mistake in map reading or gun calculations.

The first four rounds of 105mm howitzer whirred overhead, making a sound something like barrels rocketing through the air: it exploded in airbursts over the heads of the FO and his radioman, killing both instantly. The barrage then walked down the former VC trench now occupied by Marines. Shrapnel almost severed Corporal Oller's arm. Other Marines received minor wounds. All were shaken and confused by the time the last round impacted near the company's hastily occupied command post.

The "fire for effect" left the enemy unscathed.

Marines crawled from the trench after the pounding ceased, only to be met once more with accurate volumes of fire from the stubborn enemy. Snipers using the artillery salvo as a diversion had moved within 200 meters of the Americans, again pinning them down with precise rifle fire. Marines finally suppressed them with withering return fire and the employment of a 106mm recoilless rifle.

By the time the operation ended, 2nd Battalion had pulled 37 VC suspects out of their holes and destroyed their tunnels and bunkers, but it was becoming more and more clear that the enemy was effectively using strategically located and well-motivated snipers to inflict both physical and psychological damage on American troops. It was also clear that enemy marksmen could not always be silenced with superior firepower. Trying to deal with individual sharpshooters using artillery and aircraft was like trying to kill gophers with a sledgehammer.

Americans, however, were quick learners. As they fought guerrillas, they learned guerrilla tactics. Lessons from the past surfaced, brought once again to the light by the sharpshooters of Cam Ne. American troops once again brought their own sniper rifles out of storage.

CHAPTER THREE

U.S. Marine
Lance Corporal Jim O'Neill
Vietnam, 1968

My sniper partner, Bob Griese, and I accompanied a platoon of Hotel 2/4 (2nd Battalion, 4th Marines) on a recon to locate an enemy 57mm recoilless rifle that had been using the abandoned villages along the Cua Viet River to fire on our Mike boats. There were very few Vietcong guerrillas up in this area near the DMZ. We expected to find North Vietnamese Army regulars, hardcore NVA: They wore pith helmets and gray-green uniforms instead of straw cone hats and black pajamas. They discarded their helmets whenever they were in camp or lolling around their foxholes.

The platoon commander called a halt in the woods short of a fallow rice paddy that stretched flat and open out ahead in the sun for about 500 yards. On the other side of the field, beyond a line of palms, bamboo, and shrubbery, rose the rotted grass roofs of a ruined and deserted hamlet.

"Let me scope out the area before we move out in the open," I advised the commander.

Good thing I did. Through the telescopic sight of my Remington Model 700 I soon picked out green uniforms and black hair slicked back. NVA lolling around without their helmets.

"That entire tree line is alive with people," I informed the skipper.

"Who do you think they are?"

Dumb question.

"Gooks," I said. "I can see them. They're gooks."

"Go ahead and drop one," he said.

"No problem."

An easy shot. I had zeroed in for 500 yards. That meant point of aim and point of impact were the same at that range. I selected a guy sitting on the edge of his foxhole gazing absently across the rice paddies, like he was daydreaming, wishing he were back home with Suzie Nguyen eating a bowl of rice. I centered my crosshairs on his scrawny chest.

And I dropped him clean, as I had dropped more than a dozen others like him since my arrival in Vietnam six months ago in November 1967. The impact of the slug flipped him backwards into his hole. All that remained in view was his feet sticking straight up in the air.

As it happened, that was the first shot fired in the bloody battle of Dia Do. The entire enemy tree line erupted, flickering and popping as the NVA opened up with every machine gun they owned. What the platoon commander didn't know when he told me to "go ahead and drop one"—what none of us knew—was that three full NVA *regiments* were operating in the area. Every gook between the DMZ and the Cua Viet River was now rushing toward the sound of battle to close in on *us* and wipe *us* out.

The shooting went on and on as the Marines returned fire, tracers crisscrossing over the wide field. Artillery and mortar explosions slapped back and forth across the terrain like the heavy footsteps of some insane murderous giant. Every breath of air contained dust and smoke, the stench of gunpowder and fear.

Once contact was made, the battalion commander began developing the fight by inserting and positioning his companies to support us and take advantage of the terrain. It became a chess match as the NVA regiments also began to maneuver for advantage. It went on like that for the rest of the day and the night, with only sporadic fighting here and there from chance patrol encounters or from jittery grunts shooting at shadows.

Gooks promptly broke off the fight at the deserted village and left it for the Marines to occupy for the night. At dawn, the battalion commander began moving companies to the right flank away from the river to act as a blocking force. That stirred up things. The snarl and clatter of rifle and automatic-weapons fire, punctuated by the startled banging of grenades and mortars, broke out regularly from sundry points as the morning and the battle progressed.

Beyond the first village and across yet another stubble of a muddy rice field lay a second abandoned village noted on the map as Dia Do. Marines were getting hacked up like crazy, getting a real bloody nose, as we moved toward this hamlet and occupied it in the Asian peasant world's equivalent of house-to-house fighting.

I was scurrying alongside a bamboo hedge that the locals used as fences to separate their miserable little hootches when a Chicom-type grenade sailed out of nowhere and plopped onto the pathway directly at my feet.

Oh, my God! I am now dead.

It exploded, but not with a blinding flash and a deafening bang. Instead, it was more like a giant firecracker. I opened my eyes. I was still standing. The grenade had been a dud, or at least a semi-dud. It remained intact except for a smoking hole in its shell. All I could think of was that Somebody Up There must have been looking out for me.

In all the confusion and chaos, Griese and I got cut off from the rest of the company. We ran into a Navy corpsman who had set up his emergency aid station on the flanking outskirts of the village.

"I have some wounded guys over here," he said. "Machine guns are chopping us up. I could use some sniper support."

"You got it."

Griese and I had attended sniper school together back in the States, then shipped overseas at about the same time. We had been a team ever since, once I got out of the grunts where I had been misassigned. Together, we followed the corpsman until we came to a small clearing lumped with mounds; it must once have been a cemetery. Lying about the ancient graveyard were the human detritus of the ongoing battle: wounded and patched-up Marines leaking blood onto ponchos, some moaning and crying out, others simply staring. I didn't know any of them real well, since Griese and I were only recently attached to Hotel Company. The corpsman explained that this had been a wounded collection point, relatively free of hostile fire until machine guns opened up on the Marine line of battle, which now stretched from the left of the clearing toward the river.

Heavy .51-caliber slugs raked through the tops of the trees, as though to verify his observation, chopping off

limbs and sounding like bowling balls hurled at subsonic speed. Bob and I worked our way to the leading
edge of the collection point to where the woodlot and
cemetery ended at another rice field. This entire area
was a crazy-quilt design of fallow fields separated by
heavy vegetation.

On the other side of the field, about 700 yards away,
lay a second cemetery. Vietnamese often buried their
dead either sitting or standing, which left mounds about
three feet high. The NVA, not being as superstitious and
reverent of dead ancestors as their country cousins, had
hollowed out some of the mounds and planted machine
guns. Through our opticals, Bob and I pinpointed three
such nests. One contained a .51-cal antiaircraft gun that
was attempting to pick off our air support. The other
two .51s chewed away at the Marine line to our left.

This was too good to be real. Bob, acting as my spotter and security, carried an M16 with a maximum effective range of less than 500 yards. But my Model 700
was more than up to the task. Lying in the prone position, using a log for support, I began reaching out with
one accurate shot after another and touching someone.

It was bloody. It was insane. Every time I picked off
a gunner, sending him flopping, somebody else scurried
out of the bush and took his place. At the same time, a
couple of other NVA would run out from a footpath that
led straight back into the undergrowth, pick up the most
recent casualty, and start dragging him away, one on either side of the victim. Perfect targets. As soon as I
dropped one, disrupting the casualty process, the other
froze a moment in shock and disbelief, giving me the
opportunity to chamber a fresh round and wax him too.

It was a macabre process, a murderous assembly line
of ever-revolving victims: an ant trail with two lines of

ants, one rushing forward to man the machine guns, the second attempting to haul off the dead and wounded. It went on like that for what seemed hours but which must have been no more than forty or fifty minutes. Silly bastards. Even Griese with his M16 managed to pick off one of them.

I could only imagine the charnel house it must have been over there in that cemetery. I counted 24 kills before the gooks wised up, located us, and started lobbing 60mm mortar rounds in our direction. I glanced back. The corpsman and some other men were carting the last of the wounded Marines farther to the rear. A mortar shell crumped nearby, showering shrapnel and tree parts.

"We've got the wounded out," the corpsman reported. "We all gotta get outa here."

Griese and I looked at each other. "We're right behind you."

Hotel Company still occupied Dia Do itself—at least for the moment. Once we reached the hamlet's first huts, I thought if we pushed forward on this side we might get in a few more shots. A team of other snipers, Larry Thatcher and David Thompson, were working the other side.

The village had grown up from disuse, especially on its perimeters, creating green vegetative walls and thickets that even a snake would think twice about penetrating. A real firefight was under way on the forward outskirts. Bob and I trotted toward it.

A short row of hedged bamboo grew up to the side of a dilapidated grass hut with its roof caved in. As we approached, looking for a way through, rifle fire clattering fiercely from beyond, a Marine suddenly burst from the thicket, his only weapon a bayonet clutched in his right hand. Blood smeared the blade and his forearm all the way to his elbow. He was wild-eyed.

"Get the hell out!" he urged. "Gooks! Gooks everywhere!"

The battalion commander followed, crashing through the bamboo. He had a bullet hole through the hip, but he was still mobile from adrenaline and fear. After him came more Marines stampeding toward the rear, dragging or carrying the wounded with them.

"Get out of here! They're right behind us!"

I had to take a quick look for myself. I parted the bamboo. I had heard about human wave charges in Korea and in the South Pacific during World War II. But to read about them or see them in a John Wayne movie paled next to actually witnessing one when you were on the receiving end.

A wall of green-clad NVA was blitzing across the rice field. The rumble of pounding feet seemed to vibrate the earth. Muzzle flashes from their rifles flickered along the length of the fast-moving wall, like from a string of Christmas lights. This was no place for a sniper. This was no place for anyone of the enemy's opposite persuasion.

Griese and I turned and followed the battalion commander, who was hit so bad that a couple of Marines now carried him. Through a tree line appeared NVA helmets bobbing along with us. Everyone running. Good guys and bad guys all in the same direction, like a stampede. Surreal. Madness.

We ran across the other sniper team, Thatcher and Thompson. Their eyes got big.

"They're right behind us!" I shouted.

They jumped up without comment and joined the withdrawal.

Lead stung the air around my head like hornets gone maniac. It seemed a miracle I wasn't brought down. I flung a few shots with my bolt rifle into the hedges to my left, trying to slow down the pursuit. Tree branches whacked against my face. I hardly noticed. I flat ran over smaller shrubs or busted through without slowing.

Movement to the right attracted my attention. I was astounded to find an NVA soldier racing alongside me, not thirty feet away. Since I was right-handed, the barrel of my Remington pointed toward the left. The gook was looking at me and I was looking back at him, running along together almost side by side.

I pivoted abruptly to the left to gain enough distance to swing around toward him for a point-blank shot. He veered to his right, scorching the earth to get away. He was gone by the time I could get off a shot.

Out through the back of the village and on to the edge of the first rice paddy. There was nothing out there beyond but open ground, a killing field. Major Fritz, the battalion XO, and some of the NCOs were grabbing guys as they ran up and flinging them into a linear defense where there was still some cover.

I slid into home base next to Griese. Marines lay elbow to elbow on the ground while Major Fritz walked up and down the line, just as cool as could be.

"You're doing good," he encouraged. "Doing good. Now give 'em hell."

Marines blazed away at the charging human wall. The noise of rifle fire and exploding grenades was like being inside a tin barn where all the fireworks of China had been set off. The battle closed to point-blank range. It seemed nothing could stop the juggernaut from smashing through and over us.

An eternity seemed to pass before the bloody and

decimated Marines hurled the enemy back. The line held. Barely. Gook corpses lay scattered in the under-brush, along with the bodies of some of our own men.

Night was coming. The western sky looked as bruised and beaten as we felt. There would be no relief until morning. Other elements of the battalion were sur-rounded elsewhere and busy with their own fighting.

I rolled onto my back with the stench of blood and gunpowder thick in my nostrils and watched the sun die with a mixture of dread and cold fear. It had been a long day of killing and being killed. It wasn't over yet. I lit two cigarettes and passed one to Griese.

Although gooks continued to probe our line through-out the night, no further mass attacks were thrown at us. The real nightmare occurred inside the village of Dia Do. Not all Marines had made it out during the mad-ness. Some, either wounded or enveloped, had been cap-tured.

All through that long and terrible night, their cries and screams of horror and pain plucked our nerves raw, piercing the night, shredding it. *Please? Please? Oh, God, God. . . . Oh, God, no!* A few Marines on the line broke down in tears of rage and frustration and begged to be allowed to go back into the village. Although grim and strained himself, Major Fritz maintained the disci-pline that prevented even more Marine deaths.

A light drizzling rain seemed to be the falling tears of our comrades being tortured and murdered inside the village of Dia Do. Dia Do. A name I shall never forget.

The last cry for mercy shrilled out just before dawn. Then there was silence while the sun rose.

The NVA pulled back and vanished into the terrain, knowing that light would bring even more Marines and more aircraft. There was a passage of lines as 1/3, my old outfit, moved through our battered perimeter in pursuit of the now retreating enemy regiments. I begged to accompany 1/3 but was told to remain with Hotel Company to clean up the mess and collect our dead.

The hardest part was body-bagging Marines murdered in the village. They had been chopped up inside the hootches, hacked apart and dismembered piece by piece while they were still alive. Tortured as a reminder to the living and still fighting of what would happen to us if we were captured.

I burned with the urge to go out and shoot even more of such savages who would do this to helpless captives.

CHAPTER FOUR

U.S. Marine
Sergeant Chuck Mawhinney
Vietnam, 1968-70

I enlisted in the Navy Seabees in 1967. At the induction center we were divided up according to the branch of service for which we were volunteering. A Marine sergeant yelled at the Navy to move away from *his* recruits. "You pussies, get out of here."

That got my attention. I thought about it for a minute and wandered over to him. "Can I get in your line?"

He looked at me. "If you're man enough, boy."

That was how I ended up in the Marine Corps and eventually became a scout sniper with 3rd Battalion, 5th Marines, or 3/5 as it was known in Marinespeak. Although I was a trained sniper, I spent the first three months in Vietnam as a rifleman and then a machine gunner in a grunt platoon. The regiment finally moved to the An Hoa area south of Da Nang and just east of what was called Arizona Territory and the Go Noi Island sector within the confluence of three major rivers.

For years Vietcong had controlled the area with a strong communist political and military command infrastructure, providing a safe haven for both NVA and VC units. Go Noi was home to three local VC battalions: the R-20, the V-25, and the T-3 Sapper Battalion. Elements of the 2nd NVA Division were also apparently trying to reconstitute in the sector. Arizona Territory was what might be called a "target-rich environment." Sort of what Custer had at the Little Bighorn.

Regimental sniper Corporal Cliff Albury was working with my company. "If you're trained as a sniper," he asked me, "what in hell are you doing running around out here with an M60 machine gun? I'm getting short. I'll be leaving soon and we need snipers."

It took some major begging and groveling before I won a transfer. I worked with Albury for two weeks, acting as his spotter, before he rotated Stateside. I inherited his rifle, but it was all shot out. Instead of rebuilding it, the armorer issued me a brand-new M40 Remington Model 700. Then, even more to my surprise, I was assigned as a team leader with the sniper platoon since I was senior man. War through accelerated attrition has a funny way of advancing ranks and positions.

For the rest of that year and for two extended six-month tours afterwards, I operated with all three battalions within the regiment and with any company that needed help. I spent the majority of my time with Delta Company 1/5. That meant Arizona Territory and Go Noi Island. Few snipers wanted to be stuck in the Arizona because Charlie and his cousin, Nguyen of the North, owned the bush. I finally asked my platoon sergeant if he was pissed at me because he kept sending me back out there.

He laughed. "Hell," he said, "you were doing great.

You looked like you were having fun. You never complained, so we thought you liked it."

My part of the Arizona was a perfect hunting ground for a sniper: rice paddies, tree lines, rolling hills, good vegetation. You could see across ranges of rice paddies or you could set up on elevated ground for three-sixty views. A smorgasbord of kill zones.

One morning I was sitting out with Delta on a hilly staging area near Liberty Bridge, prepping for a mission, when a Huey choppered onto the site and a colonel jumped out. I had spotted movement in the paddies about 1,200 meters away and was attempting to get a handle on what it was.

"Should we call in artillery?" my partner asked.

I scoped out the targets, counted four VC watching us in a little group. Apparently they felt safe at the distance.

"Naw," I said. "Let's just shoot 'em."

It was a long-range rifle shot, but we were sandbagged and the breeze was light. I worked the bolt, seating a cartridge, put dope on the scope for a thousand meters, and placed one of the gomers at the bottom of my scope. I touched off the first round.

Miss.

My spotter called corrections. The VC had hit the ground after the first shot, but I could see them lying there in the grass. I fired a second round while the colonel and his entourage watched. The target jerked as the bullet struck him with a little puff of dust and blood.

I worked the bolt twice more, sighting and firing. A Lake City Boat Tail slammed another VC before the surviving two jumped up and broke toward a tree line.

"My God! Did you see that?" the colonel exclaimed to his staff officers. "Get my chopper in the air and finish those guys off."

The helicopter leapt into the sky and buzzed off in pursuit. From the top of the hill we watched the show as the Huey swarmed back and forth and around the tree line while the door gunner chewed up the terrain with his mounted M60. Afterwards the bird touched down where the two dead guys were and picked up their weapons. The colonel told me the range had been closer to 1,500 meters than 1,200. He wrote me up for a commendation. Actually, I was surprised I hit those guys at that distance—even more surprised that the bullets retained enough energy to kill them.

That was the longest sniper shot I ever made. My shortest-range shot occurred during a sweep of a ville when the squad with whom I was operating ran into NVA. The enemy soldiers broke and ran. My squad split up and took off in foot pursuit. I ran with them, naturally, and entered the ville thundering along the beaten path between the hootches, scattering bare-assed chickens and pigs.

I swept wide, attempting to encircle the NVA and get off a shot. I rounded a hut— and charged directly into an NVA. We bounced off each other, both of us almost being knocked down. Surprised, he hesitated with his AK. I didn't. At a range of about one foot, I didn't have to worry about muzzle energy or long-range velocity. I pointed the barrel and slapped the trigger, blowing out the center of his chest. A kill like that could truly be described as "up close and personal."

A sniper properly equipped for night work was as effective as a day shooter. The enemy often used the cover of darkness to move. If we owned the night, we also owned the kill ratio. Thirty to 40 percent of my kills were made at night with a Starlight scope mounted on an M14 rifle.

The evening of 14 February 1969 became known in Marine Corps history as the "St. Valentine's Massacre." I was working with Delta 1/5 under Captain Mike Wiley near the Arizona along the river. Another Tet offensive was under way. VC and NVA were moving troops and attacking all over I Corps.

The company dug in for the night on Go Noi Island near Liberty Bridge, about 500 meters inland from the banks of the Phu Bon Song. Just before nightfall, an observation plane flew over to check out the other side of the river. It banked suddenly and flew an orbit around an axis.

"There is a huge concentration of enemy personnel heading your way," the pilot radioed Captain Wiley. "The enemy element is pretty big—and it's headed almost directly toward your positions. They'll have to cross the river. I'll try to get you some air support, but there's a big storm rolling in and I don't know if we'll be able to fly."

"Roger," the skipper responded. "Thanks for the warning. We'll do what we can at this end."

Purple was already seeping into the landscape. Dark monsoon clouds roiling across the sky shut out the rest of the sunset. I checked a map and found a place that looked the most probable for the enemy to cross to get to us.

"Sir," I suggested, "I could take my partner and Starlight down the river and set up."

Captain Wiley recognized the wisdom in keeping the enemy from either sneaking up on the company in the dark or making a mad dash across the river to bypass Delta and head for the air base at Da Nang.

My partner and I slipped downstream to a site where the water had receded somewhat, leaving cut grooves in the bank and a shallow eddy that could be waded. We set up in good cover and concealment and waited. Overcast reduced ambient light to the point that even through the Starlight I could barely make out images on the far side. I had a twenty-round magazine of match ammo in the M14 and had dialed my scope for point-of-aim/point-of-impact at fifty meters. My partner had a Remington M40 ready to go.

The action began about an hour and a half after nightfall. "I got movement," I mouthed directly into my partner's ear. "Directly across the river. I can barely make it out."

Total silence for about twenty minutes. As I continued to watch, a shadow separated itself from the depths of the underbrush. I made out a small armed man wearing a pith helmet. He dropped to his belly in the river grass, crawled down to the water, and slithered into it like a reptile, creating hardly a ripple. This guy was a combat pro.

I kept the Starlight on him as he slowly waded across the dark river. The river shallowed again and he came out of it and crept fifteen feet up the bank and into the edge of the elephant grass. I heard water dripping off his uniform. I covered the Starlight scope with my hand to prevent its reflecting any light.

The guy was obviously scouting a crossing point for his outfit. He began to cautiously look around. He stopped about fifteen meters away. I could have almost reached out and goosed him with my rifle barrel. He moved closer. Even as dark as it was, I just knew he was going to spot me.

I locked him in my scope, my eye to the rubber eyepiece and the reticule centered on his wet chest. His head swiveled slowly back and forth as he scanned his surroundings. I slowly applied pressure to the trigger. I eased up as he turned and took a step back toward the river.

He stopped again, his senses honed and as tight as a violin string. He looked around again. I reapplied pressure to the trigger.

Then, apparently satisfied that all was clear, he entered the river and waded back to the other side. I let out a long breath that I seemed to have been holding for at least an hour.

"Things might get as interesting as hell," I mouthed into my partner's ear.

They did. Twenty minutes later, a column of NVA soldiers exited the brush on the opposite bank and worked its way single file into the river, with a space of about ten feet between soldiers. They were in full battle gear, bushes strapped to their backs for camouflage, weapons held high out of the water.

"Holy shit!" I murmured.

"What do we do now?"

"I say we shoot 'em up."

I watched the file wade directly toward us in the greenish, liquid view of the Starlight scope. The point man reached dry land and climbed out of the water. I locked the reticule on his little scope-greenish face beneath the pith helmet and squeezed the trigger.

The night exploded with the rifle shot. So did his head.

Confusion and panic gripped the NVA in the river as I began picking them off one by one, firing as rapidly as I could bolt in a fresh round and slap the trigger. As far as they knew, there might have been an entire company in ambush on our side of the bank. We had the advantage of the Starlight scope and could see in the dark. All they could see and hear were muzzle flashes and the reports from our rifles.

I took advantage of their indecision to shift my muzzle and take out a second man, a third, a fourth. They didn't know whether to continue the crossing or pull back the way they came. Those in the shallow water on their side seemed frozen in place. I kept popping off their heads, one after the other, sending pith helmets flipping and spinning into the river. I shot sixteen times. Every time I fired, another little hat went floating down the river.

We began taking return fire, finally. I didn't want to be in the AO in the event they had mortars. The NVA and VC were experts with mortars and could range in on you within a minute or so.

"Time to get the hell outa here!" I exclaimed.

We jumped up and ran. I was on an adrenaline high. The whole thing was hilarious, the way those gomers just stood frozen out there in the water like a row of ducks while I shot off their heads. I laughed and whooped all the way back, laughing so hard I had a tough time getting out "Snipers in!" to keep the grunts in the perimeter from lighting us up. I wondered later what that NVA commander's after-action report must have said about that night. He probably told his bosses he ran into an entire company of Marines.

I normally moved at night. Rarely did I move in the daytime. I wanted to be already set up when the sun rose. You had to develop tactics like you were a deer hunter. In advance of a patrol moving out into the Arizona, I picked an area where I felt the enemy might go to observe. A rise in the terrain, high ground. Then I went out before daylight and occupied the spot before the enemy got there.

As the patrol moved out and into enemy country, Charlie often scrambled to put out observers. I was often where he wanted to be. They walked right into my sights. Surprise, surprise. It was just like being on a deer stand, watching a pond for deer to come out and drink.

I stayed clear of trails, made sure I didn't leave any tracks and that I knew exactly where I was going before I even set out. There were only so many good hides in an operational area. I could use them several times, as long as I didn't return too frequently and never left evidence that I had been there. If I felt a site had been compromised, I stayed away from it because it was probably booby-trapped or mined.

On several occasions I watched Marines go into this one ville where they always ran into token resistance to bog them down while Charlie's main body scooted out the back, across a rice paddy, and into the trees. Before the next operation, I located a little hill that overlooked the back rice paddies and got set up before daylight. I was ready when the company came in at dawn and the VC tore out the back for their escape. I tore the hell out of them.

I did this three times in a row. On the third time, one of our own machine gunners opened up on my partner and me.

"What the hell? That crazy bastard knows it's us."

Then I realized what he was doing. He was shooting *over* us, not *at* us. Coming down the hill behind us, Charlie was maneuvering to get into position to take us out, having finally keyed onto what we were doing. As we didn't have a radio with us that day, the M60 gunner was warning us the only way he knew how. Thanks to him, we shagged out of the AO to continue the war another day.

Sometimes it was more like prairie-dog hunting than stalking deer. Delta Company drew sniper fire as it entered an open area. The company hit the ground, unable to locate the source of the incoming. I maneuvered to the right flank in order to observe the area from which the shooting seemed to originate. After getting tuned in, I saw the ground itself move about 300 yards away.

A "spider trap" was a foxhole with a woven brush lid that camouflaged it perfectly and could be lifted to provide a firing port for the occupant. The VC sniper loved his spider trap. He could poke up, shoot, drop down, and be still—and you would never see him unless you were looking right at the gomer when he raised up to take another shot, as I was now.

I quickly locked on as I watched a head and rifle edge into view. I popped him. The lid slammed shut. To his left, another lid lifted. Another prairie dog. I popped him too. The lid dropped, but his rifle remained sticking out.

I swept the area with my scope, detecting yet more movement in the little dog town. A trap lid eased up. A gook peered cautiously out, not sure about what was happening. I nailed him in the forehead.

The skipper called in an artillery barrage. The artillery killed no one, but when we checked afterwards there were three dead gomers, two with bullets in their foreheads and the third one through his neck. Three sniper shots, three kills.

I turned my rifle in to the armorer as required when I went on a three-day R & R [rest and recuperation].

"Don't mess with it," I told him. "The last time you did, it took me a day to get it back on target. I have it set for what I want."

While I was gone, he removed the scope anyhow to see if the mounts were tight. He didn't tell me what he had done when I returned. Suspicious nonetheless, I took my rifle out to the edge of the firebase perimeter and sat down this side of the wire to pick out a target and test to see if my dope was still tight.

As luck would have it, I hadn't waited but a few minutes before a gook stepped out of the trees about 300 yards away and looked across the rice paddies toward the Marine base. He walked boldly out to the edge of the trail and stepped up on the dike. Rules of engagement said you didn't shoot anyone unless he was armed. This guy carried his rifle slung down low along his side where it was hard to see. However, stepping up on the dike gave him away. The muzzle stuck out at an angle from his hip. Bingo.

I lined him up in the scope, aiming for his belt line. An easy shot. But when I touched off the round, he flinched and looked up toward me with a "What the fuck?" expression on his face. He looked all around, as though trying to decide what had happened or which way to run.

I cranked in another round. I knew the rifle was off now, that the armorer had fucked with it, but I didn't know how it was off. I aimed to the right of the target. That didn't work, either. He continued to stand there.

I shot to the left. I shot high. I shot low. I shot right on again.

I didn't have a spotter and there wasn't enough water in the rice to mark where I was hitting. There also wasn't enough water in the rice to slow the gomer down when he decided he might be getting shot at and that it was in his best interest to get out of Tombstone.

I was totally pissed. That bastard shouldn't have gotten away. I found out later the rifle was shooting five feet high and to the right. When I left Vietnam after 25 months in-country, I had 103 confirmed kills, 216 "probable," and one Purple Heart from a booby trap. The count would have been 104 if the armorer hadn't saved that gook's life by unknowingly sabotaging my rifle.

CHAPTER FIVE

The sniper's trade is not solely a product of modern warfare. Even prehistoric man saw the advantage of killing an enemy at the farthest possible range. Spears launched by atlatls replaced stones, which in turn were outclassed by arrows. Attila the Hun conquered much of Europe and threatened the Roman Empire with horse-mounted archers capable of accurately shooting arrows at ranges beyond 100 yards.

Samuel in the Old Testament provides the story of what may well be the first account of the single, well-aimed shot. The nine-foot-tall Philistine giant Goliath challenged the Israelites to produce a champion to face him alone on the battlefield. Winner take all.

"And David put his hand in his bag, and took thence a stone, and slang it, and smote the Philistine in his forehead, that the stone sunk into his forehead; and he fell upon his face to the earth" (1 Samuel 18:49).

One shot—one kill.

"In battle," said Theodore Roosevelt, "the only bullet that counts is the one that hits."

Each technological advancement in weapons increased the marksman's range and accuracy. Crossbows began replacing the bow and arrow in the first century A.D. The appearance of gunpowder and guns dramatically advanced a marksman's abilities. Firearms became a major part of battle in the late fifteenth century. In 1520, Leonardo da Vinci picked off enemy soldiers at 300 yards from the wall of besieged Florence with a rifle he designed himself. In 1527, another Italian inventor, Benvenuto Cellini, fired the shot during the siege of Rome that killed the enemy commander and ended the battle. Lord Admiral Horatio Nelson fell victim to a sniper's bullet at the Battle of Trafalgar.

The crack of the sniper's rifle began to punctuate wars with deadly effect. It was in the late eighteenth century, when rifles were first beginning to be used as military weapons, that the term *sniper* evolved from a rather innocuous source.

English officers in British-occupied India made sport of hunting a small wading bird known as the snipe, a difficult target because of its small size and quickness. *Sniper* gradually entered the military lexicon. The first known use of the term in its modern application occurred in a 1773 letter sent home to England: "The soldiers . . . put their hats on the parapet for the enemy to shoot it, and humorously called it sniping."

Sharpshooting riflemen came to prominence in America during the American Revolution when the Continental Congress sent out rifle-armed backwoodsmen to fight the British. Private Timothy Murphy climbed a small tree during the Second Battle of Freeman's Farm (7 October 1777), took aim on British general Simon Frazer, and drilled him with a single shot. The kill forced Frazer's troops to break off the offensive and withdraw toward Saratoga. The British surrender at Saratoga was the turning point of the war.

On the other hand, British sniper Captain Patrick Ferguson may have changed the course of history even more dramatically, and in the opposite direction, had he chosen to shoot General George Washington at the Battle of Brandywine Creek. Ferguson, ever the gentleman, could not bring himself to shoot Washington in the back when the general turned and rode away.

The American Civil War has been called the first modern war. "Rifling" in gun barrels permitted precise shooting at incredible distances of beyond 1,000 yards. Snipers on both sides of the battlefield often disrupted intended attacks by delivering accurate long-distance fire.

Indian fighters became American sharpshooters after the Civil War. Billy Dixon set a record for range that endured for many years when a band of Comanche, Kiowa, and Arapaho attacked the trading post at Adobe Wells in 1874. He picked off an Indian at 1,538 yards with a .50-90 Sharps rifle.

The wind that day was blowing at an estimated 14.3 mph, which meant a bullet deflection of 28 feet. The bullet at that range dropped 318 feet—and remained in flight for nearly five seconds. Dixon always insisted he shot what he aimed at, that the hit was no fluke.

The primary targets for snipers of both sides during World War I were junior frontline officers and infantrymen. Brutal trench warfare made sniping and countersniping common as enemies contrived to pick off each other without being picked off in return. Since the world looked upon the sniper as a sinister character employing "unfair" methods, accounts of successful World War I snipers list their number of kills without identifying the shooter. For example, several sniper stories mention "a former Canadian trapper" with 125 kills.

An American who enlisted with the Canadians to fight in the trenches formulated the sniper's skills into a science that subsequently formed the basis for all sniper training. Captain Herbert W. McBride might well be considered the father of the modern sniper's science.

Armed with a Ross rifle and a telescopic sight, he kept notes on how ballistics were affected by such externals as temperature, humidity, wind, and other changes in weather and lighting conditions. He improved upon techniques of camouflage and concealment and developed methods of fooling the enemy as to a sniper's exact location. All these techniques were passed on and used by snipers around the world.

The peace between the World Wars neglected the art and science of sniping. Shooters had always been corked up in peacetime and only released again, albeit reluctantly, when war returned. As a result, the U.S. military entered World War II unprepared to use snipers or to face them. German sharpshooters took a toll of American fighters in North Africa and in Europe, while Japanese snipers did the same thing in the Pacific. U.S. Marines were the first to recognize a need for individual marksmen.

In 1940, Marine general George O. Van Orden and Marine gunner Calvin A. Lloyd drew up a well-distributed study that concluded that snipers were necessary to a ground combat force.

"The sniper," they wrote, "has not survived merely because of the romantic, adventurous glamour which surrounds his campaign of individual extermination, the private war he wages. He is present on the battlefield because there is a real and vital need for him. It is safe to say that the American sniper could be regarded as the greatest all-around rifleman the world has ever known, and his equipment should include the best aids to his dangerous calling that the inventive genius of the United States can produce."

A number of sniper schools was eventually created to field American snipers against the Axis powers. While some offered up to five weeks of extensive training, most provided only a day's familiarization before shipping the sniper to the front. The best of these schools was founded by the Marine Corps at New River, North Carolina, and at Green's Farm near San Diego.

"Snipers can save a country, sometimes," declared Lieutenant Claude N. Harris, commander of Green's Farm.

Marine and Army snipers performed well during World War II but suffered staggering losses. Fifth Army snipers in Italy lost 80 percent of their number to hostile fire. The 24th Marine Division had nine snipers alive out of an original 24 at the end of the Battle of Iwo Jima.

The war ended—and it was cork the shooters back into their bottles. Few military leaders supported the continuation of snipers or sniper training. Headquarters, U.S. Army Ground Forces, Pacific Ocean Area, said the 8th Army found no use for sniper training. It recommended that expert riflemen at company level be issued scoped rifles only under special circumstances. As a result, both the Army and the Marine Corps considered sniping a mere peripheral activity at most.

Snipers were used in the Korean War, although no official schools existed to train special marksmen. Sniper development and training was left to commanders in the field. The Korean cease-fire in 1953 found the status of American snipers stalemated at a post–World War II level.

"The U.S. Army has no trained snipers," bluntly declared an April 1954 article in *Infantry School Quarterly.* "It has not produced snipers in the past, and it will not produce them in the future."

As late as April 1960, Colonel Henry E. Kelly reported, "Apparently, the sniper is no longer considered essential in our infantry."

A mere handful of military men in marksmanship training units and shooting teams "kept the faith" and continued to push for official recognition and formalization of snipers and sniper training. The most dogged of these was Marine Captain (now retired major) Jim Land.

"There is an extremely accurate, helicopter-transportable, self-supporting weapon available to the Marine infantry commander," he argued. "This weapon, which is easily adapted to either the attack or defense, is the M1C sniper rifle with the M82 telescopic sight in the hands of a properly trained sniper."

Late in 1960, Land set up a scout sniper school in Hawaii that for many years offered the only formal sniper training in the entire U.S. armed forces. A press release concerning the school ended with: "In this age of push-button warfare, little thought is given to the common infantryman who has nothing but a ten-pound rifle and a lot of courage. But beware of the sniper—he is deadly."

Vietnam proved to be a new kind of conflict. Although the United States had no snipers at the beginning of the war, their utilization in guerrilla warfare proved most effective on both sides. The first sniping schools in

Vietnam were set up by the 3d Marine Division and went into operation by October 1965. Captain Robert A. Russell, commander of the school, first put himself and his instructors through the course, then went into the field to try out their new tactics. One of his instructors, Staff Sergeant Dan Barker, is credited with the first official sniper kill in Vietnam.

"A USMC sniper team was formed in the Hue–Phu Bai TAOR [tactical area of responsibility]," reported the publication *U.S. Marines in Vietnam: The Landing and The Buildup, 1965.* "The team used Winchester Model 70 rifles with 8X Unertl telescopic sights and killed two Viet Cong at a range of more than 700 yards in the first exercise of this new tactic. . . . Fifty of the best marksmen were selected from each of the regiments [and] divided into four-man teams. . . . During November and December, 20–30 teams operated in the Marine TAORs daily. On 23 November a sniper team at Phu Bai killed two VC and wounded another at a distance of more than 1,000 meters."

The 1st Marine Division soon followed suit and opened its own school on Hill 55 in October 1966. Captain Jim Land was placed in charge and ordered to "train the best snipers in the Marine Corps." He recruited as senior instructor Gunnery Sergeant Carlos Hathcock, whose exploits soon made him a legend. In the school's initial three-month period, Land's seventeen snipers killed more enemy soldiers than any single battalion in I Corps.

"It's a challenge to sneak up on old Charlie in his own backyard and put a hurting on him," declared one shooter. "I like being a sniper."

In contrast to the Marine Corps, no U.S. Army sniper policy on training existed in Vietnam during the early years. An ordinary rifleman who could shoot straight was merely handed a scoped rifle and informed that he was a sniper. Even later, Army training remained largely catch-as-catch-can and was the responsibility of individual units.

The most successful Army sniper program of the war was initiated by General Julian J. Ewell, commander of the 9th Infantry Division in the Mekong Delta. Ewell's men began to train snipers in 1968. Division snipers chalked up 346 enemy KIA during the single month of April 1969.

Although he received little of the recognition awarded Marine snipers such as Carlos Hathcock, Sergeant Adelbert E. Waldron II was the war's most accomplished American sniper with 109 confirmed kills.

General Ewell described a Waldron incident: "One afternoon he was riding along the Mekong River on a Tango boat when an enemy sniper on shore pecked away at the boat. While everyone else on board strained to find the antagonist, who was firing from the shoreline over 900 meters away, Sergeant Waldron took up his sniper rifle and picked off the VC out of the top of a coconut tree with one shot—from a moving platform."

The U.S. Navy with its SEAL teams operating primarily in the Mekong Delta region south of Saigon with missions of ambushing, prisoner snatching and reconnaissance did not require sniper expertise. At no time during the war did SEAL teams include snipers. Gary Evans, who served with SEAL Team One, recalls that while SEALs were excellent marksmen, they received neither sniper weapons nor special marksmanship training. In the summer of 1969, he procured an M1D with an M81 scope and taught himself to be a sniper. He was unaware of any other SEALs who carried special scoped rifles.

By the end of the war, less than 1,200 Marines and soldiers had served as snipers in Vietnam. They killed more than 20,000 North Vietnamese Army and Vietcong soldiers, the equivalent of an entire division. They averaged one kill for every 1.3 to 1.7 rounds expended. Vietnam snipers like Chuck Mawhinney, Carlos Hathcock, Adelbert E. Waldron II, Tom "Moose" Ferran, and John Culbertson proved the "force multiplier" value of the sniper on the battlefield and helped form the profession as a permanent fixture within the American military.

"The use of snipers was not new in Vietnam," General John H. Hay Jr. wrote in 1974 as part of the Army's Vietnam Studies series, "but the systematic training and employment of an aggressive, offensive sniper team—a carefully designed 'weapon system'—was. A sniper was no longer just the man in the rifle squad who carried the sniper rifle; he was the product of an established school."

After Vietnam, and especially since the end of the Cold War, armed forces of the United States have prepared to fight smaller and more flexible wars. To the U.S. Marines goes the major credit for developing sniper training and making snipers a permanent fixture within the military structure. Men like Dick Culver, Carlos Hathcock, Jack Cuddy, Neil Morris, and Chuck Mawhinney played key roles. Snipers today are indeed recognized as "a cost-effective force multiplier," relatively cheap to train, equip, and deploy while providing options that greatly increase the ranges of infantry firepower. The importance and usefulness of sniping has become increasingly apparent in places like Grenada, Panama, Beirut, Somalia, Bosnia, and Iraq.

American snipers were used to help suppress a Cuban-supported coup on the island of Grenada in

1983. In that same year, U.S. Marine snipers targeted gunmen in Beirut in their capacity as UN peacekeepers. American sniper trainer Chuck Kramer described the action and validity of a single well-aimed shot.

"Most of the good hits were at extreme long range and most of the kills were made at 600–800 meters. These guys were getting wary by then. I got two on a motor scooter by sheer luck. I was watching this big wide avenue and sure as hell I saw this big motor scooter coming toward me about a kilometer away with two guys on it. They're both carrying SKS carbines slung over their shoulders, two shopping baskets full of food, and these canvas carriers for RPGs on the front of the motor scooter. I lined them up and . . . fired by sheer instinct. It was a classic shot. The round must have gone through the driver and then into the passenger."

Veteran Army sergeant William Lucas, who already had 38 sniper kills in Vietnam, redirected his shooting skills in the urban jungles of Panama City during Operation Just Cause. In Somalia, Marine snipers targeted heavily armed "technicals" careening around in their jeeps and pickups. Americans shot back in Sarajevo's "Sniper Alley." Confirmed kills on individual humans were made at ranges of up to 1,800 meters in the Iraqi wars and in Afghanistan. Sergeant Kenneth Terry, 1st Marine Division, knocked out a BMP armored personnel carrier at a range of 1,000 meters with two rounds from a MAC .50-caliber sniping rifle during Desert Storm.

CHAPTER SIX

U.S. Marine
Lance Corporal Roy Lafon
Vietnam, 1966

I went from a grunt humping the bush with Alpha Company, 1st Battalion, 3d Marines, to company clerk. The first sergeant had found out I could type and asked me if I wanted to be company clerk. At the time we were running ball-busting patrols in Leach Valley and Elephant Valley and in the Hai Van Pass, getting the shit shot out of us now and then.

I looked at the first sergeant like he was my savior. All I could think was: *Does a pig roll in the mud? Does a tiger doo-doo in the woods?* I jumped on the opportunity like a duck on a june bug. I saw the rear-echelon clerks back at Da Nang in the shade with their cold beer and ice, hot chow, a bunk sheltered from the rain, a good sleep every night. . . .

I was going to ride out my tour in style. That was in June. In August, Alpha received an order to send one man to sniper training. The first sergeant told me to pull the personnel jacket of every man who had at least six months remaining in-country and who had fired "Expert" on the range. There were only three: a staff sergeant from weapons platoon; a private first class; and there was—*me*.

"Why not send me?" I offered.

I must have had a brain fart, some kind of seizure from the heat. The next thing I knew, this five-seven, 145-pound, 21-year-old country boy found his volunteering ass shipped off to sniper school at Phu Bai. There went the dry bunk, cold beer, and hot chow. I went from grunt humping the bush to company clerk back to the bush again as a sniper with a long gun.

I could shoot a rifle. I was born in the mountains near Blacksburg, Virginia, where I lived with my grandfather about fifteen miles out of town until I was fourteen. Most snipers came from rural areas of the South and West. Grandfather gave me a .22-caliber varmint rifle on my seventh birthday. Shooting the rings out of those great big targets at Marine boot camp was easy compared to shooting a squirrel's head in the very top of a big sycamore on the creek.

Next thing I knew, I was issued a 30-06 Winchester Model 70 with an 8X Unertl scope and a box of Lake City match-grade ammunition and authorized to go out and shoot gooks. Mostly that meant I was back to humping the bush where I started from, getting the shit shot out of us now and then, or escorting motorized patrols on Highway 9 between Dong Ha and Khe Sanh to shoot back at enemy snipers. It was generally counter sniper stuff or targets of opportunity.

Whenever "Snipers up!" came down the column, I would trot dutifully up to point, looking important with my long gun, and take care of the problem.

The scopes on the Model 70s were prone to fog up. Later, we were issued .308 Remington Model 700s with Redfield scopes, the sweetest-firing rifle I had ever nestled against my shoulder. Until then, however, we had to make do.

I had been out in the field for a number of weeks and logged a kill or two under my belt when I teamed up with another shooter fresh out of training and on his first operation carrying a long rifle. The company had halted movement temporarily when we spotted a man step out of the jungle about 300 meters away. He wore a pith helmet and green khakis and carried an AK-47 rifle, all of which meant he was NVA. He, pooping and snooping and sniffing like a hound seeking a trail, was probably either a scout or the point man for a patrol.

My new partner opted for the shot, his first kill, since my scope was fogging over. I would act as spotter while a couple of other snipers operating with the company watched.

"Take him," I said.

He missed the first shot. Call it a touch of buck fever. He jacked in a fresh round—and missed that one too. Actually, the misses were more as a result of the scope on his rifle working loose than nerves. Whichever, his bullets came nowhere near the target. The gook didn't even flinch. Only a puzzled look crossed his face. That was the expression he died with.

The other two snipers and myself, fogged scope or not, blazed away at the same time. Call it three shots— one kill.

It wasn't a bad shot at 300 meters, scope-handicapped as I was, but I could do better.

Camp Carroll was a firebase up by the DMZ between Dong Ha and Khe Sanh. It was getting mortared one afternoon during one of my operations in the vicinity. A shell exploded not six feet from me. The concussion knocked me asshole over teakettle, but all I got out of it was a piece of shrapnel in my right arm. I was looking forward to a little payback when I returned from the hospital.

Gooks often moved up their mortar tubes under cover of darkness and prepared to shell the firebase. Patrols had detected a lot of movement on the south side of Razorback Ridge. Anticipating some action against the enemy mortar men, my spotter and I slipped out of camp after midnight so we could occupy a hide that offered a view of the ridge before it came daylight.

We crouched in the hide for five or six hours. Watching and waiting. Enemy FOs [forward observers] commonly sneaked up to the top of the hogback and radioed back targets and coordinates to the indirect fire weapons located in hiding farther down.

The sun came up red and got brighter as it moved up and over the heat-white sky. Suddenly, I detected a flicker of light through my scope. It appeared to be sunlight glinting off some object—a compass perhaps, a rifle barrel, or binoculars.

I kept looking.

Soon, sure enough, here came the mortar FO hurrying up the lee side of the hogback. He reached the top and stayed in the shadows of trees while he used binoculars to glass the base camp. I might never have spotted him if he hadn't let something he carried glint in the sun. But it was too late for his little gook ass now. He had it hanging out there, ripe for the plucking.

The range was about 900 yards. A goodly distance worthy of a sniper's skills. It was early in the morning, the air was cool, and there was virtually no breeze. A wonderful morning for killing. And, on his part, for dying.

Lying in the prone, I elbowed in a rifle rest for my forward arm and adjusted my scope for the range. I would be shooting slightly uphill, which posed an additional challenge. The unsuspecting little bastard just stood there in the shade, looking over at the Marine encampment. He had no idea.

I settled my crosshairs on the target. I squeezed the trigger. The rifle cracked and recoiled smoothly into my shoulder.

A bullet is a physical object. It doesn't instantly reach impact. Therefore, nothing happened immediately. *Now is the time for . . .* I could have quoted that much of the old typing exercise before the bullet thudded into the guy with a whack that echoed across the hills hard against the rifle's report. The punch all but knocked him out of his boots or sandals, whichever he happened to be wearing.

It was the best shot I had ever made. I was proud of that shot.

On second thought, it *wasn't* my best. There were two better than that.

I carried an M14 on the first of these because my Winchester scope had fogged over again and was in the armory for repairs. The company was out on a search-and-destroy.

"Once we cross that rice paddy," the company commander pointed out, "it's a free-fire zone and *anything* is fair game."

What he didn't know—what none of us realized—was that our point squad had already circled the rice paddy and was now approaching a little dry point of land on the opposite side, about 400 yards away in the free-fire zone. Peering through binoculars, checking for targets or signs of the enemy, I spotted a man walk out of the woods on the far side of the field and stand partly exposed to the sunlight. Black hair, black eyes, swarthy skin. Gook. I glued my front rifle post on the little hollow at the base of his neck, allowing for bullet drop at that range to nail him through the lungs and heart. This dink was one breath away from meeting his worthy ancestors.

I held a breath and squeezed the trigger. Nothing happened.

"Shit."

The safety switch was on. I pushed my trigger finger forward to release it, keeping my eye on the target.

Just then, two Marines in helmets walked into sight directly behind the gook. Only, he was no gook. He was a Hispanic Marine. Without his helmet and with his dark hair and Asiatic complexion, he only *looked* like a VC. Sweat popped out on my forehead as I realized what I had almost done. My hands trembled. I lowered the rifle to control my breathing. That poor Marine over there, a member of the point squad, never knew how close he came to dying that day.

That was a best shot because it was a shot never made.

Another shot-never-made occurred somewhat later.

Captain Starke [not his real name] was a rifle company commander in the 2d Battalion, 9th Marines, to whom I was temporarily attached for operations. He had been a poster board recruiter for most of his career. All spit and polish and shine and kiss-ass. It didn't take him long after his arrival in Vietnam to tap the animosity and distrust of his entire company.

On the last day of a three-day sweep through enemy

country, we found dead campfires and little racks the enemy built in order to sleep off the ground. It was, as commanders liked to say, a "target-rich environment." Still, we had made no contact.

We were heading back in to Camp Carroll, proceeding up this little creek because the jungle was so thick. The next day was the Marine Corps birthday. Camp Carroll was going to hold a parade and ceremony to celebrate. Captain Starke wanted his company to look good for his superiors. He ordered every man in the company to stop in the middle of the creek, in the middle of Indian Country, and wash out his web gear. I cringed. I expected the enemy to hit us at any moment while the men were knee-deep in water, splashing like a group of washerwomen.

Three guys from the company drew me aside the next time the company prepared to go out.

"That silly, ass-kissing sonofabitch is going to get us all killed just so he can look good," the group's spokesman said. "You've shot men with that rifle of yours, right? How about shooting one more? It's self-defense. You snipers are supposed to be saving Marine lives. How about saving our lives?"

The company's enlisted men had taken up a collection. I was offered $1,500 to shoot Captain Starke. I have to admit, I gave it serious consideration. Not for the money, but instead for the guys the goofy bastard was going to get killed.

The opportunity never came up. I was glad, afterwards, that it didn't, that this was another best shot never made. He got killed anyhow about a month later. I never knew the circumstances. I wasn't out there when it happened. I only heard about it.

CHAPTER SEVEN

U.S. Marine Corporal Jim Gularte
Vietnam, 1968

Things moved very fast. I got on an airliner with stews and air-conditioning one day in California and a couple of days later I was in the middle of a place I had hardly even heard of before I enlisted in the Marines—and there was a big battle under way. It was the Tet offensive of 1968. The North Vietnamese and Vietcong attacked in masses all across South Vietnam. Entire provinces were falling. There was fighting the first night of Tet on the compound of the American embassy in Saigon. The 26th Marines at Khe Sanh dug in around the airfield in an immense fortress of trenches and bunkers. Everything that could be spared was airlifted to the combat base to make sure the Marines didn't suffer the same fate as the French at Dien Bien Phu in 1954.

I was the new Hispanic kid on the block. I could be spared. I was airlifted to Khe Sanh to support in my capacity as a sniper. I had been in-country two days, maybe three. I was a "boot," as green as the jungle, and, truthfully, didn't know what the hell was going on.

I had been recruited, hooked, while still in basic infantry training at Camp Pendleton. A lieutenant and a sergeant fresh back from Vietnam gave their spiel.

"This is a great shooting war," the sergeant said enthusiastically. "This is an opportunity. If you have to go to war, the sniper MOS is what you want."

I thought of the old World War II movies of Japanese snipers hiding in the tops of palm trees. They always got waxed.

"That's Hollywood," the lieutenant elaborated. "We're a little more sophisticated now. You and other Marines like you are going to write the book on sniping because at the moment there are no formal training manuals."

The initial group of volunteers started out at 300 men. That narrowed to fifty. Twenty-five of us completed sniper training. Now here I was at Khe Sanh serving as a spotter to a more-experienced sniper. He carried the long gun, a Remington Model 700. I carried binoculars and an M14 equipped with a night-viewing Starlight scope.

We were dispatched along with an element of three grunts and a radio to a listening post about 300 meters outside the wire in dense jungle. On the west side toward the Laotian border and the Ho Chi Minh Trail. Our mission was to observe and report enemy movements. My partner and I took turns on the Starlight.

Being with a seasoned veteran—he had been in-country maybe two months—settled me in properly. I learned discipline. You didn't go out and attack any group that came along. You sized it up first, made sure you could handle it.

"We got movement, one o'clock," my partner said. It

was his turn on the Starlight. He walked me through it, whispering. "Let's see what they're doing, Gularte. Let's see how many there are. Don't jump into the fire and discover it's bigger than you thought."

We waited while he watched. The three grunts and I could barely see shadows in the darkness.

"I think this is it," my partner murmured. "I think we're going to be okay. I'm going for the last guy."

"What happens once you fire?" I asked, whispering. "Won't they return fire? What do we do then?"

"It's nothing we really have to worry about. It's only a six-man patrol."

Sounded good to me. What did I know? If it had been twenty guys, I would probably have said the same thing: *Sounds good to me. Let's take 'em on.*

The range was about 300 meters, a long shot after dark. Adrenaline coursed through my body like it was being pumped.

The enemy patrol returned fire as soon as the first kill went down. But, confused, it was shooting in every direction. I couldn't see anything through the day scope on the Remington, but I popped caps anyhow. My partner dropped a second man while the three grunts blazed away with their M16s. The night fell silent again within a few seconds, as though nothing had ever happened. Six dead men lay out there, the entire patrol. We had wiped it out. It seemed so easy, so mechanical.

The next patrol three days later turned out to be a little different. We set up on another trail about 700 meters out from the wire. The sun was going down. It was that quiet introspective time between sunset and darkness when shadows seemed to move. Some of them actually *did* move. A large enemy patrol.

The radioman called in an artillery strike while we

stayed in hiding and monitored. Somehow we must have given away our position. Within five minutes of the last artillery impact, the enemy began pelting us with mortars. Turnabout was fair play. Earsplitting geysers erupted all around, walking and stomping and filling the air with dust and smoke and deadly shrapnel hissing and buzzing with every blast.

I hugged the ground, trembling from the onslaught and scared literally half to death. I felt a bunch of bees attack my right shoulder and side. "I'm hit!" Incredulous, like this wasn't really happening. I had only been in Vietnam two weeks.

My partner crawled over to me while the shelling continued. "Hold still," he ordered, checking me out. "You'll live, Gularte. You got some splinters is all."

Choppers jerked us out of the field and I was medevaced to the cluster of Quonsets at China Beach that served as a Naval hospital. Docs removed a couple of pieces of shrapnel, declared me almost as good as new, and assigned me a rack for a couple of days of rest. A doctor came in to see me at the end of my rest period. He studied my chart.

"We're going to medevac you to Okinawa," he said.

"What for, sir? I'm fine. I'll be as good as new in a few days."

"It's for psychological exams."

I didn't like the sound of that. Did they think I was crazy?

"But, sir, I've only been here two weeks. My bubble is still on tight."

"Our policy is to send snipers out for a psych eval every time they're hit."

He paused and looked me over, looked back at the chart.

"Brand-new, huh? Two weeks?"

He thought it over some more.

"All right. We might be able to hold off on you since you just got in-country. Do you feel all right? Do you like apple pie and the U.S.A.? You're not feeling wacko or anything?"

"I'm fine, sir."

"Well, we'll let you go back to your unit and catch you next time."

As fate would have it, I would eventually be hit and sent out for psych evals four times before I left Vietnam permanently.

CHAPTER EIGHT

U.S. Marine Corporal Jim Gularte
Vietnam, 1968

I never made it back to Khe Sanh. Enemy attacks against the Marine combat base intensified until the airfield was closed. No one was getting in or out. Nothing except ammo drops and medical evacuations. I was sent back to Headquarters Battalion, 1st Marine Division, at Da Nang, soon ending up with the 7th Marines based on Hill 55, thirteen kilometers southwest of the air base in the crotch of the Song Yen and Song Nghia river junction. I was issued a Remington 700 sniper rifle and a spotter as new as I had been four weeks ago.

Staff Sergeant Carlos Hathcock was the senior man for the sniper platoon on Hill 55—a good ol' country-boy type who possessed a wealth of knowledge about shooting and the sniper's trade. Best yet, he was able to impart that knowledge without being intimidating. He was enthusiastic and anxious to keep the sniper MOS alive and well in the Marine Corps, even after the war ended.

"You can't make errors in this business," he said. "Do your job and make every shot count. You can't win a battle going up against a thirty-round AK-47 with five rounds in your rifle. Use your head. Use everything you've learned and keep a distance between you and the hamburgers so they can't take you out."

He called enemy soldiers "hamburgers," but he always respected them as warriors.

"We have a lot of people in the Marine Corps who don't believe in this MOS," he said, "who think we're an elitist bunch who should be reined in and put under restraint. Everything we're working for will go right in the toilet if we screw up out there. So—no missed shots, no shooting at animals, and definitely don't let me catch you shooting at civilians just for sport. Identify your targets. Make sure they are unfriendlies and armed. Then take them out. Let's go out there, do a job, and take it serious."

Most of the snipers under Hathcock had their stuff wired together. The sniper platoon on Hill 55 was a thoroughly professional crew. I was now part of it.

I chalked up my first kill working off the hill. A spotter and I were assigned to scout a small hamlet not far outside the wire to see what we could find. We carried weapons and enough ammo, food, and water to last at least two nights.

Nothing was going on in the ville, so we humped it past the river to set up camp in the bush for the night. Since there were only two of us, we pulled port-and-starboard watch. One slept, the other kept his eyes peeled for danger.

My wristwatch said 0300 hours, not long before dawn, when I spotted three VC moving stealthily along the road that led past us into the village. Two carried

AKs, the other an SKS. All three wore NVA-type boonie hats. Incredibly, they remained on the road. They were either inexperienced or, oddly enough, they felt safe, considering how close they were to the Marine base on Hill 55.

I nudged my partner. "I have shadow movements on the road."

He awoke instantly and retrieved his M14 with the mounted Starlight scope. The range was only about 200 meters. Moonlight illuminated the targets, providing enough shooting light for the scope on my Remington. The gooks were all in a row, like three little ducks. I sighted in on the point man while my partner took drag.

"One . . . two . . . *now!*"

The twin cracks of the rifles shattered the night as a single report. Both targets dropped like they had been hammered. I then nailed the remaining VC before he could gather his wits enough to escape.

We remained in the hide, expecting the dead guys' buddies to come out to retrieve the bodies sooner or later and thereby join them in the hereafter. The sun rose on a dry, clear day. The corpses lay in the dirt road, seeming almost to sink into it bit by bit as the day progressed and the sun arced across the sky and beat down on them. Swarms of flies gathered and sucked on blood and crawled into orifices.

Still, nobody came. Local villagers worked rice paddies only fifty or sixty yards away, but they pointedly ignored the bodies lying out there in plain view. Clearly, the dead men's buddies were waiting to ambush *us* if we went to search the corpses for intelligence while, at the same time, we waited to ambush *them*. Call it a Mexican standoff.

Darkness came again. We remained in the waiting

game. It turned out to be an uneventful night. Just my partner and me and the three dead men out there all by ourselves. We slipped out of the hide before dawn of the third morning and made our way back to Hill 55 to turn in our reports. A grunt patrol went out to find the bodies and retrieve them. They were still lying where they fell, getting riper by the hour. No one had come within yards of them for nearly two days and nights. It was like they simply ceased to exist and no one really gave a damn.

The 7th Marines prepared to launch a major operation into the badlands south of Hill 55 known as the Arizona Territory. In what may have been the first, and perhaps only, employment of its kind, sniper recon teams were sent out in advance, as a patrol unit, to probe and see what was out there. Snipers, who usually worked in pairs with sometimes a radioman attached, suddenly found ourselves in a combat element of platoon size moving off the hill and down the secured road towards the Territory while aircraft and artillery support stood by on call.

We walked past a field-battered grunt company taking a break alongside the road in the hot sun. The guys looked beaten in their faded green utilities while we snipers presented an unusual sight filing past in tiger stripes and bush hats, armed with scoped rifles. The entire company stood up and cheered.

One of the Marines called out to me, "Hey, man. Is your name Jim?"

"Yeah."

"Gularte?"

"Yeah."

The speaker was another Hispanic. "I'm your cousin," he announced, grinning. "Yeah, man. Rudy

Castro. My mom told me you were over here working with the 7th Marines in the sniper platoon."

We had never met before. He recognized me from a photo his mother sent him. Nonetheless, it was old-home week. A relative out here in the middle of nowhere. We embraced like long lost brothers.

He looked tired and weather-beaten, his outfit having been out in the field so long it was running low on water and chow. His hands were cut and bleeding from the elephant grass. I gave him one of my canteens of water, half my rations, including rice, and the new pair of gloves I had just been issued. He needed them more than I did.

We embraced again and I headed on down the road into the Arizona, one of the most enemy-infested areas in Vietnam. After a short distance, we broke off the road and entered the jungle, going combat tactical upon reaching Charlie's backyard. Perhaps, as Marines said, Charlie owned the night and the NVA owned the jungle—but our job was to make him pay for that ownership.

Sure enough, within a couple of hours we stirred up a firefight with a unit of NVA spread out across a tree line to our front. I saw tan uniforms and pith helmets. Snipers jockeyed for good firing points while the grunt radiomen attached to us got on the horn with arty and gunships. We were into a real shooting match.

I went into the prone with my spotter in some bushes and started checking out muzzle flashes on the other side of the rice. The gooks were about 600 meters away, which was seriously to their disadvantage and decidedly in our favor.

"I got a target," I said to my observer in sniper rap. "Twelve o'clock."

Tan uniform and pith helmet kneeling to fire in grass next to bamboo and palm trees. I locked his neck in my crosshairs. Neck shots offered advantages. If you erred a tad to either the left or right and experienced bullet drop because of range, you still scored a center-of-mass hit on the body. On the other hand, you risked wounding the guy in the legs or missing altogether if you aimed center of mass.

I squeezed the trigger. Since I was sighted in at 600 meters, point of aim and point of impact should be the same. I saw the bullet hit him. His neck exploded and he dropped. A solid hit.

I chambered a fresh round and searched for another target, panning across shallow jungle, tree lines, and rice paddies with my scope. Muzzle flashes flickered like spears of sunlight. I picked out another North Vietnamese soldier.

"Got another one. . . ."

By this time, my spotter was too busy fighting on his own to worry about me. He was cranking off M14 rounds as fast as he could change magazines, laying down a field of fire on full automatic. Elsewhere, caught up in the excitement and anxiety, other spotters were similarly involved delivering a volume of fire down-range.

I fired. Another neck shot and a puff of pink mist bright through the scope.

I jacked in a third cartridge. We were receiving continuing volleys of small-arms fire biting into the trees around us. Amazingly, there were no mortars yet.

I located a third target. I kept up the patter, even though my spotter was too involved on his own to listen. "He's standing behind a palm. I'm going center-shot on this one."

I wouldn't have been surprised if my spotter snapped back with something like "Who gives a shit? Can't you see I'm busy?" But he didn't. I don't think he even heard me.

A neck shot was impractical because of the man's position and his angle. I squeezed and took the recoil. The guy's chest erupted in an instantaneous red cloud and he was done.

I scanned right and then left. The jungle was suddenly empty as the NVA, sustaining heavy losses, pulled back out of contact. Such is the slow-motion effects of adrenaline that my three shots seemed to have taken forever, whereas in actuality only a few seconds had passed.

It wasn't a bad shooting match. We took no casualties ourselves. But we had put some serious hurt on old Nguyen. He had never run up against anything like this before. It was his worst nightmare. One of the snipers in the patrol ended up with eight kills. Almost everybody had at least one.

If the old saying is true that "the most deadly weapon in the world is a Marine and his rifle," that went double in spades if the Marine was also a sniper.

Nothing in an officer's training at the time prepared him to know what to expect from snipers or even how to utilize us. Carlos Hathcock always preached that we snipers needed to prove to the hierarchy that we had something exceptional to offer, that we were a valuable resource available to commanders, and that we could save American lives. Some commanders listened and were willing to be educated; they were a delight to work with. Others were arrogant and ignorant of our skills. To them, it was "Get to the end of the line. Go out and scout, if that's your job. But don't *you* tell *me* what you do. *I'll* tell *you* what you do."

Because of the tempo of the war in 1968, rest was a luxury few of us enjoyed for long. Soon I was back in the Arizona on a sweep with a platoon commander who seemed pleased to have snipers attached.

"Sir, do you know how to utilize snipers?" I always asked that question at the beginning of an operation with a new officer. "Do you know basically what our mission is?"

"You guys tell me what you need to do and how I utilize you," the lieutenant responded.

We were going to get along. He was willing to listen as his seventeen-man patrol probed deep into enemy territory. And, because he was receptive, we made it worth his while.

When the patrol made night perimeter, I explained to the lieutenant that my spotter and I would push outside the defenses for about a hundred meters and set up alongside the path to provide early warning of any intruders. I plotted it on the map and stressed that all the Marines in the outfit should know where we were and where we would cross back into lines should we run into something. A plan of action and coordination to prevent our getting nailed by friendly fire.

A hundred meters was not very far, but it was a long distance in the jungle at night. My spotter and I crept cautiously down the trail at dusk, then broke off it and burrowed into a hide that provided a reasonable view of a section of the path. We had hardly settled in before we detected movement to our left. We froze in place.

Two black-clad VC with AK rifles stepped out of thick growth not more than fifty feet away. That was only about fifteen steps. I could almost smell *nuoc mam* on their breath. There was nothing to do but wait and see what happened. It was going to be Dodge City and the O.K. Corral together if they spotted us. I trained my crosshairs on the first one, ready to shoot.

They stole out to the trail, stalking like hunters, and looked up and down it. For a moment, I thought we had been made. One of them seemed to be looking right at me. I was squeezing the trigger when he turned away in the direction from which they came.

I relaxed. We could have taken out both of them on the spot, but some little voice of caution, a sixth sense, urged me to reconsider. We might be looking at an ambush. I didn't want to trigger it.

"Let's see what's happening," I whispered to my partner.

The two men walked back into the bushes that generated them—and simply disappeared. Close scrutiny revealed a well-camouflaged cave entrance. We, and the patrol one hundred meters away, had apparently blundered into an underground complex. The enemy apparently didn't know we were near, and we wouldn't have known about them, either, if my partner and I had not scouted ahead. At least we wouldn't have known until morning movement aroused the VC and they set up an ambush. There might be dozens of them tunneled underneath us like a bunch of rats.

I turned to my spotter. "We need to get out of here."

An understatement. We waited a few more minutes to make sure things had settled down before squirming away from the location and backtracking. The lieutenant was ecstatic with relief that his scout snipers had provided him with an upper hand and possibly saved his patrol from annihilation. He hastily devised a plan for establishing an L-shaped ambush.

"We'll set up around the cave opening and see what comes out," he said.

My spotter and I led the grunts back to the cave and helped them silently deploy to cover the cave with their machine guns and grenade launchers. Both sides settled in for the night. Charlie must have slept soundly, not knowing that, for some of them, it would be their last sleep.

Fifteen VC came out of the cave just before dawn. They surfaced yakking and chattering like squirrels, seemingly in a jovial mood and behaving like schoolboys on a lark. Feeling safe in their home territory. They bunched up on the trail as they prepared to venture forth for more mischief.

They never knew what hit them. A crescendo of rifle and machine-gun fire cut through them like a scythe through wheat. It ruined their day and all their subsequent days. Not a single one survived the kill zone.

From then on, that lieutenant wanted snipers with him every time he went out. He became a real supporter of the sniper program. Carlos Hathcock was pleased. The best sign of a successful mission was when all the good guys made it back.

CHAPTER NINE

U.S. Marine Staff Sergeant
Carlos N. Hathcock, II
Vietnam, 1966-67

Long Tr'ang. White Feather. That was what the Vietcong and the North Vietnamese Army (NVA) called Sergeant Carlos N. Hathcock II. He wore a white feather in his bush hat whenever he slipped into the jungles, sometimes alone, to hunt the most dangerous game of all: man.

Hunting was good in Vietnam for Long Tr'ang. He belonged to what he called "The Vietcong Hunting Club"—the sniper detachment of the 1st Marine Division operating off Hill 55. He scored 93 confirmed kills. He figured he had at least 300 more kills that were not "confirmed." North Vietnam offered a bounty of three years' pay to the soldier who would pluck Hathcock's feather from his hat and his head from his shoulders.

Raised in the rural areas of Arkansas, Tennessee, and Louisiana—a region that has produced many military sharpshooters, including World War I hero Sergeant

Alvin York—Hathcock already knew how to shoot when he enlisted in the U.S. Marine Corps in 1959 on his seventeenth birthday. During the next few years he broke almost every shooting record in the Marine Corps and won many awards, including the United States Long-Range High-Power Championship.

It seemed only fitting that in 1966 when Captain Jim Land started a sniper school in Vietnam for the 1st Marine Division, he would have Sergeant Carlos Hathcock as one of his instructors.

"The most dangerous weapon on any battlefield," Land was fond of saying, "is the single well-aimed shot."

From September 1966 to April 1967, Jim Land's seventeen-man instructor cadre trained more than 600 snipers. During one three-month period, the sniper cadre killed more Vietcong than any battalion in I Corps. Land's snipers were often referred to with awe as "Murder, Incorporated."

But it was Long Tr'ang who stepped off Hill 55 and into the nightmares of the Vietcong. Legends of his daring and skill spread among "friendlies" and enemy alike.

It was Hathcock, according to the Marine Corps, who initiated in Vietnam the use of the .50-caliber machine gun with a 10X scope as a sniper weapon. During Operation DeSoto, the 24-year-old Marine sniper set up on a hillside overlooking a wide, flat valley near Duc Pho.

"There were hamburgers everywhere," he said. A "hamburger" was his slang for an enemy target.

From the top of the hill he recorded the longest single-shot kill ever made by a sniper. He shot a VC "mule," an arms runner, with one shot at 2,500 meters—more than one and a half miles away.

Hathcock was also the sniper who eliminated the so-called Apache Woman, a sadistic female VC platoon leader who tortured captured Marines. One night he was inside the wire of the firebase on Hill 55 when she was working. A captured Marine's screams of agony tore into raw nerves. At dawn she let the Marine go. But first she castrated him.

The young soldier bled to death before he reached the wire.

A few days later Hathcock and Captain Land were working as a team from a hiding place in the middle of the Apache Woman's area of operations when they spotted an enemy patrol cutting out of the jungle down the side of a hill. The leader called a halt, walked off to the side, and squatted to urinate.

Hathcock brought up his scope.

"It's her!" he hissed. "The Apache."

She was about 300 yards away, an easy shot for Hathcock and his Model 70 Winchester 30-06. It was a tempting shot, but the snipers decided to try for the entire patrol by calling in mortar fire.

The Apache Woman panicked when the first HE (high-explosive) rounds landed. She bolted straight toward where the snipers waited in hiding. Hathcock centered his crosshairs. When she slowed to climb over a fallen tree, Long Tr'ang fired.

"We got the bitch!" he shouted. "She ain't gonna torture no more Marines."

Hathcock viewed his bloody job philosophically, reasoning that for every enemy soldier he killed out in "Indian Country," one more Marine or GI would be going home alive.

During his first tour of duty, White Feather amassed a total of 80 confirmed kills, including seven in one day.

This number did not include an entire NVA company he wiped out in Elephant Valley, nor did it include another 100 or so enemy soldiers he killed while operating alone or who fell to his rifle in areas where it was too dangerous for anyone to go up and witness the body. A confirmed kill had to be witnessed.

"I felt a lot better in the bush than behind the wire," he remarked. "Inside the wire are uncontrolled conditions. Rockets and mortars have got your name written all over them. I had control outside the wire."

The nearest the enemy came to collecting the bounty on Hathcock's head was when the North Vietnamese sent an entire sniper platoon to the vicinity of Hill 55. According to a wounded Vietnamese woman, the best of these snipers lived alone in the jungle. She said the sniper ate bugs and rats and caught cobras with his bare hands in order to give him the edge over Long Tr'ang.

The NVA "cobra" sniper picked off several Marines on Hill 55 before Hathcock and his spotter, Corporal Johnny Burke, managed to pick up a trail. It was late one afternoon, almost dark. The trail led from the low knolls below Hill 55 to a narrow water-filled canal. Downstream, broken grass and weeds told the Marines where the NVA sniper had crawled out of the water. They followed his trail until darkness and a monsoon rain forced them to burrow into a thicket and wait for daylight.

Dawn rose orange in a clear sky. The jungle started to steam. Hathcock and Burke trailed the cobra sniper until they came upon a tiny hand-dug cave in a small clearing. Suspecting a trap, the Marines avoided the cave. They circled around and made their way toward a ridge that overlooked the clearing. A narrow draw separated the cave and the ridge. Their quarry had sprinkled rice in the draw to attract birds as an early-warning signal.

Having his ruse discovered forced the cobra sniper to scramble down the other end of the ridge. The Marines heard him in the thick cover at the bottom of the draw opposite them.

The stalk began.

By mid-afternoon, the Marines had crawled to a saddle that overlooked both the cave and the draw. As they inched their way to a large tree from behind which they hoped to get a better view, a shot cracked. The bullet grazed Burke's hip and shot a hole through his canteen.

The enemy sniper crashed down the other side of the ridge.

"He's getting away!" Hathcock murmured.

They hurried to the top of the ridge, from which they saw a brush-choked gully sloping down to the forest. Everything was quiet. The Marines lay on their bellies behind cover, waiting and scanning the gully for movement.

They waited for an hour. The setting sun was behind Hathcock's and Burke's backs. It was shining down the gully.

Hathcock picked up a flash of sudden light in his scope while Burke looked through his field glasses.

"What do you make of it?" Hathcock asked.

"It's like somebody flashing a mirror or something."

Hathcock made a decision based mostly on instinct. "I'm going to chance a shot," he decided.

Ordinarily, Hathcock never *chanced* a shot. But these were not ordinary circumstances.

He took aim on the glimmer of reflected sunlight. The crack of the Model 70 rang down the gully.

"Holy shit!" Burke exclaimed as they carefully approached the dead sniper. "Nobody's gonna believe this."

Hathcock's bullet had gone through the cobra sniper's scope and entered his eye. That meant the dead sniper had had a bead on Long Tr'ang at the instant Hathcock squeezed off his round. The difference between life and death depended upon one thing—and Hathcock had got on the trigger first.

"Most of the snipers developed a much higher level of concentration and discipline than the average infantryman," said Captain Land. "The thing that set Carlos Hathcock off from the others was his extremely high level of concentration and total awareness of his surroundings."

Hathcock agreed. "You can't let anything else enter your mind except your job," he said. "You even have to turn off your sex drive."

Hathcock took to the field with one thought in mind: killing the enemy. Traveling light, he carried a bandoleer with 84 match-grade .30-06 full-metal jacket rounds of ammo in it, two canteens, a K-bar combat knife, a .45-caliber pistol, a compass, a map, and a few compact cans of C-ration peanut butter, jelly, cheese, and crackers.

If he had a partner with him, they took between them binoculars, a radio, and a high-powered spotting scope. As soon as he returned from one mission, he prepared his gear for the next, so that he was always ready to go on a moment's notice.

Corporal Johnny Burke was with him as spotter in Elephant Valley in March 1967 when an entire NVA company blundered onto Long Tr'ang's killing ground.

Just at daybreak, the two snipers waiting in their hiding spot were surprised by a terrific racket coming from their right, out of the sunrise. As they watched, about 80 men came clanking into view from the direction of the

Ca De Song River. They ventured onto a dike that crossed the rice paddies that stretched out for nearly 1,000 meters in front of where the Marines were hiding.

The NVA troops were obviously young replacements on their way up for their first taste of war. Their khaki uniforms were fresh and new. The officer in charge walked in front and made no attempt to hide his men or have them advance quietly.

They were about 700 yards away. It was flat shooting across the valley. There was no wind, no mist, no mirages to interfere with a sight picture.

"Take the rear," Hathcock advised Burke. "I'll take the officer out front."

Long Tr'ang started the slaughter by dropping the officer. Burke dropped a soldier in the rear. That threw the rest of the Vietnamese into a panic. They scrambled for cover into the stagnant rice pond behind the dike. The dike was only about two feet high.

The snipers dumped a couple of more NVA who foolishly stuck up their heads to peek around. That panicked the only other officer with the element. He jumped up and ran back toward the river. Hathcock shot him.

Leaderless, not knowing what else to do, the rest of the company lay beneath the hot sun in the scummy water. They had neither machine guns nor radios. They were pinned down. Every time one of them stuck up his head, he got zapped.

Hathcock radioed against sending in a reaction force, since that meant a battle in which Marines were bound to be killed.

"I think we can hold them right here as long as we want them," he said.

When night fell, artillery kept the skies over the trapped Vietnamese lit up with flares. Changing positions to keep the enemy from pinpointing their location, Hathcock and Burke took turns staying awake to prevent the unit from escaping.

At about ten o'clock the next morning, eight of the recruits charged the distant tree line where the shooting originated. It was 700 yards across water. One of them made it back to the dike. Another recruit fell dead on top of the dike.

There was a fog the second night. By then the original 80 NVA soldiers had been whittled down to about 65. The fog offered the survivors their last possible chance of escape, even with the flares constantly in the air. They did not stand a chance against the snipers' deadly-accurate fire.

Five NVA soldiers, driven reckless by the heat and the death around them, charged the tree line on the third morning, their rifles blazing. They didn't cover 100 yards before all were shot down.

Hathcock and Burke kept moving their positions, not only to keep the enemy confused but also to escape the stench of death. When the enemy fired volleys at the Marines' old position, Hathcock and Burke calmly picked off two or three of them from a new direction.

Things had been quiet for a long time when about an inch of a man's head showed itself. It was at least 650 yards away. Hathcock aimed and hit the head.

Burke stared in disbelief.

"Fascinating, isn't it?" Hathcock asked, grinning.

In an act of utter desperation, about ten of the beleaguered NVA soldiers made a break for the river late in the afternoon. All ten died. The fourth day and night were repeats of the first days. When the trapped soldiers tried to get away, they were cut down. When they charged, they were dropped.

By the fifth morning there were only five or six survivors out of the original 80 men. The survivors were sick and exhausted and near death themselves from exposure. The stench from the charnel field could be detected miles away.

Since Hathcock and Burke were growing gaunt and weary themselves and getting short on ammo, food, and water, they called in an artillery barrage on the few survivors. Only a supply sergeant survived this new threat. Frightened and weak from the ordeal, the supply sergeant told his captors that he did not know who or what was out there surrounding them. He would not believe that there were only two men until he heard the name Long Tr'ang. That convinced him.

"I knew only if somebody showed himself, even a bit, he died," said the lone survivor from the Elephant Valley massacre.

Carlos Hathcock had his own list of qualities he felt a good sniper must possess in order to both accomplish his job and to survive while doing it. There were seven of them. A sniper had to be a good shot. He had to be a woodsman. He must be stable enough emotionally not to get easily excited. He must be intelligent. He had to possess good powers of observation and an acute awareness of his surroundings. He should be able to navigate using a map and a compass. And, most of all, he had to have patience.

The greatest test of Long Tr'ang's patience was not the siege of Elephant Valley. The test came only days before he was due rotation back to the States. It was his last assignment.

"You're the only man who can pull it off," he was told. "The odds on your survival are slim to none. But if anyone can do this mission, you can."

A helicopter flew for more than an hour before it let him off in triple-canopy jungle in broad daylight. For all he knew, he could have been in Laos, Cambodia, or even North Vietnam. He was told it wasn't necessary for him to know. The chopper would pick him up after the job was completed.

He was provided a piece of map with no place names on it and a detailed briefing on his mission.

"You are to sneak into an NVA divisional headquarters and assassinate the commanding general," he was told.

Hathcock made his way alone through the forest until he reached the large clearing marked on his map. He hid in the tree line and studied his objective.

The divisional headquarters sat among palm trees at an old French plantation. The low, rambling main house with its wide windows was open and airy in the French colonial style. The general's office and living quarters lay to the right of the heavy doors, behind the great windows.

The headquarters was surrounded by an open field overgrown with dry reeds and grass about three feet tall. There was not a single tree, or even a shrub until one reached the house. There were machine-gun nests stuck at strategic locations among the palms. Everything was camouflaged against an air attack. The place swarmed with NVA soldiers. From his hiding place, Hathcock saw patrols leaving and returning as they swept the open fields and surrounding jungle.

The only way Hathcock could get close enough to the general to kill him was to crawl on his belly across the open field for at least 1,000 meters. He took a deep breath to get rid of the ice that suddenly clogged his veins.

He waited until after nightfall to start. Camouflaging himself, he removed the white feathers from his bush hat for the first time. He started across the field beneath a dark, moonless sky. Lying on one side with the Winchester rifle tucked against his chest, he propelled himself along an inch at a time with one leg and his free hand. He measured progress in feet per hour. He must not let the enemy see even the unnatural motion of one grass blade. With each movement forward, he stopped and used his feet to slowly prop up the grass he had just flattened.

He hadn't traveled fifty feet from the tree line before the first enemy patrol passed within twenty feet of him. He held his breath for a painfully long time, afraid the patrol would hear it. He was afraid they might smell him. But apparently the NVA felt secure here. They were laughing and talking among themselves like squirrel hunters in their own backyards.

Hathcock inched on like a worm, throughout the night and on into the next day. He did not eat or sleep.

A second patrol sweeping on line across the field almost walked over him shortly before sunset. One soldier passed on his left, another on his right, but they, too, felt secure and did not spot the sniper in the gathering darkness.

On the morning of the second day in the open field, Hathcock was drawing near his final firing point. Several times he chanced a glimpse at the house and through the windows saw the general working at his desk. He was an old man, short and fat.

In the afternoon Hathcock came face-to-face with a green bamboo viper, a snake whose bite meant quick and certain death. The snake's ruby eyes stared into Hathcock's face not eighteen inches away. The irony of having come this far only to be stopped by a serpent did not escape the Marine. It took willpower not to jump up and run.

Finally the snake flicked its black tongue and whisked silently away through the grass. It took Hathcock several minutes to settle his nerves.

That night the sniper reached a shallow gully he had spotted on aerial photographs given him. It was only about six inches deep, but it was wide enough for him to hide in. Come daylight, he would kill the general from the gully. Then he would use its scant cover to escape to the tree line.

He lay there through the night and waited, not sleeping and still not eating, only sipping sparingly from his one canteen.

Shortly after sunrise, he unfolded a handkerchief-size cloth and laid it down so the weapon's muzzle blast would not kick up dust when he fired and give away his position. He blinked through his scope at the general, who was getting dressed behind his windows. Aides and couriers were coming and going. Someone brought around a white sedan. The general was getting ready to go somewhere. That pleased Hathcock. He waited, knowing he would only get one shot.

The morning was cool with a very light, variable wind. The range was about 700 yards. When the general came outside with his aide to get into the car, Hathcock pulled his "bubble" around him so that nothing could disturb his concentration. He no longer felt hunger or thirst or weariness. Earlier he had felt chilly from the tension, but even that faded.

The general came out onto the little porch. He yawned mightily and stretched in the morning sunlight. Hathcock lowered his crosshairs to the officer's heart.

He was squeezing the trigger, caressing it, when the general's aide stepped in front of the target.

Hathcock eased gently off the trigger and waited for a clear shot.

As soon as the aide stepped aside, exposing the general's broad tunic, the rifle jarred against Hathcock's shoulder. The Marine brought the scope out of recoil and saw immediately that the general was down and not moving, which meant a heart shot. The other NVA officers and aides were scrambling for cover.

It had taken Hathcock three days to get into position for one shot—one kill; it took him ten minutes to scramble down the gully back to the tree line. An hour later he was again deep in the triple-canopy jungle, where a chopper darted in to pluck him out of danger.

Carlos Hathcock had added to the growing legend of Long Tr'ang.

Flyers written in Vietnamese containing Hathcock's picture continued to circulate in South Vietnam for months after the Marine rotated Stateside. But by May 1969, Long Tr'ang was back on Hill 55 as platoon sergeant of the 7th Marine Regiment's sniper platoon. He added thirteen more confirmed kills to his record before the amtrac on which he had hitched a ride ran into an ambush. What the best enemy snipers in Vietnam had failed to accomplish, a 500-pound box mine did. Long Tr'ang was out of action. He suffered "full thickness" burns over 43 percent of his body and underwent thirteen skin-graft operations back in the United States.

He had amassed some 300 kills, 93 of them confirmed. Afterward, partially crippled by his burns, he was diagnosed as suffering from multiple sclerosis. Still, it was the nature of the man with the white feather not to give up.

Until his forced medical retirement in 1979, Carlos Hathcock worked with Major Jim Land in forming and organizing the Marine Corps Scout/Sniper Instructor School at Quantico, Virginia, said to be the best sniper school in the world. He also helped in the creation of the M40A1 sniper rifle, perhaps the finest weapon in existence. Today, every Marine infantry battalion has a sniper unit attached to it.

When Hathcock retired medically from the Marine Corps on 20 April 1979, 55 days short of a full twenty years in service, his commanding officer presented him with a plaque that read: *There have been many Marines. And there have been many Marine marksmen. But there is only one Marine Sniper—Gunnery Sergeant Carlos N. Hathcock II. One shot—One kill.*

Gunny Hathcock died of his Vietnam injuries and disease in 1999.

CHAPTER TEN

U.S. Marine
Corporal Jim "Levi" Lever
Vietnam, 1967-68

Sniper missions in Vietnam weren't always about using scoped rifles. We were also scout observers. A tremendous advantage we had over the NVA and VC was the ability to extend firepower by the use of communications. We could either engage directly with rifles or we could radio in requests for artillery or air strikes. Call them our "long-range sniper weapons." So much the better if we could use them to do our work for us. We saved ammo and didn't give away our positions.

I worked with the 1st Reconnaissance Battalion out of Chu Lai, I Corps, where sniper teams were given unique call signs like Texas Pete and Air Hose. We were proud of our team names and accomplishments, sort of like being on a winning baseball team. Some clerk, I suppose, picked odd words off a list or out of a dictionary and suddenly, voilà, we had a moniker.

In the Hiep Duc area south of Da Nang past Antenna

Valley rose a piece of terrain called Recon Mountain. On the map it was marked simply as Hill 452, upon which Marines had established in force Blankenship Observation Post. The hill was extremely steep on all sides, and thickly foliaged except for the denuded top. The Song Phu Bong River took a bend around the base of the hill to provide a further barrier against ground attacks or penetrations.

Normal sniper recon operations meant exfiltrating from the hill with a patrol, breaking off from it somewhere with my spotter, Lance Corporal Lance Barton, and setting up in a hide that afforded good observation, good cover and concealment, and, even more importantly, an accessible escape route in case things got hot and we had to bug out.

Things often did get hot. The river was the main supply artery for NVA and VC in the area. The hills and paddies south and west of the mountain swarmed with enemy trying to get to Da Nang. Recon's job was to spot them, identify them, and interdict—or, as Major Keating the battalion XO put it, "kill 'em." Whenever we came up with something too far away to engage, or too big to take on, we reached for the PRC-10 backpack radio and rang up arty. The entire area was a free-fire zone.

One morning my spotter and I set up on Hill 344 overlooking a footpath in the valley. I had barely checked in with Pal Joey, our commo bunker's call sign, than movement on the trail caught my eye. I later made the following notations in my sniper's logbook: *Prominent trail. 3 VC sighted 1545 hrs 29 Jan 68 moving west to east. Equipment: packs, weapons, uniform black Papa Juliets and coolie hats.*

Papa Juliets were pajamas.

I plotted the target reference: *Tango Zulu 1861, direction 6325, coordinates 8811 3779.*

Tango Zulu was the angle in distance from the observer to the target: 1,861 meters, out of range for a rifle. The direction, 6,325 mils, was calculated on the 360 degrees of a compass divided into the mil scale of 6,400 mils for artillery usage. The direction 6,325 was therefore almost due north. The coordinates, eight digits, indicated location on the map within ten meters.

I rang up Quebec, our designated artillery battery.

Received 6 rounds high explosive in fire-for-effect from 175-millimeter gun battery, salutation Quebec. Excellent coverage of target. 1 probably KIA.

The arty strike evidently failed to scare off the bad guys. There was more activity forty-five minutes later.

We got a hootch with 6 VC and 2 NVA sighted 1630 hrs 29 Jan 68. Congregating around hootch. Equipment: weapons, and NVA have AK-47 rifles. Wearing gray utilities.

Back on the horn with Quebec.

Target reference, Tango Zulu 1863, direction 6250 mils, coordinates 8784 3828, fire for effect.

Always upon setting up a hide, I advised the artillery battery Fire Direction Center of my coordinates. The FDC therefore knew my exact position and could plot his fire accordingly from a known point without my giving myself away to any enemy radio interceptors operating in the area. Normally the cannon cockers did an excellent job. However, my log reflects disappointment in this particular mission.

Receive 6 rounds-in-effect from Quebec. Poor coverage of targets. No probable.

A couple of days later I noted a particularly successful mission: *Spotted probable VC bunker. Two VC sighted with weapons. . . . Enemy concentration approaching, 20 VC sighted with weapons and packs. . . .*

Received fire from salutation Quebec, 12 rounds mixed fuse, excellent coverage of target. Three confirmed KIAs with 10 high probable.

Subsequent patrols produced similar mixed results. On a patrol with call sign Lucky Lark, we spotted over 100 NVA moving east from southeast of Hill 344.

Enemy concentration. Came toward our position wearing gray utilities, web gear with mixed weapons. Lucky Lark called air strike and artillery. We were not given BDA [bomb damage assessment].

The valley was full of enemy soldiers. A following entry stated: *VC hootch sighted. Fifteen NVA moving in and out of hooch. . . . Received 6 rounds-in-effect, excellent coverage. Hooch destroyed. Secondary explosions. Two confirmed KIAs, 12 probable.*

That was an instance in which the NVA were entering the hooch and changing into black pj's to better blend with the civilian population. Obviously they were preparing to infiltrate the air base at Da Nang for a sapper attack. The secondary explosions were satchel charges going off.

Lucky Lark might have saved a lot of Marine lives that day.

CHAPTER ELEVEN

U.S. Marine
Corporal Jim "Levi" Lever
Vietnam, 1968

I never kept a running total of my confirmed kills. To me, it was like counting your winnings while the money was still on the poker table. I simply turned in my "confirmed and probable" report and forgot about it. In some of the other units, snipers had to almost go up and step on the body or watch it and not see it move for hours before the kill was "confirmed." Some got to the point where they brought back ears and said, "There's your confirmed kill."

The region south of Da Nang along the Song Khedienne River was an excellent hunting ground. In hunting there, or anywhere else for that matter, I used the lay of the land to my advantage. The best hide I ever used was in a blind next to a small stream that flowed into the river. Shooting from the north toward the south, I had an excellent point of view to the river's opposite bank. Plus, the river itself offered protection. Shooting across an obstacle like a river while maintaining good cover and concealment could be just as good, if not better [than], . . . shooting long-range across open ground. You either kept distance or an obstacle between yourself and the engagement area, a buffer zone against the enemy's reaction from the kill zone.

It was only 200 meters from my blind across the river to the opposite bank. My spotter and I worked the hide several times. You could do that if you were careful and didn't overdo it. We scored several kills from that location before we moved on.

I was still quite new in-country at the end of January 1968 when enemy activity began increasing all over our AO [area of operation]. Tet, the Vietnamese New Year, was approaching. Although no truce had yet been declared for the holidays, we expected one. Reports of VC and NVA moving in massive units toward the cities, prominent capitals, and military bases made everyone edgy.

Spotter Art Luna and I were burrowed into a hillside position on the afternoon of 31 January when Art espied a lone VC stopped next to a trail. "Levi, check this out."

I focused crosshairs on him and through the scope saw a young Vietnamese man in black pj's and a floppy boonie hat. He carried a satchel and an AK-47 and had paused to light a cigarette. It would be an easy shot, only about 500 meters, but the angle downhill was a steep thirty to forty degrees. The "high-low angle rule" applied.

Rifles are sighted in on a flat range. The bullet leaves the muzzle and flies downrange in a parabolic curve, dropping a given number of inches per hundred meters due to gravity, friction, and loss of energy. A rifle sighted in at 300 yards for point of aim/point of impact will shoot low at ranges beyond that and high at closer ranges. You have to adjust for it. For example, a .30-caliber round drops twelve feet at 1,000 meters. A 1,000-meter shot means you either adjust the scope or, if sighted in at 300 yards, set the crosshairs two and one half times the height of a man over the target.

Shooting at a down-angle or up-angle is more complex. Shot downhill, a bullet drops less than if shot level and quite a bit less than if it is shot uphill. The "high-low angle rule" states: Shooting down, aim low; shooting up, aim high.

Whispering to myself, "All right, I'm going to hit high," I dropped my crosshairs to the guy's nuts and squeezed off a round.

The bullet punched through the foliage two feet above his head. He jumped and took off like a rabbit. He was gone, *gone,* by the time I worked the bolt for a second attempt.

That night, the enemy launched surprise attacks all over South Vietnam. The biggest enemy offensive of the war began, Tet, 1968. Out on Hill 452, Blankenship Observation Post, we thought the war had simply intensified in our area. We didn't know about the fighting in Hue and Saigon.

Sappers struck about midnight, moving in on us through the wire without a sound until their satchel explosions began going off. After that, the hill lit up with tracers and the white-hot strobes of mortar and artillery rounds detonating. The firefight raged until Spooky showed up.

Spooky—sometimes called "Puff the Magic Dragon"—was a C-130 gunship armed with a 105mm howitzer, 20mm Vulcan cannon, and 7.62 miniguns. A formidable air battleship that orbited in the darkness overhead and unleashed all its fury against the enemy surrounding and attacking the outpost. Solid undulating streams of red fire lashed out of the sky and whipped back and forth, chewing up everything in its path and leaving a thick haze of smoke and dust in its wake, like a giant tiller ripping up a garden.

I hugged the ground, terrified, even though I knew it wasn't shooting at me. *Just imagine,* I thought to myself, *imagine how those gooks out there bearing the brunt of such destruction must feel. Imagine* us *if they had a weapon like that.*

Finally, Spooky banked off and flew away. Silence, total silence, settled over the battlefield. No shooting, no yelling, no sounds except the hissing of a few fires. The last parachute flare sizzled out of the sky, allowing darkness to descend once again. The attack had been broken.

Security patrols were sent out at dawn to sneak and peek. My observer, Mark Doss, and I went out to see if we might find some action. I chose as my weapon a shotgun loaded with double-aught buck, since I expected any shooting would have to be done at close range.

"I gotta take a whiz," Doss said, moving over next to a tree to wet it down.

I waited for him.

I heard a sudden *pop!* I felt a stiff jolt, like someone had stumbled into me. Then the pain, excruciating pain, burning like molten steel thrust into the veins and capillaries of my left thigh. The sniper's round had struck a CS tear gas grenade I carried, shattering it. Fragments ripped into my flesh. Chemicals in CS were an extreme irritant on mucous membrane and open wounds.

"Over there!" Doss yelled, opening up at the same time with his M14.

I pumped my shotgun, blasting away until it was

empty. The sniper was less than fifty yards away, dumb bastard. We shredded him with bullets and double-aught. His entire body when it hit the ground was red-speckled with bloody wounds.

I caught a medevac chopper to Da Nang. It stopped several times on the way in, like a bus ride, to pick up other wounded from other firebases. I knew by the activity at Charlie Med, the thumping of helicopters coming and going, that something big was going on. A lot of fighting. Wounded Marines were literally stacked up for triage. As doctors worked on a leatherneck my medevac picked up from Hill 55, I heard one of them comment, "They got VC bodies piled up on a bridge like cordwood. They got into Dog Patch. Our guys are still trying to root them out."

Dog Patch was a slum on the outskirts of Da Nang infested with VC and VC sympathizers.

The next morning, the walking wounded were armed and placed on guard duty to ward off any attack against the hospital. I convalesced wearing blue hospital pajamas and carrying an M14. After a few days, I returned to the teams.

On 5 March, my old recon team, call sign Texas Pete, was hit. The team leader, my friend Lieutenant Pat McClary, lost his arm and was evacuated from Vietnam. I never learned the details of the action, but one of the recon members, Private First Class Ralph Johnson, received a Medal of Honor for throwing himself on a grenade.

We were briefed to be on the lookout for "a big blond guy" traveling and fighting with the enemy. Rumor had it that he was a Russian—or that he might even be an American deserter. Every sniper in I Corps longed to get the sonofabitch in his crosshairs.

Major Keating, the Recon Battalion XO, went out with one of the teams, then split off with me to act as spotter while we covered a cart trail used as an enemy supply route. It was a direct offshoot of the Ho Chi Minh Trail that ran past just across the Laotian border. I located a hide on the other side of a muddy stream where I could observe a goodly distance down the trail.

It didn't take long before we had activity. A column of NVA spaced out well and moving like veterans. I scanned for the blond guy, not seeing him. Instead, I detected a high-ranking officer. He wore gray utilities and carried a side-arm instead of a rifle. They stopped in a clearing. Two or three of the soldiers approached him and bowed. I would take him in compensation if I couldn't get the blond man.

I made a good clean hit. A few days later a sniper in 3d Platoon shot the Caucasian. He turned out to be a former French Legionnaire who had been with the VC since the 1950's.

Spotter Mark Doss and I were working with a recon team in the Phu Bui area near Phu Loc and were moving into "harbor" position near nightfall when I began hearing movement in the surrounding forest. *Damn,* I thought, *these guys are making a lot of noise for a small element.*

I glanced at Doss, who had frozen in place. Then I noticed that the rest of my team had also gone to ground, their eyes bulging with sudden fear. My heart went on double-time when I caught a glimpse of men moving about in the trees nearby, their forms diffused by darkening shadow but nonetheless recognizable as NVA soldiers. I dropped instantly into hiding. I don't think I moved as much as a little finger for the next several hours. I was almost afraid to breathe.

An entire company of NVA had stumbled into our immediate AO and was also getting ready to bed down for the night. They were all around us, shuffling about and spreading out ground mats and making beds for themselves out of fronds and springy tree branches. It was so dark, however, by the time they got settled in that we could have slept literally side by side and not noticed each other. Fortunately, the gomers were disciplined troops and built no fires or turned on any lights.

That was the longest night of my life. None of us in the recon team so much as closed an eye. Some of the gooks slept so near I heard them snoring. Occasionally my heart skipped beats when one of the enemy soldiers got up and walked off a few paces to take a leak. I thought they might step on one of us.

The NVA company stirred before dawn, saddled up, and moved out like seasoned troops. By daylight they seemed to have all gone. We were moving out, too, when I saw a gook rushing back down the trail toward us. He was still about 200 meters away. Had he lost or forgotten something? He would notice us in another moment.

I dropped him in his tracks. We were in triple-canopy jungle, which covered our movements as we cleared the area before the NVA could come back and find us. Although I never knew how many confirmed kills I made, I took the shoots whenever I had the chance. What mattered to me was that the shots I made saved Marine lives. Those were the shots that really counted.

CHAPTER TWELVE

U.S. Marine Corporal Gary Reiter
Vietnam, 1966

Toward the end of April 1966, I received word to report to Headquarters Company. Phu Bai at the time was still a 4th Marine tent city in-country, but Seabees were starting to construct semipermanent structures. Hardbacks or plywood facings with canvas covers and screened-in windows to keep out some of the mosquitoes. I wended my way through the OD-green slum ville until I found the designated tent. I took a deep breath, stepped smartly inside and snapped to attention.

A captain and a staff sergeant, lean men with somber faces, sat behind a field table with a service jacket opened before them. Mine? I must have really fucked up somewhere big time. For the life of me I couldn't figure out which of my minor transgressions they might have found out about.

The captain half-smiled, like he could read my mind. Uh-oh. I was in for it.

"At ease, Corporal," he said.

I went to a modified parade rest. How was I supposed to relax with these two looking at me like I had swallowed the colonel's canary or something? They introduced themselves as Captain Russell and Staff Sergeant Side. Criminal investigators?

"Yes, sir." Puzzled.

The sergeant asked me several questions about my combat experiences since I arrived in Vietnam. What did they expect me to say? I landed at Red Beach in March. Sometime within the eight days of sailing from Okinawa to Vietnam on APA-248 (Attack Transport), I was designated as an assistant gunner for a 106mm recoilless rifle and driver for the little mule vehicle that carried the big gun around. Back home in Washington state, I had had fifteen different vehicular accidents before I turned eighteen and enlisted in the Marine Corps. Now, here my Marines issued me a federal driver's license.

"God, this is really cool. Plus, I got this mule to pack my stuff around in."

I convoyed with the mule up to Phu Bai, where I promptly discovered there wasn't much use for a 106 driver. I found myself tossed into regular grunt duty with a line company. Day patrols and night ambushes in the bush.

"Do you have any reservations about fighting the enemy?" Sergeant Side asked.

Still puzzled, I assured him I had none.

Forty minutes more of rapid-fire questions followed.

"Would you like a chance to kill more gooks?"

"Could you pull the trigger while looking into his eyes?"

"Would you like a little revenge for some of your fallen Marines?"

They took notes and from time to time whispered to

each other. They finally stopped talking and asking questions. I grew even more uneasy as they stared at me.

Finally, to my surprise, Captain Russell asked, "How would you like to be a sniper?"

I was immediately transferred to the Scout Sniper Platoon, issued a Winchester Model 70 .30-06 rifle with an eight-power Unertl scope, and sent to sniper school for two weeks, where I learned to love the recoil of the Winchester into my bruised shoulder.

Each shooter was allowed to choose and practice with ammunition of his choice. I selected a heavy 180-grain silver-tipped round that the platoon sergeant ordered from Okinawa or somewhere. These babies made quite an impact. I carried them in a leather bandoleer worn underneath my utility jacket.

It was still early in the sniper program in Vietnam and there were only seven shooters in Scout Sniper Platoon. Hardly any of the unit commanders knew what to do with us. We each were provided with a two-page typed document that commanders could use as a guide in deploying us for action. Some COs pored over the papers and shrugged. Others growled, "I don't need to read this shit." That was why they were always trying to get us to climb trees, like they had seen Japanese do in World War II movies. Didn't they also see how those Japanese were always getting shot out of those trees?

As a result, most snipers ended up doing foxhole and night-ambush duty with the grunts. I found it decidedly uncool—and a little impractical—sitting in a hole at night with a bolt-action rifle and scope. We snipers were always looking for something to do within the parameters of our skills.

R. J. Johnson and I partnered occasionally and were always ready to volunteer. He was a tall, slow-talking, anecdotal kind of typical Texan who loved open country and telling stories about his home state. I heard a lot of his stories when we were sent to Hue for a couple of weeks to guard a rice shipment in a building on the edge of the Perfume River. It sat right across from the Citadel where gooks, most of them undoubtedly VC, were always coming and going. Naturally we weren't allowed to pop any of them because the Citadel was off limits and protected. The ancient fortress later played a bloody role in the 1968 Tet Offensive.

A month passed and I still hadn't seen any business. Third Battalion Recon requested a sniper for a snoop-and-poop on the Ho Chi Minh Trail along the Laotian border. I was duly impressed with these guys. Over in my recon, we didn't even have camouflage face paint. We scorched pieces of sandbags and used the ash to blacken our faces. It was tough on the skin, but it worked.

Third Recon, on the other hand, had *everything*. Supply opened its arsenal and told me to select what I wanted from an array of grenades, pistols, detonation cord, C4 plastic explosives. There were carbines and Thompson submachine guns, .45s and old metal-stock grease guns from World War II. I strapped on a .45 Colt pistol and inserted into the bush with my Winchester strapped to my pack and a grease gun hanging on a strap around my neck. I was prepared for action.

A pair of Hueys lifted seven of us out of base camp and choppered out over enemy country, a green expanse of jungle-covered hills along the border. After several false insertions to confuse any bad guys who might be watching—they wouldn't know on which insertion we unassed—we bailed out on the fourth. It was my first experience with elephant grass. The first two Marines ahead of me leaped out of the bird while it hovered and promptly disappeared in grass taller than they. I followed, dropping like a rock and hitting the ground so hard I went to my knees. I couldn't see shit through the grass, even when I regained my feet. An ocean of razor-edged green closed around me, almost blotting out the morning sun.

For the next two or three days we humped up and down mountains so steep that when we slept for a few designated minutes we had to straddle trees to keep from rolling off the earth. There was no talking. All communications began and ended with sign language as we observed enemy movements on the Ho Chi Minh, taking notes and making sketches. I couldn't shoot even when we spotted targets because the report of the rifle would give us away and cast us into deep doo-doo.

I made one more mission before I said to myself, *This is no place for a sniper. There ain't no rifle action here.* Even though the line commanders didn't know how to use us, I had a better opportunity of burning a silver-tipped round with them than sneaking around in the woods trying to avoid contact. I was a sniper who had never made a kill.

R. J. Johnson and myself, along with the partners Ed Kugler and Mike Hutchison, were reassigned to 3d Battalion, where once again we ended up patrolling and hiding in foxholes with our bolt-action long guns. One afternoon the four of us were in transient with a daylight sweeping force, moving along a well-worn path bordered by tall trees and undergrowth, ditty-bopping along, clanking and rattling like a tank, announcing to every gook in the AO that the by-God badass U.S. Marines were on the prod. We snipers were staggered in location throughout the column.

Suddenly, heavy fire ruptured from the right side of the trail, hammering hard in a solid fusillade. An ambush, but one prematurely sprung. Muzzle flashes sparked all through the trees. Marines dived and rolled for cover. I found myself belly-down between two trees next to R.J. A hail of automatic weapons fire clipped small branches and showered us with a green snow storm of leaves.

Fierce return fire broke the ambush. The firefight quickly disintegrated into little pockets of yelling and movement. Foolishly, I stood up next to my tree to take a look around and maybe get off a shot. A scoped rifle is almost worthless at such close range.

A bullet meant for my head cracked into a branch a couple of inches away. Marines always said you never heard the one that got you, so I obviously wasn't "got." Only the limitation of gravity prevented my hitting the ground faster than I did.

R.J. chuckled when he saw I wasn't hit. "That was slick, Reiter. Slick."

"And smart too."

I sighted through my scope to where I thought the shot came from the base of a tree less than 100 yards away. I panned across the underbrush, seeing nothing but a maze of green overcoated with a misty veil of gun smoke. I glimpsed movement at the base of the tree. I took a second look and studied it more closely. The immediate chaos seemed to fade into a distant dull roar as I directed my entire concentration at that single tree.

The widening of the trail there provided me a longer, relatively open field of fire. After a moment, clear and sharp through the scope, I detected a flash of a black-clad arm and part of a shoulder. I drew in a deep breath to steady my nerves and went into the sniper's "co-

coon." I waited with surprising calm, marveling at how my heart returned to almost its normal rhythm.

The gook's bare head popped out from around the tree trunk. Hadn't he ever heard that curiosity killed the cat? It was a young smooth face with short black hair topping it. Dark eyes gazed in my direction, almost as though we were standing looking at each other face-to-face. Maybe he thought he had shot me and was checking.

I recalled what we had been told in sniper school: how there was a big difference between shooting at running, dodging shadows in the heat of a firefight, shooting at anonymous targets, and deliberately, coldly selecting a man for extermination—looking him directly in the eyes when you squeezed the trigger. A lot of guys, we were told, couldn't do it when it came to that point.

The gook stretched his neck a little farther out, like he had trouble seeing what was going on. At this close range, I froze my crosshairs on his chin. I was zeroed in for 200 meters, which meant I had to shoot low at one hundred. I dropped the hairs to his neck, but I could still look into his eyes hovering at the top round of the scope. I took a last look into his eyes. He was nothing but a target now. I squeezed.

The rifle cracked and the butt jarred into my shoulder. The 180-grain silver-tipped bullet eradicated his face. When I pulled down out of recoil, nothing remained through the scope except an ephemeral pink mist where the guy's face used to be.

Call it a body count, a first kill entry for my sniper's log.

CHAPTER THIRTEEN

U.S. Marine
Lance Corporal Tom "Moose" Ferran
Vietnam, 1967

"Awright, ladies, listen up," the sergeant major shouted. "We ain't got enough deuce gear to go around yet, but be patient." Combat 782 gear, better known as deuce gear: pack, harness, helmet, etc. "Operation Rio Bravo is going on. There'll be plenty of gear coming back from the field. The previous owners won't need it anymore."

I didn't like the sound of that. But, sure enough, the dead and wounded began arriving. Their gear was stripped off and issued to replacements. Some of it was crusted with blood. I had already heard that the roads to hell were paved with the bones and good intentions of second lieutenants and the Marines who followed them.

I was nonetheless anxious to get on with it and get out to my unit with 1st Battalion, 7th Marine Regiment. "Cool your heels, Moose," the sergeant major said, sizing up my six-six frame. "It's going to be a long war. You'll get your chance soon enough."

I was big enough all right to be a moose. The name stuck. Upon graduation from Brooklyn's St. John's Prep, I had been voted the "most rugged" on the football team. As a tackle, I ate up quarterbacks. When I enlisted in the Marine Corps, I brought the big, bad, tough persona with me. Perhaps it was because of that that I volunteered for sniper training once I reached Vietnam. I had qualified "Expert" on the range. Besides, being a sniper seemed preferable over humping the boonies with the grunts—endless combat patrols, sweeps, search-and-destroys, night ambushes, hole watches. What had I got myself into?

"Numb nuts, you're jumping out of the frying pan into the fire," my platoon sergeant warned.

"At least I won't be having some dumb second lieutenant telling me to charge a hill."

Captain Jim Land and Sergeant Carlos Hathcock were running the Division Scout Sniper School on Hill 55. It was a two-week school at the time. Mostly it was shooting, shooting, shooting. After which, basically, we were issued new M40 sniper rifles—Remington Model 700s with heavy barrels and Redfield 3x9X variable "Accu-Range" scopes—and told to go out and kill something. Patience, hell.

My first teammate was a young, hard-charging Marine named Ed Pool. We were sent together back to the 7th Marines at Chu Lai, Mike Company of the 3/7. Mike Company was having a bit of a problem with an enemy sniper. This guy had brass ones the size of basketballs. He boldly moved around in the open below Mike's hill, but always out beyond the 1,000-meter range where the Marines couldn't reach him with their rifles. He dug his spider holes and sniper positions within full view of the Marine perimeter, then settled in with his rifle and scope to pick off anyone within the firebase who tried to move about. Even mortars had been ineffective against him. He heard the pneumatic *pop!* as they were fired, saw the rounds coming at him in flight, and simply moved out of the way.

The Marine sniper program was still new in Vietnam. This guy had not yet encountered a counter sniper.

Ed Pool and I waited for him. Soon he showed up, digging his hole in a tree line about 1,300 meters away from the top of Mike's hill. The maximum dope I had on my rifle was for 1,100 meters. The "come up" or the "hold over" was based on logarithmic mathematics, on the aerodynamics of a bullet in flight not making a perfect parabolic curve. The farther the range, the more quickly it dropped at the far end due to its expending energy and due to gravity and air resistance. Since I knew the "come up" from 300 meters to 600, and from 600 to 1,000, I simply extrapolated the triangular formula from 1,100 to 1,300.

Ed turned his spotting scope a quarter-turn out of focus to allow him to pick up the bullet's vapor trail and call the shot. In the prone, I rested the rifle and brought the scope to my eye. I discovered I was sweating as I took up trigger slack. I held my breath and settled the crosshairs onto what I thought might be the proper elevation above the target's head. I squeezed off the round.

"You're low and to the left," Ed corrected. "Come up five and right five."

My first shot after sniper school was a miss. I worked the bolt. The target had wheeled around to face the hill when the first bullet struck near him. I fired again. My second shot after sniper school slammed him backwards.

I heard cheering. In my concentration, I hadn't noticed a large group of Marines gathering to watch events unfold and to applaud when the company's nemesis finally got his due. A squad was dispatched to drag back the body, thereby coining a new infantry term: *Fetch!* It was great sport in a black humor sort of way.

I momentarily rejoiced in my first kill, flattered by applause from the grunts. However, the enormity of what I had done slammed down on me in the privacy of my pup tent. I had killed a fellow human being. I had looked directly at him, and then I destroyed him as he turned to look at me. That made the war very personal and, sometimes, guilt-ridden because of my Catholic-school upbringing. I didn't know if I was cut out for this new work or not. I suppose, as it turned out, I was.

There was no rest in Vietnam, for the weary or anyone else. During Operation DeSoto, a joint Army-Marine effort, Mike Company worked the Duc Pho area against Vietcong guerrilla forces. One afternoon, Ed Pool and I were in a hide when we identified a squad of VC moving in a tactical patrol formation across a rice field. I crosshaired the last man in the patrol, intending to start there and work forward. The sound of a rifle shot from 700 meters, indistinct and muffled, could sometimes go unnoticed, as did the falling of the last man in a formation.

I dropped the last man. Then the man in front of him. I came right up the line like that, firing as rapidly as I could chamber fresh rounds, aim, and fire. A third man. A fourth. By the time the fifth man fell, the survivors had gathered their senses enough to flee for the nearest tree line. They went to ground, undoubtedly trembling with fear at the unseen bolts of deadly lightning out of nowhere.

We weren't finished with them yet. I radioed for a fire mission, requesting 25-meter VT, variable time-fused 105 howitzer rounds in air bursts. The first high explosive blossomed directly over the hiding VC, killing all those who remained.

"Cease fire! Cease fire! Mission accomplished," I radioed.

"Say again. Did you say 'Cease fire'? Over."

"I say again: Cease fire. Round on target. Thanks. Out."

It was likely the only time the artillery battery destroyed a target with a one-round fire mission. I could almost see the puzzled looks on the gunners' faces.

A patrol later confirmed seventeen kills. It made me realize that the best sniper rifle was in fact the 105mm howitzer. One shot—a dozen kills.

After a month in the field running daily combat operations and search-and-destroy missions, Pool and I received orders to report to General LaHue at 7th Marine headquarters. Both of us blanched. There must be some kind of dire emergency. That was the only way you got out of an operation, short of being wounded or going back in a body bag.

The monsoons had started and Vietnam was being pummeled by daily heavy rains. Dark gray cloud cover shrouded the tops of hills and mountains, and wet fog seeped through valleys and clung to stream courses. Since aircraft were grounded most of the time, making resupply difficult, body bags full of Marines stacked up in the battalion's rear areas, awaiting transportation out, and there was a blood drive going on because med choppers couldn't get in often enough.

When the weather finally broke, Sikorsky CH-34 helicopters lined up on the makeshift airstrip at battalion. Ed and I caught a bird already loaded with eight Marine bodies in bags. Pool crawled inside next to the bodies and prepared to get a little shut-eye during the flight. The pilot calculating weight and balance looked me over.

"How much do you weigh with all your gear?" he asked.

"Sir, about three hundred pounds with everything."

He was calculating gross payload down to the last pound. "Okay. Sit at the edge of the door. If we can't get off the ground, I'll give you the word to jump out."

The big radial engine wound up. The bird vibrated as the four rotor blades engaged and reached takeoff rpm. It rested up to its wheel hubs in mud. For a minute it appeared it wouldn't be able to shake loose from the ground's grip.

Then, slowly, it lifted, hovered and drifted slowly forward above the ground. I got the word to stay aboard as it began to climb. Pool wrapped himself around his knees and dozed off next to the body bags. The door gunner crossed his arms, leaned over his pintled M60 machine gun, and closed his eyes.

Apprehensive over why we were being summoned to headquarters, uncomfortable with flying in such marginal weather in an overloaded bird, I remained alert and vigilant sitting in the open doorway. The chopper entered soup so dense I saw nothing outside except the gray insides of clouds. I knew other aircraft were also flying in this stuff; that also made me nervous.

Staring idly out the doorway, I suddenly became aware of a dark shadow underneath. It moved ominously into clearer view, a hulking large shadow. It was rather like floating on an air mattress in the ocean and spotting a shark directly underneath.

Alarmed, I woke the door gunner and pointed. His eyes bulged and he did a double take before he screamed hysterically into the boom microphone mounted to his helmet. The pilot responded with a sharp left bank, thereby averting a midair collision with another CH-34. The unexpected maneuver threw me back inside the aircraft. I would probably have been tossed out into space had the pilot decided to bank right.

Had I been asleep like everyone else, the other chopper's blades would have chewed into our belly. I could almost have been jealous of the eight fallen Marines in their bags; they wouldn't have been called upon to die again.

I was still shaken when we reached the regimental command post on Hill 55 south of Da Nang. Gunnery Sergeant Wilson greeted us. "You guys stand by. You're going to see the general tomorrow."

"What's this all about?" I asked.

The gunny smiled. "The general wants to touchy-feely real Marine snipers."

He explained how Pool's name and mine kept showing up on the morning report as we generated a body count. The general was going to decorate us. Was that all it was? I let out a sigh of relief.

"Be in proper uniform," the gunny concluded.

Right. All I had were the jungle utilities I wore in. When we finally reached Da Nang, the general's adjutant came to us.

"The general had intended to give you guys Bronze Stars, but we're out. The last Bronze Star went to the postal officer for his end-of-tour award. So he's going to give you combat promotions. The general wants to know if that's all right with you guys."

What were we going to say?

There was a little ceremony and the general wanted a photograph of himself posing with snipers. Somebody handed me an M40 sniper's rifle as a prop. The general was about five-foot-four, so I towered over him by a foot. The photographer told me to squat down because the general didn't like that. He took the photograph, the general shook our hands, Pool and I went back into the field.

I was assigned a new teammate, a Marine named John Wendling—"Windy" for short. He and I worked as well together as Pool and I had. Early in our partnership, we set up on a brushy hillside, good vantage point over a vast tract of terrain. We lay in hiding all day. Nothing happened.

Toward nightfall, as the light was seeping out of the sky, five men dressed in black appeared walking across a rice paddy. It was the dry season and the field contained only a few isolated puddles of water. These guys should have stayed in the trees. They were probably lazy and wanted to take the shortest route between two points.

I waited until they were near the middle of the very large open field. I engaged the point man first. I fired. As my rifle came out of recoil, I saw that I had scored a direct hit. The punch of the heavy bullet actually lifted the guy off the ground.

I swung back to the tail man and knocked him down before the others went to ground behind the dike. Now it became a waiting game. A sniper had to have patience.

About ten minutes passed before a head popped up. I expected it. It was like squirrel hunting. All you had to do was sit still and wait long enough and the squirrels started looking out again to see what was going on.

I fingered the trigger, settled the crosshairs on the head, and fired.

"You're low. You hit the paddy dike," Windy said, watching through his spotting scope.

My scope was set for 600 meters, but the zero could change from banging the rifle about. I came up a click on the scope, about six inches at that range.

Shortly, another head shot up. His head exploded in a crimson mist, like a watermelon. We had now narrowed the number of the patrol to only two.

The waiting game continued. Another head raised just at sunset. I nailed him. That left one.

The remaining gook was smart enough to stay down until after nightfall. He escaped—but four out of five wasn't bad.

The troops of Charlie Company, 1st Battalion, 26th Marine Regiment, were totally demoralized. All because of an NVA sniper known as Zorro. Grunts didn't mind so much going out on combat patrols, running night ambushes, and conducting normal missions. That was their job. However, the prospect of getting their heads blown off from afar by a sniper whom you could not engage, whom you never even saw, definitely zapped morale. Zorro had already killed a number of Marines, eight of them out of one company.

The 26th Marines occupied the fire base at Khe Sanh. My spotter, John Wendling, and I were jerked out of the field with the 7th Marines and sent to Khe Sanh for a briefing. Snipers from all over I Corps were present when we arrived. Something big was up.

"We're bringing in sniper teams from all over the area," confirmed the briefing officer, a captain from S-2 Intelligence. "We're using our own regimental teams—plus any others we can beg, borrow, or steal from other regiments—and we're massing them in this area."

He pointed at a large map of Khe Sanh as he spoke.

"We're after one NVA sniper. He's bad news. The sonofabitch has been killing our Marines and we want him taken out."

He passed around a dossier on the intended target, a master sniper with the rank of lieutenant in the North Vietnamese Army. An all-around type guy who also ran the propaganda machine in northern I Corps and was officer in charge of the land-mine warfare unit.

"After you familiarize yourselves with his file," the captain resumed, "you'll be assigned to units and operational areas to hunt down this guy. The team that gets him will be given a week's paid R & R to your choice of ports of call." He grinned and offered a further incentive. "Plus, the shooter's rifle will go to the Marine who kills him."

It was going to be an interesting hunt. Snipers fight snipers—and snipers fear other snipers. Every Marine sniper in Vietnam had a bounty placed on his head equal to a month's pay for an NVA soldier. A fellow sniper and my friend, Eddie Ernest, fell prey to an enemy sniper. He was the first of us killed in Vietnam when the enemy shooter selected him out of an element because he carried a long rifle. A sniper was an automatic priority target. I always felt like a walking bull's-eye. It made you cautious, wily.

There were three antisniper weapons of choice: bombs, artillery or mortar rounds, another sniper. Zorro first had to be found. That required knowledge and savvy, a man on the ground with a rifle.

Zorro wasn't aiming for bodies when he shot. He was making a statement by picking an impact area between the top of the target's flak jacket and the bottom of his helmet, a target of about six inches. The masked Zorro of television fame carved the *Z* on his opponents; *this* Zorro made his mark via a bullet through the skull.

I interviewed Marine squads who had suffered casualties to Zorro, trying to get a handle on the guy and his one-man operation.

"How much time was involved," I asked them, "between the crack of the bullet, impact on target, and the pop of the rifle?"

From their responses, I calculated an average of two seconds, which put the shooter out at about 700 to 800 meters. This guy was good. Marines were apprehensive of leaving their perimeter out of fear of this guy; I felt a quickening of my own heart at the thought of going up against him one on one.

Not only was he obviously more experienced than I, and a more skilled shooter, he was also an officer. I was a lance corporal. Did that make him smarter, shrewder, more cunning and calculating? It seemed he had other advantages as well. In fact, it seemed like he had *all* the advantages.

I was operating in his backyard. He knew the terrain. I didn't, as this was my first time in the Khe Sanh AO. He knew and was comfortable with the villages and local people. A fish in the sea. I was the new kid on the block, a stranger from a foreign land.

Sniper teams were splayed out all over the map to hunt for Zorro. Most of us held a tremendous respect for this lethal phantom—but he still had to die. Windy and I were initially assigned to a watchtower that overlooked Charlie Company's area of responsibility; Charlie had been most hardest hit. The tower gave me time to study the map and relate it to the surrounding terrain.

On the second day, a Marine patrol encountered a superior NVA unit. The sniper wasn't involved, but the

Marines were taking a pounding. They called the tower for air support, as they were out of artillery range.

There were two radios in the tower, one set to the company and battalion net, the other to the dedicated air support channel. I had never called for air, but these guys out there needed help fast. I requested a fire mission on the air freq. Air knew I was the tower and where I was located because of the tower call sign.

"Roger," replied a raspy voice. "There will be a bird in your vicinity in two or three minutes."

Three minutes later, sure enough, an F4 startled hell out of me by zooming so low over the tower, outrunning the roar of his own jets, that it shook like a leaf. He broke and pulled up, trailing exhaust.

"Okay, Marine, where am I?" he asked.

"Sir, you are at my twelve o'clock."

"First of all, don't call me sir. Now, where am I? I'm not at your twelve o'clock because I'm moving."

"Yes, sir. You're still at my twelve o'clock."

"Okay, son, calm down. Where are you in relation to me? In other words, where off my wing?"

I was still rattled. "I see, sir. I'm at your nine o'clock."

"Thank you," he responded, realizing I was new at this. He began walking me through the fire mission.

"Give me the azimuth and the grid to the Marines out there."

I settled down and fed him the information. He banked, climbed into the clouds, and roared back over the tower in the direction of the azimuth I provided.

"Is this the location?" he asked.

"Roger," I acceded, eyeballing through my binoculars.

He had the Marines in sight. I relayed to him where

they wanted the ordnance. He made another pass and dumped right on target. Smoke and dust rose out of the hills in a boiling cloud. The NVA broke contact.

That was the only action Windy and I saw from the tower. In the meantime Zorro was still hunting, still leaving his telltale bullets in the head. We finally concluded that we should split up. Windy would stay with the tower, observing, while I accompanied fire teams or patrols into Zorro's hunting ground.

I studied maps and pinpointed the locations where Zorro had previously struck, trying to predict where he would hit next. Trying to think like him. To *outthink* him. Where were his best fields of fire? Where would he stalk a Marine patrol sent out as bait? Where would he hide? Then I went out with elements and dropped off to set up in those likely spots to wait for him to reveal himself.

My knees were knocking, as I was definitely encountering a serious fear factor. I couldn't help thinking that he was hunting *me* while I was hunting *him*. Playing hide-and-seek out there in the bush, with violent death the outcome for one of us. I kept feeling his crosshairs on me.

Zorro moved out of Charlie Company's AO and began operating in a new sector. I hunted and stalked but to no avail.

Not every saga ends in the dramatic Hollywood shoot-out at the O.K. Corral. Real life simply does not follow a script. While Wyatt Earp—me—was sneaking and peeking elsewhere, Zorro took a last shot. He killed yet another Marine, but he was careless enough to let himself be seen.

Marines closed in and discovered a spider hole. They opened up with automatic weapons in a vengeful fury, seeking payback for the weeks of terror he had inflicted upon them. More than a hundred rounds literally ripped him apart and destroyed the rifle that we snipers had coveted as an ultimate trophy. I thought it was an ignoble death not befitting his status. Sniper versus sniper would have been more appropriate.

Nonetheless, I breathed a sigh of relief. I had feared he would get me before I got him, a feeling I later learned I shared with every other Marine sniper out in the field during those days we stalked Zorro from the North Vietnamese Army. All I knew was that I didn't want to die as he did.

Windy and I ended up with Delta Company 1/7 working the aptly named Arizona Territory south of Hill 55. Delta moved out in a massive on-line sweep. As afternoon shadows lengthened, a six-man detail led by Lieutenant Gagnon, and including Windy and me, was dispatched to conduct a secret mission into a nearby village to either snatch the village chief, the local coordinator for guerrilla and NVA operations, or take him out with a long-range shot. We crawled out of the immediate area on our bellies to avoid being observed, then held up alongside the banks of a narrow river to wait for darkness. Unknown to us at the time, we were burrowed in alongside a main NVA supply route.

Delta diverted attention away from the village by sweeping away from it to clear a couple of pockets of resistance. Then it withdrew into a perimeter for the night while the hidden snatch team waited in thick brush on the near side of the river.

Near dusk, the metallic sound of a rifle bolt being seated startled me. I recognized it as an M14 rifle used by Marines and friendly ARVN units. It came from somewhere across the river. The stream was only about twenty-five meters wide. I scanned the north bank with binoculars and soon detected movement as a line formation of soldiers cautiously approached the river. Their uniforms and field gear gave them away: NVA. One of them must have taken an M14 rifle from a dead Marine.

They were likely the recon point element of a main body. They prepared to cross directly into our faces. As we watched, ready to trigger a hasty ambush, our original mission now a moot point, the bad guys produced a small sampan and sent four men paddling across. They landed twenty-five feet away.

They climbed the muddy bank to the edge of the undergrowth and split up. Two waited on the bank while the other two scouted in opposite directions. The near one crept to within fifteen feet of where I lay. Shadows were long and darkening by this time and we were well camouflaged. He looked around suspiciously but failed to see me. My heart pounded against the ground. He returned to the sampan, where his leader signaled the main body to cross over.

Using hand and arm signals, we devised a quick plan to let the main body reach the middle of the river before we opened up. They waded into the water. I transferred my attention from them to the point men who were already on our side and posed the most immediate threat. My scope was set on nine power; all I saw of my target, since he loomed so near, was his entire face filling out the view. As I was turning it down to 3X to get a wider field of view, I froze in consternation at the click of a Marine M16 safety being switched to the "fire" position. That sound betrayed us. The NVA point man knew exactly what it was.

My target disappeared from the scope as he swung

his AK-47 toward us. I paused, trembling from a sudden acute case of nerves. I jerked the trigger. To my surprise, the round blew off his face. He dropped his unfired AK.

Bedlam erupted as the ambush sprung. A hailstorm of bullets boiled the water around the wading NVA. A couple of them sank, then bobbed up again, dead, leaking out streams of red into the brown of the river. The surviving point men scrambled to hide in the woods, fleeing for their lives.

A bolt-action rifle is nearly worthless at such close range. I jumped up and ran into the kill zone, where I snatched up the AK the man I killed would no longer need and added its fury to the chaos. Sometimes we do dumb things in the heat of battle.

When the firing ceased, four NVA floated in the river and the fifth kill lay sprawled on the bank where I dropped him. One of the dead was a woman, an NVA "playgirl" sent out to the units for morale purposes. Bullets had literally torn her apart, even amputating one arm at the elbow. She floated peacefully in the river, her dismembered hand and arm floating over her face in one of those ghastly images produced by warfare.

WP bags carried by the enemy officers contained important documents pertaining to operations in the Arizona. We recovered them for intelligence purposes, along with weapons and other items. Later we learned the papers included the names of 42 VC spies and the location of 57mm recoilless rifles and 82mm mortars. The information was valuable enough that the northern soldiers apparently didn't intend to let us get away with them without a fight. There was still daylight left and we heard activity on the other side of the river.

Lieutenant Gagnon got on the guard channel and requested emergency backup from the company. The six of us redistributed ammunition and got ready to hold off the NVA until Delta elements reached us to pull our bacon out of the fire. A Bird Dog, a Cessna spotter plane, who happened to be cruising the skies in the vicinity overheard the radio chatter. He banked, dropped lower to the south of us, and flew back. He came up on the channel.

"I see enemy elements across the river," he reported. "I'll mark them with red smoke."

We watched him through field glasses. That Air Force pilot was one ballsy dude. He nosed the tiny plane down, came in hard, and swept on through the tracers blasting out of the forest at him. A red puff of smoke marked one end of the enemy's flank.

He then marked the other flank. Through binoculars, I saw him extend his arm out the window of the Cessna as he made his pass, a .38 pistol in hand. Green tracers webbed the sky all around the little plane as the gooks unleashed everything they had at him—and he returned fire with a *pistol*. A guy with courage like that, I would have kissed his ass in Macy's window.

He made a final flight over our position, wagging his wings in a salutation for luck. He took off for base, out of smoke and likely out of bullets for his revolver. I could almost see that pilot reporting in to Da Nang with his little puddle jumper all shot up, having engaged the North Vietnamese Army with a handgun. He probably received a Distinguished Flying Cross along with an ass-chewing.

Marking the enemy positions aided Delta Company in its rescue effort. While the enemy soldiers maneuvered against my small detachment, Delta Company maneuvered on them. Alarmed, the NVA threw valor to the wind, abandoning their efforts to recover their lost papers, and disappeared like ghosts into the darkening jungle.

The information from the bags triggered a major battalion-sized operation the following day to take advantage of the intelligence while it was hot. Disappointed, I had to turn in my AK-47 war trophy as "confiscated ordnance." It later found its way to the wall of the 1st Marine Division headquarters at Camp Pendleton, above a plaque that read: *Captured August 1967 by Delta 1/7 from a reconnaissance unit in the vicinity of An Hoa, triggering an ambush which resulted in the capture of enemy equipment and names of 42 ARVN spies.*

I asked the commanding general if I could have it back. I didn't get it.

CHAPTER FOURTEEN

U.S. Marine Corporal Gary Reiter
Vietnam, 1967

Hill 51 took up a square in the middle of the Co Bi Than Tan Valley between Camp Carroll and what Marines called The Rock Pile. Leathernecks were just beginning to secure the AO. A company-size element of entrenched Marines and a few tanks occupied a firebase on top of the hill. It was hairy on the mound in the beginning. VC slammed it with mortar fire day and night until F4s started flying air cover and put a crimp in the enemy's activities. The entire area was a free-fire zone, which meant open season on anything that moved out there.

Five snipers were assigned to the hill, with an extra rotating in now and again. I was one of them. The others were a big blond kid we called Water Bu, short for "water buffalo;" "Von Zipper," a former biker whose real name was David Schemel; Robert "Greek" Divoti, a lanky kid two inches over six feet tall; and Ed Kugler, whose exploits in sniping later made him known as "The Phantom of Phu Bai." We were all vets with body counts. Mine was approaching 50 kills.

We made daily grunt patrols with the line until we secured permission to conduct our own search and recons. That was when the real hunting began.

One afternoon Greek, Zipper, Bu, and I were down in the valley dinking around when we came upon a sampan pulled up on the bank of a small waterway. Kugler had gone on R&R. Bu tossed a grenade under the boat so it couldn't be used again. The explosion flushed out an iridescent green bamboo viper, ol' Mister Two-Step. And was he pissed. According to the tales, two steps were all you got if he clamped his fangs into you.

Two-thirds of his body stuck straight up in the air like an exclamation point while the remaining one-third propelled him toward the invaders like a vengeful streak of green mercury. Laughing, we jumped out of its way until Zipper took off its head with a single shot from his M14.

"Did you know snakes don't die until the sun sets?" Greek announced.

"Bullshit," I said.

"I'll prove it."

We wouldn't have long to wait. We took the headless and still-writhing snake to a deserted farmer's hooch and sat facing each other in a circle so we could see in all directions, with the snake in the center. While we waited for it to stop squirming, the subject of our forming a hunter-sniper team that could go about anywhere and do what we were good at—hunting gooks—came up. Kugler and I had discussed it before.

That was how TOADS formed: The Order of Assassins and Demented Sadists. Who else but a bunch of 20-

year-olds given weapons and the authority to shoot any-thing that moved could come up with shit like that? We were the baddest and most predatory cats in the valley.

Incidentally, the headless snake stopped moving after the sun went down.

From then on, reveille was at 0300 hours on the hill for the TOADS. Up and at 'em for another day of fun and games. It became almost a ritual. We planned the night before which way we were going, where, and what we intended to do. We got up, burned sandbags for face camouflage ashes, stuffed chow and extra ammo into our packs, and slipped out through the wire while it was still night. Gooks never expected round eyes to come out and fuck with them in the dark.

Before I deployed to Hill 51, snipers in the 4th Marines were ordered to turn in their Winchester Model 70s in exchange for the new .308 Remington 700 with a Redfield 3X9 scope. I didn't trust the Remington. I went back to a scoped M14 with as much ammunition as I could carry. You definitely wanted ammo if you were going to do this kind of work.

The TOADS soon made a real impact on the dink population in the valley. Those sorry fuckers were spooking at shadows and jumping at noises. They never knew from where or when the next shot might come. I felt like a ghost, a Halloween apparition out there haunt-ing no-man's-land.

It took the incident of the lime tree to bring us back to earth a bit.

A half-dozen or so hooches in a little deserted ville lay about a mile and a half from the base of Hill 51. They hadn't been lived in for quite some time. Dry grass roofs were caved in and a few weeds and vines had taken hold around the doors and windows. A thicket of bamboo grew on the outskirts, in the midst of which stood a lime tree laden with fruit.

The four members of the TOADS—Kugler was still on R & R—were gleefully peeling and eating limes like a troop of rock apes when someone heard a twig snap on the other side of the nearest ruin. We dropped where we stood and froze, rifles at the ready.

After a breathless moment, we watched a gook ease around the edge of the dilapidated hooch. Scrawny fella with black pj's, straw cone hat, and an AK-47. He skulked up to the building and peered through the window opening from the outside. Because our side of the hut had collapsed, he looked all the way through, concentrating on the bamboo around the lime tree. Like he sensed something wrong but couldn't quite make out what in the shadows.

Bu and I, facing him, slowly shifted the barrels of our weapons toward him.

He detected the slight movement. His eyes popped out of his head like a cartoon character. He seemed to run in place, his legs engaging while the rest of him remained in place. Then he was gone down a path that led back into the jungle on the opposite side.

Greek jumped to his feet. "I'll get him, Corporal!"

He darted into what was left of the hooch and fired three times through the window. The gook dropped hard on the trail.

Well and good, except that there was a *beaucoup* of his buddies in the bush. They threw every fucking thing at us except the proverbial kitchen sink. Flying lead harvested more fruit from the lime tree than we had. It was Greek's turn to do the bug-eyed cartoon character. He ran back considerably faster than he had gone.

"They're out there!"

No shit, Dick Tracy.

We attacked in a different direction, with haste. Marines don't retreat. Covering each other in short, fast rushes while blasting back at the enemy. Across an open grassy field to a mound where we might put up some kind of defense. On top of it was a Buddhist shrine, worn and gray and lichen-coated with age. Hitting the dirt around it for cover, we threw some major rounds back in the direction of our pursuers. They went to the hole, not knowing the size of our force. The firefight died down into an unexpected silence while each side took stock of the situation.

"Corporal, I'll look for a way out the back," Greek volunteered. He was a helpful kid.

"Go!"

He scurried off, lanky body bent over like a pretzel. A minute later he called out from the bush.

"Okay, guys. There's a way—"

That was as far as he got. A sharp explosion obliterated the rest of his announcement. Holy shit—a booby trap! I leaped to my feet and darted toward a faint trail leading from the back of the Buddha's mound. Bu and Von Zipper remained on defense.

Smoke from the detonation clotted the trail and clung to the surrounding foliage. Through it, I spotted Greek lying flat on his back. Stunned, he stared at me with pain-filled eyes. His boot and the bottom of his foot still in it appeared to have been blown off. A bloody awful mess.

I took a step toward him before I realized what I was doing. An entire field of Chicom mines seeded the trail, their tops sticking up from where the rains had washed away the soil. A buddy-fucking garden of death. Greek hadn't noticed it in his haste to find an escape route.

I took a deep breath, kind of sucked my balls into my throat, and carefully made my way through the mines, walking in Greek's footprints. I knelt next to him.

"Okay, buddy. Let's get you fixed up and out of here."

I slashed the sleeve off my utility jacket with my knife and used it to fashion a tourniquet for his lower leg. I put his boot back on and tied everything together with a field bandage.

In the meantime, Bu and Zipper maintained the standoff with the gooks. Bu got on the radio and requested backup. A tank and a minesweeper were dispatched. The VC didn't wait around for them. Not knowing what they had stumbled into, they withdrew and faded into the jungle from whence they came. Greek was soon on his way back to the world. The war was over for him. The TOADS had suffered our first casualty, penetrating the self-imposed myth of our invulnerability.

The TOADS—later Rogues, when Battalion HQ found out what TOADS stood for—continued to conduct semi-independent operations in the valley. We planned missions a bit more carefully after the lime tree shitstorm and were not quite as cavalier in our operations. Nonetheless, we were still out there on our own.

The north end of the valley had been shot all to hell. The Sierra Club would have had plenty to bitch about. Moon craters where 250-pound and 500-pound bombs had exploded pockmarked the mountains on either side. Tank guns had made toothpicks and splinters of entire forests. Napalm left charred stretches. Lines of relatively undamaged forest, like Mohawk haircuts, remained standing every hundred yards or so apart, blocking observers on Hill 51 from seeing enemy movements. It looked like prime hunting territory for snipers.

After the predawn ritual of burning sandbags, rubbing ashes on our faces, stuffing packs, and checking weapons, five shooters slipped out of the firebase to set up on stands before light came and gooks started sniffing around. Water Bu, Zipper, and I were joined by two other guys fresh out of sniper school. Just like a party of deer hunters.

"Oh, a-hunting we will go . . . a-hunting we will go. . . ," Von Zipper hummed softly as we got ready, to show the new guys his nonchalance.

We worked our way north in the dark, then up the side of the mountain to where we commanded a shooter's view of the valley past some of the Mohawk hair tree lines. A 500-pound bomb crater, almost like the opening of a small volcano, provided a hide. The bottom of the crater contained about three feet of semiclear water in which, as dawn arrived, we saw big-ass green leeches waiting greedily for a warm-blooded meal. Bu made a disgusted face.

We waited for something to move as the sky lightened, scanning the tree lines through scopes. Sniping for the most part was a boring job. Tedious. You could wait hour after hour and not see squat. Still, you couldn't let your guard down. You got lax, so many bad guys might show up so suddenly that you got your ass in a crack. You also had to be careful about your targets. If you could help it, you never shot into a two-man point element for a company of gooks that was going to wax *your* ass.

This territory was rich enough in game to prevent monotony. I spotted movement shortly after dawn. We were looking south from our north side of the valley when a party of five soldiers skulked across an opening toward a tree line that was probably forty yards wide and 300 yards long. Pith helmets and gray-green uniforms marked them as NVA. VC usually wore black.

I estimated the range at 500 yards. Perfect shooting.

"This is too good," I murmured.

Sure enough, it was. A second patrol of five gooks began crossing the clearing from the foothills to the tree line as the first element reached the woods. I waited until the second batch was deep in the open.

"Good enough," I whispered, knowing we had backing in force on Hill 51. "On my command."

I centered my crosshairs on the point man. Everyone took a bead. The little bastards would never know what hit them. Lightning from the sky.

"Fire!"

Two of the gooks dropped in their tracks. Their buddies grabbed them and dragged them into the tree line on the run. We held further fire, not wanting to give away our position.

It was time to add pieces to the show. Bu radioed the hill and reported we had gooks in the tree line. He looked up.

"They're sending us some tanks," he said.

Outstanding. We waited on the tanks and for the NVA soldiers to make another appearance. Nothing moved anywhere until, suddenly, a soldier jumped up directly in front of our crater, not thirty yards away. He ran directly across our front from left to right.

"Get him!"

High-powered rifles spat. Unscathed, the gook vanished. Lucky sonofabitch.

Then, too late, it occurred to us that we had been suckered. The gooks had been maneuvering on us all this time and we hadn't seen them. The run from left to right had been a Vietnamese ruse to make us fire. Rifle signatures gave us away. A crescendo of AK fire rattling savagely from the nearest tree line confirmed our suspicions. They had us zeroed in. A hail of bullets chewed up mud and dirt around the rim of the crater.

Fortunately, they couldn't get to us right away because we held the high ground. But—and this was the other side of the coin—we couldn't get out of the crater either.

It was a standoff. Gunfire dwindled off from both sides as the Viets crept about, seeking an opening, and we kept our eyes peeled. Soon the advantage shifted toward us as a pair of tanks rumbled up from Hill 51, creeping along the napalm burns and sniffing around like a pair of prehistoric predators. One of the new snipers blew a breath of relief. Zipper cheered softly. Using the radio, I directed the behemoths toward the threatening tree line below our defenses. The tanks cautiously entered the trees, one leading the other, and disappeared from sight.

Immediately we heard the fierce rattling and banging of small arms, followed by an explosion. The tanks scuttled out of the forest the same way they went in. Hill 51 promptly informed me the tanks had confronted an undetermined force and would have to pull back. I stared dumbfounded at the radio.

"What about support?" I demanded. "We're taking fire out here."

Hostile shooting immediately broke out from farther to our left, as though to underscore the point. We were being triangulated. The enemy hoped to trap us in a crossfire. I hunkered down over the radio next to the leech pool while rounds snapped overhead and thudded into the crater's rim. We had to get out quickly—or we might not get out at all.

"How do we get back?" I demanded, my voice thin with terror and anger.

The response sent a chill through my blood. "Get back the best way you can."

In other words, we were expendable. Snipers were merely attached to outfits, always on a temporary basis, and seldom belonged to an integral unit long enough to make friends. It seemed no one on Hill 51 really cared about us. As incredible as it seemed, we were going to be left out here on our own with the hostiles. I blinked. Had such a thing ever occurred in the history of the U.S. Marine Corps? Abandoned?

I stared at the drawn faces of my comrades. They looked as stunned as I felt when I broke the news to them.

There was no time to wallow in disappointment and temper. We had to do something quickly before the pissed-off gooks charged us. I looked around, making an assessment as team leader and weighing our options.

The crater lay about 60 yards or so below the crest of the ridge, up a rather steep but brushy incline. There were two ways back to Hill 51, as I saw it. We either charged through the bad guys below, or we scrambled to the top of the ridge, over it, and hotfooted our raggedy asses the three miles back to the firebase. That wasn't much choice, but you worked with what you had.

Jesus. I studied the incline. For at least part of the way we would be exposed to fire from below.

"Anybody got a better idea?" I solicited.

"Dorothy's red slippers," Bu cracked. "We could tap them together and make a wish."

"Funny," I said. "Good luck, guys."

One of the new guys volunteered for the first dash while the rest of us laid down cover fire. I heard him clawing shale rock. A mini-avalanche showered down on top of us. I heard the thunk of lead seeking his flesh. He made it to the top and called back down.

Bu was next. The gooks knew what to expect now and were ready. Gunfire crescendoed as he threw himself out of the crater and started to the top. Bullets made a clanging metallic noise as they struck his radio backpack and spun him off his feet. He slid down the crater wall until he sank knee-deep in the leech pond.

"All right, Bu?"

"Yeah. But the radio is fucked."

It had been hit from the side, which indicated the enemy was about to cut off our escape route. That meant we all went at once from the crater, in a single quick rush that hopefully confused the enemy—or we might not go at all. I lay on my back a moment, looking up at the sky and blistering it with a stream of profanity aimed at the cowardly tankers who had hauled ass to leave us out here and the even more chicken-livered officers on Hill 51 who told us to get back any way we could. Chances were that not all of us was going to make it.

Bu shed the shattered radio pack and we got ready, crouching below the edge of the rim. If one quail jumped, a hunter concentrated solely on it. If a covey flushed, it took a second's hesitation for the hunter to select one and shoot. I was counting on that hesitation.

"Go!"

It was a mad free-for-all to get to the top. Soaked in sweat. Dust boiling. Mini–rock slides. Zigzagging. Sucking air. On hands and knees part of the time. Bullets slapping the ground all around. Every muscle from

my heels to the top of my head tensed against an expected impact.

Zipper threw himself over the top, followed by Bu.
The last new guy and I sailed over the crest together. Incredibly, by some miracle, not a one of us suffered so
much as a scratch. But there was no time for congratula-
tions. We ran every step of those three miles back to Hill
51. I kept playing in my mind what I was going to say to
the sonofabitch who refused to send help to Marines
who needed it.

CHAPTER FIFTEEN

In November 1965, Lieutenant Richard Regan's platoon of the 9th Marines fell prey to a VC sniper concealed at the edge of the village of Giang Dong. The sniper's first shot missed, snapping through bamboo near Lance Corporal Craig Roberts and PFC Roland O'Brien. A second shot struck Lieutenant Regan in the head, sending his helmet flying and killing him instantly. A third shot drilled the machine gunner, Gonzales, through both calves.

The VC sniper abandoned his hide after three shots and made a run for it. He had occupied a spider hole next to a small Buddhist temple. As the figure in black and sandals made a run for it, Roberts brought him down with a burst from his M14. Other Marines lay down a bitter fusillade of lethal fire to finish him off.

The significance of the kill would have been negligible except for one thing. The little man was armed with a Moison Nagant 7.62mm Russian sniper rifle equipped with a telescopic sight. He and other enemy soldiers like him were employing their trade against American troops with deadly effect, proving the value of such shooters in combat. At the time, U.S. forces were fielding no snipers. The Marine Corps program was just getting off the ground.

"The Vietcong would maneuver through the tall grass and the rice paddies until he was within the effective range of the weapon he was armed with," Marine Captain Robert A. Russell recalled. "He would fire a shot or two, then disappear. We eventually determined that the Vietcong would simply melt into the countryside by hiding their rifles and playing the role of pacified farmers. . . . At that time, Charlie, as he was known, roamed the battlefield almost at will. As a result we lost a number of men from small-arms fire."

Marine commanders eventually decided that the VC snipers had become such a threat problem that companies in the field required a solution. Colonel Frank E. Garretson, regimental commander of the 9th Marines, summoned Captain Russell to division headquarters at Da Nang. Russell met with Colonel Don P. Wyckoff, 3rd Marine Division operations officer.

"You're Russell, huh?" Wyckoff said. "Fine. Start a sniper school. Let me know when you're ready to go."

Russell is credited with starting the first in-country sniper school in Vietnam. He opened training at the ARVN range near Hill 327 outside of Da Nang in mid-1965 and began sending snipers to line units later in the year. They were trained according to an early definition: "A Marine who, by the aid of a telescopic sight, could observe the battlefield, deliver accurate rifle fire, and 'see' far better than the average rifleman."

The captain began searching for the right weapon. Marines were issued the standard M14 semiautomatic rifle, with a full-automatic version known as the Mark II. No sniper rifles as such were available. Units scrounged up anything that would mount a scope. Special Services, where servicemen could check out sporting equipment like volleyballs, swim fins, fishing rods, and hunting equipment, were stripped of deer rifles. Most were Winchester Model 70s. Sometimes officers and NCOs were sent to Okinawa to buy .30-caliber bolt-action Winchesters and various scopes—Tascos, Redfields, and others—out of the post exchange. A few World War II and Korea-era M1D and M1C Garands were also broke out of dusty warehouses Stateside.

Such efforts failed to fill the growing need for properly trained and equipped snipers to counter the communist sniper threat. The North Vietnamese Army was way ahead in its sniper program.

According to Gunnery Sergeant Jack Childs in *Sea Tiger* magazine, the commander of an enemy sniper platoon surrendered to a village chief north of Da Nang and was turned over to U.S. Marines: "The officer, a 35-year-old lieutenant, carried a Russian-made sniper rifle and scope (Model 91/30 Moison Nagant with a 3.5 power PU telescopic scope). Word of his surrender reached Major Robert A. Russell. . . ."

"I was extremely interested in obtaining information on their activities," Major Russell said. "He was very cooperative. He told me that with the exception of their officers, each man was a volunteer. Their families received extra rations if they volunteered, since snipers were considered elite troops."

That amounted to about twenty piasters a month (approximately twenty cents). The lieutenant's sniper company had deployed nine weeks previously. Each sniper squad was guarded by a VC platoon. No squad operated within three days' march of another in order to assure dispersement and survivability.

Formal training for an NVA sniper lasted three months. Eight hours a day was spent snapping in (dry firing). The range utilized man-size targets at ranges up to 1,000 yards. However, due to conservation of ammunition, each student was allowed to fire only three rounds every five days. Nonetheless, the training produced superb marksmen who targeted officers, NCOs, and radiomen once they went to the field. U.S. forces had a distance to go in order to catch up.

The first dedicated sniper rifle employed by Americans in Vietnam in numbers was the Winchester Model 70 target rifle that had been in the supply system for over three decades. It was known as the Van Orden rifle after Brigadier General George O. Van Orden, who had written the original specifications for the military version:

Rifle, .30-06 Sniper: 24 inch medium heavy-barrel precision grade, mounted in the Winchester M70 special clip-slotted receiver; barrel mounted with bases for Lyman 77A Front Sight and Lyman Super Target Spot sighting telescope. . . .

Tested with Western .30-06 Super Match 180 grain Boattail Handload to assure zero and grouping within requirements of national competition; final assembly inspection and test under supervision of experienced ordnance and target practice techniques; delivered complete with operating instructions, ammunition handbook, metallic and telescopic sight manuals and warranted ready as received for competition without further modification or adjustment other than the determination of the user's zero.

The rifle changed slightly as time progressed. The Unertl 8X scope replaced the Lyman for issue in Vietnam on the standard sniper rifle. A Headquarters Marine Corps memorandum dated 27 November 1965 outlined weapons-issue requirements for the Marine Corps:

> The total requirement for the entire Marine Corps, including the active forces, schools, mobilization structure, 20 division months supply block, and attrition factors is approximately 550 rifles complete with telescope, equipment and repair parts. The following items have been shipped to the 1st and 3rd Marine Divisions:
>
> 20 M1D caliber .30 sniper rifles (3rd MarDiv);
> 53 Model 70 Winchester rifles, caliber .30-06 (3rd MarDiv);
> 59 8X Unertl telescopic sights (3rd MarDiv);
> 20 M1D caliber .30 sniper's rifles (1st MarDiv).

The Unertl scope could be adjusted for elevation and windage by micrometer knobs on the rear scope mount. Instead of having internal crosshairs adjustment, the scope physically moved in its mounts. It was also "free-floating," which meant it likewise traveled forward and backward in its mounts to partially absorb recoil. Original scopes possessed a "battery return spring," or recoil spring, that surrounded the scope tube and was designed to serve as a shock absorber, returning the scope to its rear "battery" position automatically after a shot was fired. The spring proved problematic and was removed from rifles shortly after they arrived in Vietnam, thereby requiring the shooter to manually pull the scope to the rear after each shot. This proved awkward in a situation demanding quick action.

The Model 70 with Unertl scope, however, was carried quite successfully by such notable shooters as Carlos Hathcock (93 confirmed kills). Eventually they wore out.

"They were junk," Hathcock noted. "Just plain worn out. We needed something new, something more modern, that would and could survive the heat and moisture of Vietnam. The Winchesters were good sticks in their time, but they weren't built for Vietnam. They were built for target ranges and competition back home."

In an effort to answer requests from Vietnam, Headquarters USMC ordered the Marksmanship Training Unit (MTU) at Quantico to come up with a lighter off-the-shelf rifle and scope that would be cost-effective, suitable to replace the Model 70, and obtainable in short order. After testing several commercial bolt-action rifles and scopes in December 1965 and January 1966, the MTU decided that the Remington Model 700 mounted with the Redfield 3x9 variable power scope (known as the "Accu-Range" because of its integral plastic range finder) was "superior to items now in use." Winchester fell by the wayside due to its cheaper "post-1964" design that failed to hold up under combat conditions.

The Remington 700 also fired 7.62-millimeter NATO rounds, which made it compatible with current ammunition supply capabilities. It could fire both M14 and M60 machine-gun ammunition if no match-grade ammo was available in the field. The specific nomenclature for the new weapons system was officially described as "7.62 mm bolt-action Remington rifle with short action receiver and heavy sniper's barrel. Rifle has a magazine consisting of five rounds, dull oil finish stock, military (Parkerized) finish, military sling swivels; clip shot in receiver, and aluminum butt plate."

Life expectancy of the system was listed as ten years. With several modifications, however, it has survived until the present era in the current M40 series.

The USMC sniper program took permanent roots after the Vietnam War with the establishment of the Sniper Instructor School at Quantico. Improvements to the battle-proven M40 began.

Marine officers and NCOs of the school—Major Dick Culver, Gunnery Sergeant Carlos Hathcock, Captain Jack Cuddy, Warrant Officer Neil Goddard, among others—tested and developed a custom sniper rifle made of hand-assembled parts. The final version became known as the M40A1. It consisted of a Remington M700 action, an Atkinson stainless-steel barrel, a McMillan fiberglass stock, and a modified Winchester trigger-guard assembly.

None of the current telescopic sights met the specifications of the "ultimate sniper rifle." Since the Marine Corps worked on a limited budget, no major manufacturers wanted to participate in a development program to produce a limited number of scopes. Unertl, however, finally bid on the job.

The Unertl 10X mil-dot ranging telescopic sight is still in use today. It is constructed of steel rather than aluminum alloy for rugged use in any climate. Optical lenses are coated with a light-gathering substance known as HELR (high efficiency, low reflection), which permits at least 90 percent of available ambient light to come through the scope. A sniper can operate out to 600 yards with the scope under moonlight or flares.

The scope weighs two pounds, three ounces, and is twelve and a half inches long with a half-minute-of-angle elevation and windage adjustment. It has a mil-dot duplex reticule (crosshairs) for range estimation and for calculating the lead on moving targets. Designed for use with M118 Lake City Match Ammunition, the scope allows point-of-aim/point-of-impact out to 1,000 meters.

In 1996, the USMC began designing a replacement for the M40A1. The result, slowly phasing its way into service as the A1 wears out, is the M40A3 equipped with a Harris bipod and accessory rail and a new McMillan A4 stock with adjustable cheek and length-of-trigger pull. Built by USMC armorers at Quantico, Virginia, the A3 is an extremely accurate rifle, very rugged, and was designed from the start to be a superb sniper rifle. Combined with the new M118LR ammunition, the system is ranked as one of the best in the world.

In the meantime, the U.S. Army was also developing a successful sniper program and a rifle to go with it. Although the Army has not been as dedicated to utilizing snipers as has the Marines, several sniper programs have been successful up to the present time.

In Vietnam, the Army retained the semiautomatic rifle as its sniper weapon: the XM-21, a match-grade or accurized M14. Various scopes were mounted, the most notable being the ART (adjustable ranging telescope) developed by an Army lieutenant named Leatherwood. A cam mechanism at the rear of the scope tube allowed the user to range-find a target and shoot point-of-aim/point-of-impact, provided the ammunition was that specified for the scope settings. This system was used very successfully in Vietnam and remained in service afterward as the M21.

Noting the Marine Corps success with the M40 and its later versions, the Army eventually saw the value in a dedicated bolt-action sniper rifle. As the Marines had, the Army chose the basic Remington Model 700 and made it heavier and more "military" than the standard off-the-shelf weapon. The result is the M24 Weapons System.

This rifle mounts a 24-inch heavy barrel chambered for the 7.62mm NATO round, with a few versions chambering the .300-caliber Winchester Magnum. It weighs twelve pounds and mounts a Leupold 10X42X Ultra M3A telescopic sight with a mil-dot reticule. In the hands of a trained sniper, the M24 is capable of making consistent 1,000-yard shots.

Because of size and bureaucracy, Army planners stress "combat power" and "firepower" over the marksmanship of individual soldiers—a "spray-and-pray" mentality: Spray rounds downrange and pray some of them hit. It is therefore in the Army elite units that the sniper programs exist and flourish. U.S. Army Special Forces, Rangers, the 10th Mountain Division, Delta Force, along with certain Airborne and other Special Operations units, all have programs with dedicated, well-trained, and well-equipped snipers and counter-snipers.

It is among such units in the Army, and in the Marine Corps and Navy SEALs, that .50-caliber "sniper rifles" can be found. Most of these heavy bolt-action, semiautomatic models are made by Barrett. The M107 SASR weighs 22 pounds unloaded, has a magazine capacity of five rounds with a ten-round version available, and is equipped with a variety of telescopic sights, including the Leupold and Unertl. The recoil is dampened by a special dual-chamber muzzle break and a specially designed recoil pad. The weapon is used to disable vehicles and aircraft and to eliminate obstacles. Explosive Ordnance Disposal teams employ it to clear unexploded ordnance.

A sniper from Desert Storm, the 1991 war against Iraq, described the rifle's knock-down power: "If an enemy sniper was in a building and we couldn't get to him with our sniper rifle, we called up the SASR guy and he simply blew the wall away."

The longest sniper kill recorded to date was made by a Canadian sniper in Afghanistan using a .50-caliber rifle.

Other experimental versions of "sniper" rifles are currently being examined and developed by U.S. forces. The U.S. Army Marksmanship Unit at Fort Benning, Georgia, took a standard M16 lower receiver, mated it to an Armalite M4A1 flattop upper receiver, and called it a "Designated Marksman Rifle." "Special-purpose rifles" (SPRs, either basic M16s or AR-10s modified) come equipped for Special Operations duty with Leupold M3LR 3.5x10X telescopic sights and OPS Inc sound suppressors. Some 150 SPRs painted desert tan were manufactured in 2000.

Technology will continue to advance sniper weapons systems. Early in the Vietnam War, night "sniper scopes" of Korean War vintage consisted of a lamp assembly, a scope, and a large battery pack worn on the belt. The shooter first turned on the infrared lamp to observe the target area through the scope out to about 100 meters in a hazy green glow. If he spotted a target, he aimed using a little white dot and hoped he got off a shot before the battery went dead. Such devices were expensive and too fragile for extended combat duty.

The AN/PVS 2 Starlight scope arrived later in the war. It was a bulky but useful first-generation light-gathering scope, "passive" in the sense that it gathered ambient light and therefore did not require a lamp assembly and large battery pack. Snipers made many kills at night in Vietnam using this device mounted by the Marines on the M14 or by the Army on its M21. Famed Marine sniper Chuck Mawhinney killed 16 NVA soldiers in one night as they crossed a river while using this device.

Today's sniper possesses the generation-3 night-vision system that provides a shooter with a view that is almost as good as daylight. Instead of fuzzy green speckles and patterns, the sniper sees his prey with crystal-clear clarity. He can identify friend or foe out to 300 meters and shoot much farther. Now, at night as well as day, it is one shot—one kill.

It is not unforeseeable that future snipers will be equipped with computerized telescopic sights that can be used day or night, that will read ranges by means of sonic or laser beams, and that will self-adjust for point-of-aim/point-of-impact. They will have FLIR (forward-looking infrared) heat-detection capability and be pressurized and waterproofed for deep diving depths. They may even have IFF (identification friend or foe) capability. Rifles will become lighter using new composites. They will shoot farther, harder, and more accurately using improved ammunition.

And they may well fire almost without sound. Various "silencers" have been fielded since Maxim introduced the first one during World War I. Some are used today by Special Operations soldiers. There are two basic varieties, integral and supplemental. Supplementals are those that screw or clamp onto the end of the barrel. Integrals are built into the barrel as part of it. Knock-down power is substantially reduced by either version, especially at distances, but it is not inconceivable that a sound suppressor will be developed for snipers within the near future.

Yet, what no amount of technology can replace is the basic American rifleman, the shooter with skills to survive and succeed on the battlefield. The sniper is more than a man with a fancy rifle: He's a wolf, a predator, a scout, an observer—and he is a weapon in his own right.

CHAPTER SIXTEEN

The U.S. invasion in 1983 of the tiny Caribbean island of Grenada, Operation Urgent Fury, ended four years of Marxist control. It was the first time since before World War II that an avowed communist government was replaced by a pro-Western one.

Grenada in the southeastern Caribbean, only 90 miles from the South American coast, is a small, comma-shaped island of 133 square miles of mountains and forested volcanic earth, with a population of about 110,000 people. It gained independence from Britain in 1974. Five years later Maurice Bishop seized power, established the leftist Provisional Revolutionary Government, and then turned to Cuba and the USSR for support. The United States became concerned when Bishop, with Cuban aid, began constructing a 9,000-foot-long runway capable of accommodating strategic bombers from the Soviet Union.

On 13 October 1983, Deputy Prime Minister Bernard Coard forced himself into power in the name of the Provisional Revolutionary Army (PRA) and placed Bishop under house arrest. He considered Bishop too moderate. Coard wanted Grenada to convert to a communist government right away. This second coup signaled an expansion of Soviet power in the Caribbean, which had been held in check since the Cuban Missile Crisis.

On 17 October in the capital, St. George's, the PRA opened fire on a crowd that had forcibly freed Bishop and other members of his former government, killing over 50 people and wounding that many more. Bishop and four of his ministers and three of his supporters were taken to nearby Fort Rupert and shot on 19 October. A shoot on sight curfew was extended over the entire island.

About 1,000 Americans were living on the island, of whom some 600 were students at St. George's University Medical School. The U.S. State Department held an emergency meeting. The National Security Council ordered the Joint Chiefs of Staff to prepare for a military rescue of U.S. citizens on the island. President Ronald Reagan expanded the mission to taking over the island and rescuing Grenada's former governor-general, Sir Paul Scoon, who was being held under house arrest by the new regime. Joint Task Force 120, code-named Operation Urgent Fury, was assembled under the command of Vice Admiral Joseph Metcalf. The operation was to be carried out in complete secrecy, with no press notified.

It was to be the most massive American invasion since the Inchon landing of the Korean War, involving thirteen ships, hundreds of fixed-wing aircraft and helicopters, and more than 7,000 men. Elements of the invasion force consisted of parts of SEAL teams Four and Six; U.S. Army's Delta Force; the First and Second

Ranger Battalions; the 82d Airborne Division; the First Special Operations Wing of the Air Force; and the 22d Marine Amphibious Unit (MAU), which had been on its way at the time to relieve the 24th MAU, which was in Beirut, Lebanon, at the time.

The general plan called for a simultaneous two-pronged attack from the sea and from the sky. Marines would make an amphibious landing to seize the northern half of the island while Rangers and elements of the 82d Airborne secured the southern half by parachuting onto the airfield at Point Salines. Five missions were identified: take and secure the runway at Point Salines to enable C-130s to land on the island with troops and supplies; rescue American students trapped on the nearby medical school campus; rescue Governor-general Sir Paul Scoon from imprisonment at Government House; take and hold the Radio Free Grenada radio station at Beauséjour; free any political prisoners remaining in custody at Richmond Hill Prison.

Marines began choppering ashore at 0520 Tuesday, 25 October 1983, in coordination with Rangers parachuting onto the Point Salines airfield in the south. Fighting continued for several days, but most of the defenders either surrendered or fled into the mountains. By mid-December, U.S. combat forces were on their way home while a pro-American government took power in Grenada. Official casualties for the operation were listed as 19 Americans dead and 123 wounded. Forty-nine Grenadians and 29 Cubans were killed, with several hundred wounded.

The United States utilized snipers in the operation, but in a rather limited capacity.

CHAPTER SEVENTEEN

U.S. Marine Corporal Carey Fabian
Grenada, 1983

Two days out to sea, five troop ships loaded with Amphibious Ready Group leathernecks bound for the Middle East to relieve the ill-fated 24th Marine Amphibious Unit (MAU) in Lebanon were suddenly diverted to a new and more pressing concern. I was puzzled when the battalion S-2 passed the word to unit commanders, who then relayed it down the line: "Get all your people together on the 02 deck in fifteen minutes." We had just learned of the suicide bombing in Beirut that claimed the lives of 241 Americans and the wounding of 70 others. What could be so urgent after that? we wondered, as Marines packed the decks of the transports in loose platoon and company formations. Marines on all ships received the same basic briefing.

"As you can probably tell," the S-2 began with The Big Picture, leaving subordinate leaders the task of fleshing out individual operations orders, "the ARG has turned on a southerly heading. That's because we're steaming toward Grenada. Tomorrow morning we're going to invade the island of Grenada."

I exchanged a startled look with Corporal Jeff Graham. Grenada? I had never even heard of the place. And we were going to *invade* it? Marines identified *invasion* with Tarawa, Iwo Jima, and Okinawa; with bloody pictures of gyrenes charging ashore against heavy defensive fire and sustaining enormous casualties. Graham and I had done a tour in Beirut earlier in the year and were on our way back for a second. How quickly life and times changed in the Marine Corps.

Confronted with the sudden unknown, the ship turned somber and remained that way throughout the long night that followed. Few of us slept much, even though we had the time for it. Briefings on our missions and rehearsing actions on the objective took up much of our time. Squads and platoons and teams huddled over maps while armorers and weapons people inspected and issued rifles and equipment. In their spare time, guys drew up last wills and wrote letters home.

"Don't do anything stupid tomorrow," buddies cautioned each other.

Graham and I were NCOs in charge of the battalion STA [Surveillance and Target Acquisition] platoon. We farmed out sniper teams to rifle companies that foresaw the most action, that might be most apt to utilize long guns in the offensive. He and I, along with Biddle and McClellan, linked up with Echo Company for what was intended to be a beach assault but which actually became a helicopter vertical strike to seize, secure, and hold Pearls Airfield on the extreme northeastern tip of the island. Rangers and the 82d Airborne would parachute-assault onto the airfield in the south at [Point] Salines.

At dawn, nervous cooks attempting to be jovial sang out as combat Marines clambered down to the mess galley. "Steaks and eggs, Marines!"

"The last meal of the condemned," cracked a company first sergeant and Vietnam vet, grinning.

Echo's CO, Captain Henry Donigan III, sat down with the snipers prior to scrambling aboard helicopters. Cubans behind the militarization of the island, he said, had dug in mortar and antiaircraft positions all over Pearls Point. He pointed out the airport on a map.

"It'll be fast and furious," he said. "After the helicopters insert the company, I want the scout snipers to kick out about a thousand meters and run the flanks for us. Move to the far end of the airfield. If you engage something you can't handle, give us a call. We'll move up."

Simply put, our mission was to serve as Echo's eyes and ears in the junglelike growth that surrounded the airfield, engaging targets of opportunity and preventing a surprise enemy counterattack.

The first birds lifted off the various assault ships at 0615 hours that bright 25 October morning. The early quiet of the sleepy island was suddenly interrupted by the distant buzzing of approaching aircraft, followed by the cyclic barking of antiaircraft guns. Marine-laden CH-46 Sea Knight helicopters sprang off the decks of the assault ships like swarms of bees in the rosy dawn light. The enormity of it, the *reality,* set in immediately as I gazed apprehensively out the side door of my chopper crammed with battle-geared leathernecks. I watched as mother ships receded against the incredible blue of the sea. Graham semi-crouched next to me, also looking out, hunched forward, his face as sharp and grim as a hatchet.

He flinched as the door gunner opened up with a

burst from his M60 machine gun, test-firing into the water below. The crew chief stood up in the front of the compartment. After a remarkably short time, he began waving his arms to attract attention.

"Marines, lock and load!" he shouted.

From my limited vantage point, I glimpsed badass Cobras growling past in streaks. They were the hornets of the bee swarm. As land appeared, I heard them grinding away with their 20mm nose guns. A couple of mortars or rocket rounds exploded somewhere in the distance. A war had started down there.

The heavy Sea Knights dropped out of the sky with dizzying suddenness and flared over the designated LZ, a clearing in the jungle not too far from the airstrip. They spat out gobs of green-clad Marines, who spread out rapidly into a hasty defensive perimeter. I found myself running, *running,* with my M40A1 sniper's rifle firmly in hand, racing for the nearest tree line while the helicopters put some gone under their tail fins, clawing for altitude.

Two Cobras worked over a round forested hill that rose above the jungle like a hairy tit at the far end of the runway, laying heavy fire on it while it seethed with smoke and flame. I heard the throaty, jarring *crump* of rockets detonating, the fierce, explosive chatter of machine guns. The Cobras buzzed in circles, making their ordnance runs and leaving contrails of gun smoke inscribed behind them in the brassy air.

One Echo platoon established security, ticking like clockwork as squad and fire-team leaders designated sectors of fire and areas of responsibility. The rest of the company consolidated and began working toward the airfield. It was so good it looked scripted.

Graham and I broke off to one flank of the movement

while Biddle and McClellan took the other flank. The company had hardly started, however, before an enemy soldier suddenly popped up in headlong flight. It appeared he was stripping out of his uniform even as he ran. I snapped my rifle to shoulder and dropped to one knee for stability. I caught a single fleeting glimpse of him behind the crosshairs before he vanished into the forest.

Caught up in the heat of the moment, I jumped up to pursue. The platoon leader stood nearby. He shook his head. *No, no! Don't chase the guy.*

No resistance met Echo on the airfield. The strip lay abandoned. The enemy even left some of his weapons and equipment lying about. Captain Donigan ordered a platoon to secure and occupy the hairy-tit hill, the most commanding piece of terrain in the area.

"Take two of the snipers."

There had been no mortar or machine-gun fire from the hill since the beginning when the Cobras, now gone elsewhere, had worked it over. Thin wisps of smoke curled out of its crown, like it was a miniature volcano seething to erupt. In smooth overwatching elements the platoon approached its objective. Graham and I ranged out on the flank, ready and pumped up for action.

The Cobras had scorched the crown of the hill, knocked down a few trees still smoldering, and put a hole in the ground here and there. Otherwise, the "seething volcano" was dormant, as abandoned and peaceful as the airfield. I was almost disappointed. As far as I knew, not a shot had yet been fired by the invading force.

Marines below on the airstrip established a full perimeter defense while the platoon on the hill consolidated and dug in. By this time it was getting late in the afternoon. I wondered if the war elsewhere was as slow as it was on Pearls Point. The company commander trudged up to take a look.

"Fabian, here's what I want the snipers to do," he said. "Set up in the most advantageous position. You're not concerned with the airport because we've already ringed it with a three-sixty. We're not concerned with what's behind us, either: the ocean. The jungle out there is what we're concerned with."

Aye, aye, sir.

A grunt in combat rarely sees or comprehends The Big Picture or what is going on with a war or battle in general. The war for him is either good or bad according to what he sees within the vicinity of his own foxhole. Although occasional rumors floated by, I had little idea of what went on elsewhere with the invasion. I had seen no fighting at all, other than when the Cobras attacked the hill. This was more like training than actual combat.

I settled in with Graham as darkness approached. A counterattack failed to materialize. I rummaged in my ruck for a ration and enjoyed it with a hearty appetite as the quick purple of the tropics spread out over the island like spilled ink.

A couple of nervous rifle shots went off shortly after nightfall, snapping the line to alert. I borrowed Graham's M16 with its attached PVS/2 nightscope and peered through the green liquid of the lenses, scanning the surrounding forest. Considering how quiet things had been, I was surprised to discover a silhouette skulking in the trees directly to my front.

I pegged crosshairs on the figure, not wanting to miss a second opportunity to utilize my skills. I held off and waited for him to emerge into better light. He peered from behind a tree, then shot out into the open, bent over at the waist and sneaking like a thief. What was the poor bastard up to? Like he thought he hadn't been seen in the darkness.

I took up trigger slack, held a breath, and . . . some other Marine with a night vision device must have also spotted the intruder. A grenade went off with a blazing explosion that magnified itself through my scope. I dropped the rifle as the pain of the flash pierced to the brain and momentarily blinded me.

The grenade cued the FPL, the final protective line, and it fired off automatically. M16s and machine guns crackled and sparkled all along the black crest of the hill. Muzzle flashes stabbed into the night and tracers skittered and weaved, piercing the jungle. Disgusted and frustrated, I leaned back in the hide I shared with Graham and waited for the platoon to call cease-fire.

"We blew that sonofabitch to hell," someone concluded.

Right. The rest of the night passed uneventfully. A patrol went out the next morning to make a body count. There was nothing out there. No body, no blood trail, no weapons. No shit.

No action, either. I waited on the hill, bored in the somnolent heat. Some invasion this was turning out to be. Around noon Captain Donigan came up to me and said, "I've written this op order. Take a look. We have intel that some of the leaders of their military are holed up in this house. How does it look to you, Fabian?"

"Looks real good, sir. All you need are a couple of snipers to round things out."

"That's why I showed it to you. Get Graham and let's go."

I trotted off down the line to the far edge of the hairy tit to fetch Graham. We might get some action after all.

"We're going on an op," I informed him.

We hurried back to the CO.

"We're not going," he said.

"Why not, sir?"

"They've already given themselves up. Some civilian told another outfit about them. So the outfit went up to the house and yelled, 'Come on out with your hands up.' And they did."

Our objectives for the invasion had been secured—and all we had done for the most part was sit on our asses in the heat for the past two or three days. The Army's 82d Airborne and 101st Airmobile were going to relieve us. Blackhawk helicopters appeared out of the morning sky, buzzing in fast and furiously. Troops poured from the chopper bellies onto the airfield and hurried into a combat three-sixty. Textbook stuff. Like they expected banzai suicide attacks.

I was chilling out underneath a coconut palm next to the airfield with Corporal Biddle and Corporal Pogatez. We watched with wry amusement.

"That's real pretty, isn't it?" I cracked sarcastically.

Other Marines around the airfield were also watching and grinning, taking the opportunity to poke at the soldier boys. An Army lieutenant colonel leading a short little warrant officer marched off one bird, looking *strak* and businesslike. I stood up at attention to greet him as he approached.

"Where's your command post, Marine?" he snapped.

I pointed. "Sir, it's up on top of that hill."

"Do you have a jeep I can use?"

"Sir, the only jeeps we have are on perimeter security around the airport."

He looked as though he didn't believe me.

"We're Marines, sir," I expounded. "The only way we get around is on foot."

His eyes shifted to the top of the hill a goodly walk away.

"We'll be able to find it, sir," the warrant said. "Ready, Colonel?"

I couldn't help getting in a final dig. "By the way, sir," I said innocently, "this airport has been secured by the U.S. Marines for the last four days."

CHAPTER EIGHTEEN

U.S. Navy SEAL Team Six
Grenada, 1983

In the early morning stillness of 25 October 1983, Governor-general Sir Paul Scoon, the Queen's representative to the island of Grenada, alerted to the noise of aircraft engines and the staccato beat of helicopter rotor blades. His guards, Grenadian police who held him under house arrest in his home at Government House, became excited and ushered him, his wife, and members of the household staff to the cellar.

The invasion had begun. Aboard two of the nine dark green Sikorsky UH-60 Blackhawk helicopters were 23 members of the U.S. Navy's elite counterterrorist unit, SEAL Team Six. These two birds banked out of formation and streaked toward Government House. Their mission: to rescue the governor-general.

The overall plan for the U.S. invasion of Grenada called for Marines to make an amphibious landing to take the northern half of the island; plans were later changed to make it a helicopter insertion. Rangers and elements of the 82d Airborne would secure the southern half by parachuting onto the airfield at Point Salines. Navy SEALs were tapped to perform four missions.

First, operators from SEAL teams Four and Six would clandestinely infiltrate on the night of 23 October to pave the way for the airdrop onto Point Salines in the early hours of 25 October; SEAL Team Four would recon the Marines' proposed beach landing site near Pearls Airfield on the island's northern end; other operators were assigned to capture the Beauséjour radio station at St. George's; SEAL Team Six's primary mission was the rescue of former Governor-general Scoon from Government House on the outskirts of St. George's. SEAL Commander Robert Gormly would lead the attempt.

The mission seemed simple enough. However, a series of setbacks and snafus soon turned the mission into what military men called a "clusterfuck." First of all, the predawn assault, scheduled to commence with the landing of Marines in the north and Army paratroopers in the south, failed to become airborne until after daybreak. Soon the rattle of machine guns and small arms and the explosions of grenades and mortar fire awakened the tiny island. Surprise had been lost.

An early sense of confidence and determination among both air crews and SEALs quickly dissipated. The objective, which should have been easy to locate, especially in broad daylight, proved elusive. The white-columned two-story mansion sat on a hilltop surrounded by several manicured acres and a stone-and-wire fence. "Night Stalker" pilots of the Blackhawks had been briefed to look for a turnaround circle in front of the entry that would distinguish it from other large houses on the hill. As they drew near and cut airspeed to search for the landmark, they began receiving ground fire.

The sparkle of muzzle flashes from around the house and from nearby Fort Frederick, along with the bright arcs of tracers, intensified as enemy gunners found the range. A hail of bullets slapped into the choppers' metal skins. Holes suddenly appeared in spears of dust-laden light. SEALs jerked with quick pain and shock as they were struck.

Several perilous moments passed before pilots picked out Government House. Stately old trees studded the lawn, making it impossible for the two choppers to land as intended, one in the backyard, the other in front. Only two possible insertion sites presented themselves: a tennis court toward the rear of the residence, and a small garden in front. Neither place was large enough or sufficiently uncluttered for the birds to actually touch down. The SEALs would have to fast-rope to the ground.

The helicopters streaked in low and fast, coming to a sudden brake to hover above each site. The chopper over the tennis court was hardest hit. The pilot shouted through the radio that his copilot was hit hard and that the aircraft itself may be going down. With Commander Gormly and its load of SEALs still aboard, it leapt back into the air and returned to its sea base, trailing a thick mist of gearbox fluid. It crash-landed on the deck of the USS *Guam,* a Marine helicopter assault carrier standing by offshore.

In the meantime, the second bird full of SEALs flung cotton ropes out the door and SEALs slid down them like firemen on greased poles through a hailstorm of bullets. During the landing melee, a round struck and destroyed the team's radio; the thirteen SEALs who made it into the little garden and raced toward the house were left without communications. The Blackhawk screamed back toward the *Guam.*

Bullets sought flesh as the valiant SEALs thundered across the green of the Scoon mansion, returning as good as they got, their automatic weapons chattering fiercely. A couple of men were dinged. Nothing serious. They burst through the front door in a mob and slammed it against pursuit, were any Grenadians so foolishly inclined. Police constables inside, intimidated by such a violent show of force, gave up immediately and threw down their arms.

Lieutenant John Koenig and Lieutenant Duke Leonard were now officers in charge of the rescue, since Commander Gormly had failed to make it down. They hurriedly distributed their men to defend the house against assault while a team cleared the rooms, working from the first floor to the second and then into the basement, where they found Governor-general Scoon, his wife, and nine staff members hiding in terror.

"Americans!" the SEALs shouted. "We're here to rescue you."

Later, after Governor-general Scoon had assessed the situation—thirteen American commandos surrounded by scores of hostiles—he murmured, "But who's going to rescue *them*?"

The plan had called for the governor-general and his staff to be freed and either ushered to a helicopter waiting outside to be flown to safety or to wait at the mansion for ground forces to arrive. Obviously, the firestorm and the inability of choppers to land made the second choice mandatory.

Koenig and his SEALs prepared to hold out against overwhelming odds for as long as required. The loss of their radio left them out of touch with the rest of the invasion force.

Among the thirteen SEALs was a petty officer with

sniper training. Lieutenant Koenig assigned him and a spotter to the second floor as Grenadian troops, aroused by the activity, rallied their forces. A Soviet-built BTR-60 armored personnel carrier on which was mounted a devastating 12.7 heavy machine gun cranked up in the garrison at Fort Frederick and rolled toward the action. Two more joined him.

Moving from window to window on the second floor, picking off whatever target presented itself, the sniper and his spotter were the first to see the APCs rattling up the hill toward them. The steel monsters sealed off the front gate, from which position they covered southern approaches. At the same time two groups of infantry moved in from the north and across the tennis courts. The SEALs were surrounded. Although they could hold off a good-size infantry force, they hadn't the weapons to deal with the BTRs. Not for long anyhow.

Within minutes, the enemy launched a determined counterattack. The incessant cracking of Kalashnikov assault rifles and the deep-throated hammering of turret-mounted machine guns on the BTRs generated a pall of gun smoke that settled over the mansion's well-kept grounds. Bullets pockmarked the walls of the stately residence.

SEALs returned fire. The well-placed sniper shooting from the second floor, nailing virtually anything that moved, dissuaded the enemy from pressing the attack with too much fervor. Even the APCs chose caution over valor and pulled back to continue the assault from a safer distance. The SEALs remained in charge of the battleground.

Although without a radio, Lieutenant Bill Davis discovered to his surprise that the telephone system on the island was still in operating condition. He dialed the airfield at Point Salines, where American airborne and Rangers were already in control, and asked for gunship protection. Two Sea Cobras responded. Antiaircraft emplacements from Cuban military headquarters at nearby Fort Frederick shot both of them down, killing three Marines.

Salvation arrived in the form of an AC-130H Spectre gunship from the U.S. Air Force's 1st Special Operations Wing. It bristled with guns that included two rapid-firing 20mm Vulcan cannon capable of spewing out 2,500 rounds per minute, a 100-rounds-per-minute 40mm Bofors cannon, and a 105mm howitzer. Like a hawk over prey, it circled the sky 10,000 feet above the mansion, out of range of Cuban antiaircraft guns, keeping an eye on developments with its special cameras and infrared equipment.

When the BTRs summoned enough courage to venture through the front gate and charge the house, the Spectre nailed the first one only twenty feet from the front door. Like thunder in the heavens, like a flying dragon, the aircraft belched fire and death. It was a terrifying sight for both friend and foe. Streams of missiles screamed earthward, marked by a solid fire path of tracers shattering the air, ripping into earth with deadly accuracy.

The other APCs fled for their lives, followed by the infantry. What began as a counterattack deteriorated into a stalemate. The two remaining armored vehicles prowled the vicinity waiting for the cover of nightfall. Soldiers went to ground. Inside Government House, SEALs settled in to await the enemy's next move. Only the sniper and his spotter remained fully active as they dissuaded the most foolhardy or the bravest from becoming too aggressive.

The C-130 circled over Government House for the rest of the day with its massive firepower, like a guardian angel. As the day wore on and evening approached, sporadic small-arms fire began to build in intensity. The Spectre went into action a second time later that night. SEAL lieutenant Bobby McNabb watched the show from a second-floor window. He described the action:

"The BTR was probably fifty to seventy-five yards away. He wasn't shooting at us. He was trying to hit the plane. You could hear the plane, kind of see it outlined up there. The plane shot the 20mm at him. Every time one of those rounds hit, they kind of gave off a spark. Well, he was hitting dead on top of the APC. The Spectre hit the APC so many times it had a hellish glow over the top of it. You could see the bodies getting blown about. Oh, man, it was brutal!"

The gunship coupled with marksmanship and sniper action from the encircled mansion kept enemy forces at a respectful distance throughout a nerve-wracking night. The anticipated ground force relief still failed to arrive. SEALs expected the PRA to move in on the house. Yet, nothing broke the stalemate. Sir Paul and Lady Scoon spent an anxious day and night amid broken glass and spent cartridge casings.

During the night, a company of Marines held in reserve landed at Grand Anse Bay near St. George's. A second company crossed the island by helicopter from Pearls Point to reinforce it. At 0300 hours on 26 October, the two forces linked up and, supplemented by five M60A1 Abrams tanks, descended upon the governor-general's mansion. Grenadians besieging Government House fled.

SEALs inside the house were relieved at 0712 hours

and the governor-general, his wife, and his staff were quickly evacuated. A rescue mission projected to occur with complete surprise and lightning execution had taken over thirty hours to complete. The SEALs had suffered no serious casualties during the day and night of battle at Government House. However, four had been killed when they made an at-sea paradrop prior to the start of operations.

CHAPTER NINETEEN

The sniper, often neglected between wars, misunderstood by his commanders, not appreciated for his special craft and skills, has not always been looked upon as a legitimate addition to the brotherhood of arms. The rise to his proper place in the profession of warfare has not been easy. Although he saw the rise of the nation, it was not until after the Vietnam War that the sniper was finally accorded full peacetime status and accorded an MOS (military occupational specialty) of his own. Prior to that, snipers were ushered out onto the field when the shooting started, then locked away in the closet again when the shooting stopped, as though they were something of shame.

The U.S. Marines were leaders in recognizing the full potential of battlefield snipers and in sniper training. Under the guidance of Marines like Jim Land, Dick Culver, Jack Cuddy, and Carlos Hathcock, the first permanent scout sniper training school was established in Quantico, Virginia, in 1977. Two other Marine divisional-level sniper schools were subsequently established at Camp Lejeune, North Carolina, and Camp Pendleton, California. These schools trained students from the Army and Navy, and even the FBI, until these branches created their own training programs.

The U.S. Army followed the Marine Corps in developing peacetime sniper training. An Army sniper school was set up at Fort Bragg, North Carolina, in the 1980's, under the direction of the XVIII Airborne Corps' Army Marksmanship Training Unit. The Army finally organized its own permanent sniper school at Fort Benning, Georgia, in 1987.

At about the same time, U.S. Navy SEAL (sea-air-land) teams created a nine-week sniping course similar to that of the Marines, only modified somewhat to suit the special covert nature of SEAL operations in counterterrorism and behind enemy lines.

Finally, the U.S. Air Force got into the game on a much smaller scale in the 1990's with its Countersniper School at Camp Joseph T. Robinson in Arkansas. The course, only two weeks long to accommodate reservists, was not designed for traditional snipers who crawl around the terrain hunting enemy targets. Rather, it taught countersniper tactical shooting to be used by security personnel in perimeter and airfield defense.

There is a broad similarity in all the schools, no matter the military branch. Modern sniper training is essentially a consolidation of lessons learned from as far back as the French and Indian War and the American Revolution up through Vietnam and the Iraq War of 2003. It was Vietnam, however, that stamped the definition of sniper, as expressed in the training manual *Infantry Training—Skill At Arms: Sniping:* "An infantry soldier who is an expert marksman and observer with the ability to locate an enemy, however well concealed, then stalk up or lie in wait to kill him with one round. He is able to observe, interpret and accurately report enemy movement. He can observe without being observed—kill without being killed."

Selection of a potential sniper is of the greatest importance, since only good soldiers make good snipers. Selection boards look for specific qualities in an individual: already-established marksmanship; good physical conditioning; good hearing; excellent vision; intelligence; initiative; common sense and patience; a mature personality to cope with the stress of calculated, deliberate killing; good observational skills; attention to detail.

"When students showed up for the first day of sniper school," noted USMC Master Sergeant Neil Kennedy Morris, senior sniper instructor, "we inventoried all their gear to make sure they had everything on the check-in list. If it was on the list to have two canteens and they only had one, we dropped them right there for lack of attention to detail."

Lieutenant Colonel Randy Smith, commander of the Marine Sniper School at Camp Lejeune, looked for superior judgment in a student. "If we say to a Marine, 'We want you to crawl out there in enemy territory and not be compromised and engage the enemy threat in such and such a manner,' he's going to do exactly that. If we say, 'The rules of engagement are such and such, you are going to shoot this kind of target only,' that's exactly what he's going to do. If a new commander has a sniper who he thinks is a rogue, who's going to take shots as he sees fit, he's not the kind of guy you want."

While the original Vietnam sniper vets—Jim Land, Dick Culver, Jack Cuddy, Carlos Hathcock and others— were the most instrumental in launching full-time sniper schools and stamping them with the potential for success, Master Sergeant Neil Kennedy Morris is probably responsible for most sniper training standards currently used by all branches of the military.

Morris began his career in the Army as a Ranger. He then switched to the Marines to begin a twenty-four-year career spent primarily in sniping and special operations. After participating in real-world sniper operations on at least four continents, and in teaching the lessons he learned, he retired in 2001 as senior Marine scout sniper, master sniper, and one of the most experienced snipers and sniper instructors in the history of the Department of Defense. He was the first and, to date, the only Marine to hold senior instructor/operator billets in all three U.S. Marine scout sniper schools. He assisted in writing the current curriculum for the Marine, Army, and Navy basic sniper qualification schools and authored the USMC Advance Scout Sniper course.

As chief sniper instructor for the 1st Marine Division at Camp Pendleton, he drafted a successful POI (program of instruction) based on a logical progression of phases from basic to advanced proficiency. Concerned that the school at Quantico was moving away from the proven fundamentals introduced by Jim Land and others, he took his POI to Quantico in 1987 to be reviewed by a course curriculum review board composed of instructors from all three Marine sniper schools.

"We wanted to get back to training snipers and get away from all that gee-whiz commando bullshit," he explained. "The infantry battalion doesn't need a ninja warrior running around in a black flight suit. What the sniper does is already a special skill."

All three Marine schools went with the POI Morris

had already implemented in the 1st Marine Division. That same POI, with certain modifications, has since been adopted by the rest of the U.S. military.

Although sniper courses vary somewhat in structure, three broad areas are emphasized: marksmanship; field craft, to include camouflage and concealment; and tactical employment, or stalking. Stress and ardor are typically built into a course.

"Being a scout sniper is extremely stressful business," said former sniper school commander Captain Tim Hunter. "The school shows us how a future scout sniper will act and react under pressure. If he can't handle that stress in a school situation, there is no way he will be able to cope with it on the battlefield."

Each of the three phases in Morris's POI progressively builds upon the previous phase. "By the time a student gets into the second phase, for example," Morris explained, "he is well versed in the weapons systems and understands how the bullet flies and has a lot of experience calling the wind."

The POI was created for an eight-week training period. The first four weeks, phase one, concentrate on known distance marksmanship; reading aerial photos; map reading; land navigation; mission planning and employment; and communications, with emphasis on calling for mortar, artillery, and air strikes. There is little field craft or stalking during this phase.

Students begin constructing their "ghillie suits," a procedure Jim Land called "part of the passage into the sniper community." The ghillie suit was developed by Scottish gamekeepers called "ghillies" during the nineteenth century for stalking on the great Highlands estates. It is still the most effective personal camouflage in temperate regions. However, as a practical matter, it has rarely been used under combat conditions, especially in its full form.

The ghillie suit is nothing more than loose overalls in a camouflage pattern to which netting is firmly secured. The front of the suit is reinforced with heavy cloth or canvas and padded at the knees and elbows. Hundreds of long burlap strips are attached to the netting, especially on the back, to cover the sniper in an irregular pattern in the prone. Headgear is a bush hat or hood similarly festooned, coupled with a mask or face veil. A sniper in a ghillie suit is a startling apparition, a "bog creature."

Marksmanship training continues during the second three-week phase of the course: unknown distance shooting; firing from supported and unsupported positions; field expedient positions while standing, kneeling, sitting, or in the prone. To the shooting are added field-craft skills in tactical employment, stalking, concealment, approach and withdrawal routes, intelligence gathering, survival and escape and evasion, and utilizing a "hide."

As an aside note, Navy SEALs have added an extra week and an additional phase to sniper training to accommodate the special nature of snipers in the Navy Special Warfare role. Almost forty hours are devoted to naval gunfire support, across-the-beach operations, sniper operations involving parachute drops and helicopter insertions, shooting from helicopters, boarding of potentially hostile vessels at sea, and other similar skill demands for us in low-intensity conflict.

The third and final phase of Morris's POI is a one-week field tactical exercise during which surviving students are evaluated in the actual performance of everything they have been taught. They are expected to accomplish a variety of simulated missions under conditions as close to the "real world" as possible: sniper patrol orders, construction of positions, the stalk, target reduction, and the final shot. In order to pass, the student must be meticulous in every detail, invisible to his foe, and capable of delivering forcefully, without fail, when his moment comes to squeeze the trigger.

"He's a well-rounded package now," said Master Sergeant Neil Morris. "He's progressed through all three phases. He's good with his weapon, he can navigate, he can call for fire, and survivability in combat is going to be increased greatly."

All that remains is going out and doing the job under actual combat conditions. Sniper Chuck Mawhinney (103 kills in Vietnam) offered one final tip that the new sniper should learn quickly once he reaches the field:

"I had the advantage of having served as a grunt for three months before I became a sniper," he said. "Grunts work harder than anyone else. They carry twice the load, march farther, get less sleep, and work on less sleep than anyone else in the military. The grunt goes out, works day and night, and eventually comes back alive, if he's lucky. Because of my knowledge of what it was like, I made sure I gained the trust of all the grunts I worked with. I didn't want them to think I was some kind of prima donna puke just because I was carrying a different rifle or wearing camouflage.

"Every sniper, and every damned so-called specialist out there, should learn this lesson. It's the most important lesson they can learn. You take care of your grunts, and they'll take care of you. If you get compromised or in a jam, the grunts will bail out and come to help you, no matter what. You have to gain the respect of the units you work with and work every day to keep it."

CHAPTER TWENTY

Because of the Arab-Israeli war of 1948, thousands of Palestinian refugees fled to Lebanon and settled in Beirut, feeding the conflict between Christians and Muslims. Yasser Arafat's Palestine Liberation Organization (PLO) set up headquarters in West Beirut in 1970 after being expelled from Jordan. The PLO launched several raids into Israel using Lebanon as a base, after which the Christian-dominated Lebanese government attempted to stop any further PLO military actions. That prompted Arafat to side with the Muslims against the Lebanese government and the Christians, declaring with the Muslims a "broader Pan-Arabism."

Open warfare broke out between the Christians, the Palestinians, and the Muslims in 1975. Muslims and Palestinians took over West Beirut, while Christian groups fortified East Beirut. Fearing an Israeli invasion as violence escalated, Syria sent 20,000 troops to Beirut "to prevent destruction of the Christian community." Shortly thereafter, in June 1982, Israel invaded Lebanon in hopes of driving out Palestinian forces. After a series of "full-scale attacks" by Israel, Yasser Arafat and his PLO hastily evacuated West Beirut.

The withdrawal changed the devil's equation in Beirut but little. Although the Christian militia and the Lebanese Army maintained order in East Beirut, religious fanatics and different and often rival Muslim factions in the other half of the city turned it into a hellhole of anarchy that left much of the central city in shambles.

The United States had sent 800 Marines to Beirut in August 1982 to oversee the evacuation of the PLO. The Marines withdrew afterward, only to be redeployed as the 32d Marine Amphibious Unit (MAU) in late September following the assassination of the Lebanese president-elect and the massacre of Palestinians at the Sabra and Shatilla refugee camps by Christian militiamen. Two days after their arrival, on 30 September, Marines suffered their first casualties when one was killed and two wounded while clearing unexploded ordnance.

On 30 October 1982, the 32d MAU was relieved by the 24th MAU, which extended a presence in Beirut to the earlier Christian sector. Marines patrolled the "Green Line" that divided the city and helped the Lebanese Army regain and maintain order. From September 1982 to 19 October 1983, seven Marines were killed and 64 wounded in a war that was never declared a war.

On 23 October 1983, a suicide truck loaded with 12,000 pounds of explosives destroyed the Marine headquarters building and barracks at Beirut International Airport, killing 241 Americans and injuring 70 others. A simultaneous suicide attack against a building occupied by French paratroops resulted in 58 casualties.

It was into this chaotic and confusing anarchy of Beirut that U.S. snipers were inserted to operate as counter snipers in a "peacekeeping" role with the United Nations.

CHAPTER TWENTY-ONE

U.S. Marine Corporal Frank Roberts
Beirut, 1983

You had to see Beirut in 1983 to appreciate the ferocity and utter destructiveness of the internecine warfare that had engulfed the city for the past ten years, and which continued with no relief in sight. Israel bombed and mortared it. The LAF [Lebanese Armed Forces] bombed and mortared it. We shelled and mortared it. In between all this bombing and mortaring, about a dozen different warring clans shelled and mortared it and each other. The result was basic World War II urban bombing rubble: blown-up hulls of buildings, streets blocked by the burnt remains of vehicles and crashed aircraft, shattered cement with rebar sticking out like old bones. . . .

At first, the rules of engagement for Marines sent to the city to regain the peace were very strict. You couldn't return fire unless first fired upon. After you assessed the incident to make sure the incoming was in fact directed at you, you called for permission to shoot back. The request went from the man with the rifle to his supervisor, to the lieutenant, to the S-2 [Operations], to the commander, to Germany, to Washington, D.C. . . . Your target could die of old age by the time you received permission.

That procedure began to change after the Israelis pulled out. For two days an endless procession of Israeli tanks, APCs, half-tracks, and other vehicles rumbled out of Beirut on the Sidon Highway. They left a huge vacuum between the Marines, the British, the Amal, the Druze, the Christians, and whatever other groups were all mixed up inside that armpit of the world, shooting at each other.

The LAF, which were basically Christians, moved up from the Mediterranean and through Marine lines to establish themselves in the void left by Israel. The Druze began to advance from the Shufan Mountains. Amal was already in the city. Hundreds of other fighters drifted in to the refugee camp at Hasalom, which was next to the library and barracks controlled by U.S. Marines. Naturally, shit started to happen. Small-arms fire went on nonstop, along with rocket and artillery explosions. You almost had to have a score card to determine who was fighting whom. I basically figured out that *everybody* was fighting *everybody else*.

The Druze had Soviet radar-controlled antiaircraft batteries. They promptly took out the entire LAF Air Force. About twenty ancient jets fell out of the sky like wounded birds as the Druze advanced, pushing the Lebanese back to the International Airport, which U.S. Marines held. With the LAF behind us and the Druze in front attempting to drive all of us into the sea, rules of engagement relaxed.

I suspected they relaxed or tightened according to how many Marines died or were wounded on any particular day. As a scout sniper in a bunker at the airport, I maintained commo with the S-2 and therefore received all the intel about casualties. The S-2 might call one day and say I didn't have to ask permission to return fire *if* the target was firing at me. He might call back after a couple of Marines were shot and snap, "Shoot the bastards if they need shooting, whether they're firing at you or not."

I was armed with the new Remington M40A1 with a Unertl 10X scope, a real sweet-firing weapon. On a wall about 425 yards away from my bunker hung three large posters of the Ayatollah Khomeini; the Iranian holy man was a local hero of the radical Muslims. The posters made perfect targets for zeroing in our weapons. Snipers shot noses and ears and punched out eyes.

Sporadic incidents occurred. Some nut would show up out there in all that city war rubble and take potshots at the Marines lines around the airport. He and his buddies were accustomed to spraying bullets and not hitting shit. On the other hand, sniper teams who engaged them fired one shot and a guy dropped. They weren't used to that.

Of course, it was tough to verify our work, since none of us volunteered to go out there and take a look. However, you generally knew you had accomplished your mission and made a hit from all the shrieking and screaming that followed.

One afternoon a guy loosed a few random shots and then went into hiding. Scanning the ruins with binoculars, I spotted him peering out through an aperture in his homemade bunker. That was all I saw: eyes. It was enough. I placed a bullet through the slit. A moment later, a woman appropriately dressed in black ran out flailing her arms and weeping and wailing. I must have shot her boyfriend or her husband. He should have stayed home.

That was the way it went for the first month or so I was there: us sitting out there at the airport in our bunkers while they winged shots at us. Morale suffered. The commander decided to give it a boost through a "Marine of the Month" program. The winner went before a board to be meritoriously promoted. I was selected. The commander's jeep picked me up at 0630 to deliver me to headquarters. On the way in, the convoy to our rear was ambushed as it left the airport perimeter. One Marine was killed and two others wounded.

Instead of going before the board and getting promoted, I hopped a jeep with a driver and another sniper named Forbush. The driver agreed to take us as close to the airport as he could. A fierce firefight continued to rage around the ambush site. Artillery rounds whistled above the city and detonated with jarring bangs, hanging a curtain of smoke above bombed-out buildings.

The nervous driver finally balked at going any further when we were within about 1,500 yards of the airport, a little less than a mile. "I'm going back."

I couldn't blame him. Any vehicle, and especially an American military vehicle, was a prime target in this savage, battered city on the seacoast. I looked at Forbush. He looked back at me and shrugged. We grabbed our rifles and trotted off through the ruins of Beirut toward Charlie Company and the relative comfort and safety of our bunker.

It took us about an hour and a half to work our way through the maze of wasteland Marines called Hooterville. The home stretch required us to cross the wide street where the convoy had been ambushed and where a fight was still going on. Exactly who was fighting whom was unclear, as the Marines had already withdrawn.

Stray bullets whacked into the sides of buildings like horizontal hailstones, adding to the pockmarks of countless other fights. Dust and haze hung low in the street, clogging the nostrils and tasting dry and ancient. Brush fires smoldered in the weeds and brush outside the concertina wire that enclosed the airfield, contributing to the overall murkiness.

I looked outward from the airport and up the street before I took a chance on crossing. I made out the smoky outline of a rolled jeep and a couple of other vehicles left behind as wreckage following the ambush. Forbush and I would have to rush across the boulevard under heavy fire in order to reach the outer concertina and wriggle underneath the wire to our own lines. I hoped headquarters had informed our guys that friendlies were coming in. We had no radio or other means of communication.

"Cover me," I said to Forbush.

I bunched my legs underneath, took a deep breath, and sprung into the street, my legs already blurring like those of the cartoon Road Runner character. I made it about two-thirds of the way across before some asshole started zapping bullets my way. I combat-rolled into a shallow ditch and got so low that the only thing that prevented my getting even lower were the buttons on my utility shirt.

I lay there panting, one eye on the wire—which offered relative safety beyond in the bunker complex, and which seemed a moon's distance away at the time—and the other eye trying to pierce the fog of battle to pick out the bastard shooting at me. Forbush's weapon remained silent; apparently he was also unable to locate my assailant.

While I was thus engaged contemplating the peril of

my position, a tiny incongruous bundle of fur and mange suddenly appeared from nowhere. Wriggling the tail half of its body and drooling with friendliness, the tiny creature launched itself at my face and damned near drowned me with puppy kisses. It scampered about with joy, letting every hooter in Hooterville know exactly where I was.

A second rifleman hidden in the debris and smoke honed in on me, skipping bullets off the concrete within inches of my head. Too late now to shoo the puppy away, even if I could have broken the bond he already seemed to have formed with me. It was only a matter of minutes, even seconds, before a bullet skittered into my flesh.

Fuck it. I couldn't just lie there with the dog jumping back and forth over me like some kind of a circus act. I bounced to my feet and bolted for the wire, with the barking puppy and Forbush racing after me. All three of us, miraculously unscathed, flung ourselves underneath the concertina. Good thing those fuckers out there couldn't shoot for shit.

During the lull that followed that night, three sniper teams were deployed in bunkers nearest the outer perimeter to pound the hooters a little payback for the ambush. My partner Rick David and I took the center. Tom Rutter and his partner occupied the bunker to my right while Forbush and Moore took the farthest to my left. We engaged targets intermittently during the night as they crawled around in shattered buildings out there in the wasteland. It was a bit like plinking rats in a city dump. The crack of a high-powered rifle would ring out and the target would disappear. No one was going to walk out there to see if the guy was dead.

Shortly after daybreak, following a long respite in the action, I was surprised to see a group of five men venture out of the city and into the open about 400 yards away. They obviously thought they were far enough away from our lines that we couldn't reach out and touch them. All sported new crisp Soviet Bloc camouflage uniforms. No typical blue jeans and sneakers for these guys: They were *important*. The leader, the one giving all the orders, had a German shepherd on a leash and carried an AK-47 slung over his shoulder.

Curious, I watched them through my scope for about fifteen minutes as they measured wall craters made by Marine M203 grenade launchers. I assumed they were checking for penetration to determine how much cover their men required. It soon became more apparent that they were assessing fields of fire and selecting avenues of approach for a planned assault against our positions.

Time to put a stop to it.

I dispassionately measured the target on my scope's mil-dot scale, laid crosshairs almost dead on him at this range, and squeezed the trigger. As the stock recoiled into my shoulder, the target dropped like God had reached down with an invisible sledgehammer and poleaxed him. The startled dog lunged against its leash, broke free from the dead man's hand, and fled for cover with the deceased's comrades. The body lay unmoving where it fell. He didn't look so important now.

A squad of raggedy militia arrived twenty minutes later to engage me with counterfire. The way the streets were laid out, such as they were, attackers were limited to using alleys that opened up directly in front of the airport and Marine lines. I returned a shot or two with uncertain results, whereupon the aggressors entertained second thoughts and withdrew from my sector.

above: Lance Corporals Thomas D. Ferran (left) and Edward F. Poole (right) show Brigadier General Foster C. La Hue, commanding general, Task Force X-Ray, the sniper rifle used to kill five Vietcong in a two-week period during Operation DeSoto, 50 miles south of Chu Lai, Vietnam.

left: Tom "Moose" Ferran, USMC Scout/Sniper, 7th Marines, 1st Marine Division, Vietnam.

Gary Reiter with Winchester Model 70 in Phu Bai, Vietnam, May 1966.

GARY REITER

GREG KRALJEV

Greg Kraljev with Winchester 700 7.62mm (.308) in Vietnam.

Jim Lever with the 1st Marine Division with Remington 700 with Redfield 3 x 9 x scope in Vietnam, November 1967.

Jim O'Neill with Remington 700 with Redfield 3 x 9 x scope in Vietnam.

NEIL MORRIS

above: Neil Morris in camo with ghillie net.

left: Master Sergeant Neil Morris, USMC, at Quantico with M40A3 sniper rifle.

NEIL MORRIS

Neil Morris giving instructions to DEA.

TOM RUTTER

Marine sniper, Corporal Tom Rutter, sights through Unertl
scope atop his M40A1 sniper rifle in Beirut, Lebanon.

EARL SCHOOLEY

Operation Just Cause, Panama, 1989. Front row (left to right)
Corporal Earl Schooley, Sergeant Thomas Dewitt, Corporal Michael Tagle.
Back row (left to right) Corporal Louis Dimoff, Lance Corporal Abrash,
Lance Corporal Tim Hagen, and Lance Corporal Kevin Sloss.

FRANK GALLI

Frank Galli (right) and Paul Webster
at Camp Casey in Korea, 1989.

Sergeant Michael Carr in Somalia, 1994.

Carlos Hathcock (left) and Craig Roberts in 1988 at the Tulsa Police Department range during sniper training.

White feather still adorning his hat, Carlos Hathcock evaluates a target for the Tulsa Police Department's Special Operations Team snipers, 1988.

Major E. James Land, USMC, who started the 1st Marine Division sniper school on Hill 55 in 1967. Land was Carlos Hathcock's commanding officer.

The dummies. They shifted to my right and attempted the same tactics in engaging Marines there. Rutter knocked off one of them, perhaps two.

They still hadn't had enough. A half hour passed, then firing broke out on my left. Forbush and Moore knocked down two more as the blitzkrieg sneaked down an alley. That did it. The would-be commandos hauled ass back into the ruined city from whence they came.

Force having failed, they now resorted to guile, negotiation, and bitching. A rattletrap Land Rover flying a white flag pulled up to the north end of the airport perimeter. A guy got out and introduced himself as a representative of Nabih Berri, chieftain of the Amal militia. Apoplectic with rage, stamping his feet and flinging his arms, he demanded to see the commander of the Marine forces. How unfair it was to employ sniper fire against them!

My bunker lay within earshot of all the yammering. I stepped outside with my scoped Remington M40 crooked into my elbow. I leaned casually against the side of the door, wanting the militiaman to see me. He stared, his eyes wide and mouth agape at beholding one of the sharpshooters who had rained death upon his men. After a moment of permitting him to inspect me, I turned without a word and reentered my bunker.

I later learned what transpired when Nabih Berri's agent met the Marine commander.

"Make your snipers stop," the Amal militiaman badgered.

"Our snipers are doing exactly what I tell them to do," the commander responded. "And until you guys conform with the peace process here, we're going to continue doing it."

CHAPTER TWENTY-TWO

U.S. Marine Corporal Tom Rutter
Beirut, 1983

Lance Corporal Thomas Gregory Rutter waded ashore from the "Mike" boat that deposited him in Beirut. He carried in its protective case a Remington M40A1 sniper rifle with attached Unertl 10X scope. Like the Marines who landed in Lebanon in 1958 to quell the insurgency that threatened the pro-Western government, the men of 1st Battalion, 8th Marine Regiment, found themselves caught in the middle of a civil war.

Beirut was a city in ruin. High-rise buildings that formerly stood out as jewels in the Mediterranean sun were now burnt-out hulks. Battle scars and bullet holes pockmarked nearly every wall. Rubble creatively fashioned into roadblocks and sandbagged bunkers dotted the neighborhoods as armed men from different groups and factions dug in and laid claim to their turf in the city. Amal Shiite Muslims, the Christian Militia, the LAF (Lebanese Armed Forces), all clung fiercely to their own sectors and defended them against any who encroached, while the Israelis in the urban area called Hooterville shot it out with Yasser Arafat's Palestinians of the PLO. It was one confusing mess.

United Nations peacekeeping forces—primarily U.S. Marines—occupied a middle ground at Beirut International Airport. The BLT [battalion landing team] building, which harbored battalion headquarters, barracks, Intelligence and Operations, backed up to the airport and was conveniently located near various other government and university buildings manned by Marines. Half the snipers of the STA [Surveillance and Target Acquisition] platoon, six men, remained at the BLT while the other three teams of two, including Rutter, were dispatched to the Lebanese University. The snipers' mission was to cover terrain that rifle company grunts with their M16s couldn't reach.

A sergeant was supervising a working party on the roof of the main four-story university building when the snipers arrived. He surveyed the young Marines toting their hard-shelled rifle cases.

"You snipers?" he asked.

"Yes, Sergeant."

The sergeant wiped sweat from his brow and squinted in the blazing sun. "It's a hot sonofabitch," he said. "We gotta build a bunker on the roof so we can cover the surrounding area. The bad guys have RPG-7s. If they put a rocket into the side of the bunker, we want to be well protected. That means at least six sandbags thick."

Rutter scanned the surrounding countryside with his professional sniper's eye, calculating ranges, possible avenues of approach, and "hides" for the bad guys. Toward the north lay the area controlled by Christian Militia, to the west were Hooterville and the mountains beyond. Between Hooterville and the university stretched an open field about 500 meters wide and covered with scrub brush and ditches.

Another 500 meters to the south began the city. Buildings pocked by bullet holes and rockets straddled streets cluttered with burnt cars and piles of rubble. The roof of the BLT building rose beyond several abandoned high-rises.

"This place is a mess," Rutter said, putting his binoculars aside.

"These people have been fighting for a long time," the sergeant said. "If this war ever ends, someone's gonna make a lot of money in the construction business."

Roof bunker built, the university Marines settled into a boring routine of standing watches, cleaning weapons and relaying reports to headquarters. A team of two snipers was required to be in the bunker at all times, which meant little downtime for the six shooters.

Everything remained relatively quiet as long as the Israelis manned nearby positions in Hooterville. Fighting in the city avoided this sector, for good reason, as the Israelis were quick to respond to any aggression with overwhelming force. One night Rutter was watching when a group of Amal crossed into the open field between the university building and the Israelis. The Muslims went down a ditch until they were within range. One of them fired an RPG rocket at an Israeli bunker. Israeli soldiers instantly blasted back with machine guns and tanks. The Amal hastily retreated, running for their lives. Things settled down again.

"Don't mess with the Israelis, especially when they have tanks," Rutter's partner commented wryly. "Those guys don't have to get *permission* to fire, like we do."

"It's kinda nice having the Jews around," Rutter said.

The Israelis, however, didn't stay around long. Politics. Israel pulled out of Lebanon. The atmosphere around the university changed immediately. Amal Shiites took over the former Israeli strongpoints and occupied Hooterville. AK-47 gunfire rattled away in the streets. Rutter watched through binoculars as guerrillas ran wildly through the city, spraying buildings with their assault rifles and pushing out the LAF.

At an intersection, ambushing Shiites swarmed like ants onto a pair of Lebanese armored personnel carriers. The back doors on the APCs dropped and the LAF crews jumped out into the street with their hands up. Guerrillas took over the vehicles' mounted .50-caliber machine guns and swiveled them toward their huddled prisoners. The guns blazed death, crumpling the captives like so many paper targets and contributing another pile of shattered blood, flesh, and bone to the city's litter.

Horrified and helpless to intervene, Rutter snapped at his partner, Corporal Jonathan Crumley, "Get on the hook and tell S-2 what just happened."

Crumley grabbed the handset. "This is Spyglass One with a SITREP. We just saw a bunch of ragheads take over a couple of APCs and execute the LAF troops. They had green, white, and red flags and carried AK-47s."

After a brief radio conversation, he replaced the handset and turned to Rutter. "They said it's the Shiite militia. It seems they're getting real bold, now that the Israelis have split."

"I wonder just how bold they'll get."

He soon found out. Amal showed up a day or so later with bulldozers and began constructing berms, bunkers, and fortifications on the far side of the field facing the Marines. Knowing the Marines couldn't shoot at them unless they were first fired upon, they brazenly went about their business of cordoning off UN forces into pockets, the better to eventually attack and wipe them out.

Rutter watched with contained frustration and anger. There was nothing he could do unless the Amal attacked. Even then, he had to seek permission from BLT headquarters before he could so much as slap a loaded magazine into his rifle.

Completing the fortifications emboldened the Amal to start taking on the Marines. Sporadic AK-47 rounds whipped around the university building and slapped into its walls. Although fired outside their maximum effective range, they were nonetheless potentially dangerous and certainly annoying. Plus, the lack of response by the Marines further encouraged the Amal.

One watch period seemed to run into the next as tired and frustrated Marines manned their posts and ducked rifle shots from the gleeful and persistent guerrillas. It soon became apparent that the situation was about to deteriorate into open warfare. The guerrillas seemed to hold nothing but contempt for the impotent Americans. They stood in full view on top of their bunkers and waved their arms before unleashing magazines of bullets at the university.

Finally, the U.S. command had had enough. Word came down the pipe that the discretion to shoot should be with the men on the firing line. The Marines, at last, could shoot back.

"We finally get to play the game," Corporal David Baldree commented, locking a full magazine into his sniper rifle.

Rutter grinned and patted his M40. "This is really going to give them a shock."

Two days later, Rutter and Baldree were on duty at the roof bunker when a burst of bullets whined over their heads. Since scout snipers were the battalion's eyes and ears, Baldree immediately reported the incident to the BLT's combat operation center.

"We got incoming fire, over."

"Roger, Spyglass One. Can you suppress?"

"That's affirmative," said Baldree, nodding at Rutter.

Rutter radioed line company Marines on the ground floor. "Send the STA Platoon guys up," he said. "We got targets."

The other snipers scrambled to the roof and took positions at firing posts. They soon pinpointed a lone gunman hiding behind a berm at about the 600-meter range. He poked his head up quickly, fired his weapon at the Marine bunker, then ducked down again before changing his position along the berm and repeating the process.

"I'll keep an eye on him until I get a shot," Crumley proposed. "Rutter, see if anyone else is shooting at us."

Rutter continued to scope the wasteland. He sweated profusely underneath the mid-August sun and had to keep blinking and wiping it away. He concentrated on every detail of the shattered terrain as he slowly glassed across it.

Movement caught his attention in the firing revetment of a sandbagged bunker at the open end of a Hooterville street. A muzzle flash winked at him as he took a second look. He settled his reticule on the target and fired. Shooting from that position ceased.

Crumley refused to allow himself to be distracted by his bunker mate's rifle shot. He continued to watch the berm through his scope while he timed the shooter and determined his pattern. He read the range from his mil-dot scale and set his dope for 600 meters. The next time the man stuck up his head, Crumley was ready. Payback time. He fired.

A puff of dust kicked up in front of the unknown assailant's face and his head exploded in a crimson mist. He flipped over backwards out of sight. A few minutes later a red and white ambulance raced up to the berm and stopped. Two men jumped out and lifted the corpse into the ambulance, then drove off again without a second look at the university.

That began the macabre cat-and-mouse game of sniper and countersniper, with the advantage held by the expert marksmen in the sandbagged bunker on top of the building. It was almost ritualistic, almost suicidal in a macho sort of fashion, the way the Amal rifleman played the strange game. Individuals or small groups would dart out of hiding and fully expose themselves long enough to fire a quick and inaccurate burst or two, then dodge back to cover. A bit like taunting the bull. The Marine snipers obliged them.

It became Rutter's habit to carefully check the terrain each time he reported on watch. Had anything changed since last time? Anything new out there? Once he was satisfied, he entered a notation in his log and settled down to await developments.

1730 hrs. All quiet. No new obstacles or positions, he jotted down one late afternoon in the third week of August. The setting sun cast long shadows through the streets of distant Hooterville.

He had hardly begun his watch than a string of machine-gun rounds blasted into and past the bunker. Baldree and he instinctively ducked, then peered out, seeking the source.

Another burst. Then another. The firer was at least

smart enough not to use tracers, which would have marked his position. It was the gathering darkness that soon proved his undoing.

"I got something," Rutter said, concentrating through his scope. "That building at two o'clock. Back in the shadows."

The window of the darkened room flickered and cast a momentary glow each time the machine gun chattered.

Baldree homed in on the site. "We can't get an angle on him from here," he concluded. "Let's put a little teamwork on this asshole."

Crumley ran downstairs to help Marine M60 machine gunners pinpoint the enemy. He rang on the field phone when he was ready. Rutter and Baldree locked tracer rounds into their Remingtons.

"Ready?" Rutter asked.

"Ready," said Baldree.

Twin red streakers cut through the darkness and snapped through the targeted window, marking it. Marine M60 machine gun fire instantly ripped apart the night. Angry red tracers filled the raghead's lair with a brief unholy glow. There could be no further question about who outgunned who.

By late September, things had quieted down at the university. Marine snipers and supporting line company leathernecks had taken almost complete command of the battlefield. Amal couldn't get close enough to cause damage without sustaining casualties. S-2 at the BLT called to say there might be work for a sniper at the airport.

"Cut cards for it," Rutter suggested. "Low man goes."

Rutter lost. A CH-53 helicopter dropped him at Beirut International Airport shortly after dawn the next morning. Heat waves already danced on the ramp. It wouldn't be long before the desert sun burned off the last of the night's chill. Another sniper from the STA platoon, Rock, met him in Operations.

The intel chief, Captain Walter Wint, conducted the short briefing. "First Platoon of Charlie Company has been taking excessive amounts of small-arms fire and RPG rockets at their sector of the airport," he said, stabbing a finger at the map. "Yesterday a staff sergeant was driving down the road in front of their positions and the Amal opened up on him. He was killed. Charlie Company is pissed and so are we. You two get over there tonight and see what you can do. I'll see that sentries are notified that you'll be moving across the runway. Watch your asses."

Rutter and his new partner picked up their equipment and started for the door. Captain Wint stopped them with a grin.

"One more thing, Rutter. You'd better get some new stripes. Your promotion came through. Corporal."

The two shooters reported in to Charlie Company. From 1st Platoon's bunkers, Rutter analyzed the terrain and the boundaries and picked a bunker that seemed to give them the most advantageous command of the area. In the morning sun toward Charlie's front and across a field sat a small square mud building proclaiming itself to be Danielle Café. Even this early there was quite a lot of activity in and around it.

On the wall of a building across the street from the restaurant hung a large poster of Ayatollah Khomeini. Dark eyes from the poster stared at Rutter. The sniper settled his crosshairs between the Ayatollah's glaring eyes.

"*That's* the bastard I'd like to drop," he murmured.

The café was obviously a weapons cache. Amal militiamen entered it unarmed and came back out with weapons to take up hurried positions in bunkers and behind roadblocks. A few isolated bursts of gunfire sailed over at the Marines in the late afternoon, but the shooters judiciously stayed under cover. By nightfall, all was quiet.

The same scene of Amal arming themselves at Danielle Café replayed itself at the next dawn. This time, however, they made a big mistake due to overconfidence. They came out of the restaurant with guns blazing, running around out in the open.

"I'll take the first one," Rock said, drawing a bead on a moving rifleman wearing a green uniform and helmet liner. "He must be an LAF deserter."

The Remington recoiled. The green helmet liner sprang into the air, tumbling as it fell to the street. The deserter's head snapped grotesquely to one side as brain matter erupted in a pink puff and he collapsed in the street. Horror on their faces, his comrades bolted around the corner out of sight. The street was empty except for the dead guy lying in the road.

Two minutes later a little red foreign car darted around the corner and stopped in the street. Three men jumped out while the driver slumped low behind the wheel and kept the engine gunning. Two militiamen ran to the fallen soldier and began dragging him toward the car. The third sprayed bullets toward the Marine positions.

Rutter had already taken a bead on one of the two dragging the dead man. He squeezed off a single round. The target slammed backwards into the side of the car, his chest skewered.

"Two down, three to go," he quipped as he worked the bolt.

The second litter bearer dropped his burden and dived into the backseat of the car on top of the gunner.

Another Marine sniper positioned nearby, Corporal Frank Roberts, shot the driver through his windshield. The glass and the man's head exploded just as he slammed the little car into reverse. The roaring engine spun the car, the two surviving Amal, and the dead driver around a corner out of sight. Two corpses now lay in the street.

An elderly woman stepped out of a building across from Danielle Café and stared. She began yelling and pointing.

"Wonder what she's bitching about," Rock said.

"Probably wants the mess cleaned up. Keep Beirut clean: Bury a Shiite."

The poster of the Ayatollah continued to glare disapprovingly. Rutter couldn't resist the temptation. Rock grinned and joined him. Cement dust geysered and the poster split as a pair of bullets struck square in the middle of the angry man's forehead. *From America with love—scumbag.*

On 23 October 1983, a Shiite Muslim drove a truck laden with explosives through the gate of the Marine complex and detonated it. The blast collapsed the building and killed 241 American Marines, soldiers, and sailors, including most of the command staff. The explosion awakened Corporal Rutter at the airfield. He rolled out of his sleeping bag and looked toward the source of the discharge. A massive column of black smoke encircled in a second ring curled into the morning sky. The BLT building, normally seen from Charlie Company's positions, was gone.

CHAPTER TWENTY-THREE

U.S. Marine
Lance Corporal Carey Fabian
Beirut, 1981

The U.S. Navy and the U.S. Marines evacuated civilians from Juniyah in Lebanon because of the civil war crisis that had been raging inside that country for well over a decade. After we dropped them off in Cyprus, an operation that went off without a hitch, the task force steamed a holding pattern in the Mediterranean for about a month, creating a "presence" and doing little else.

Word finally came down the pipe that the Navy and Marines were returning to Lebanon, this time to Beirut with an international force to rescue the PLO [Palestine Liberation Organization] from the Israelis, who had stormed up from the south to surround the Palestinians in the city. Yasser Arafat and his guys were screaming for help. Personally, I would have preferred it if the Jews knocked off the murdering old terrorist and saved everybody a lot of grief—but I was a U.S. Marine, and a disciplined Marine followed orders.

.. in 1981—and for any number of years after-
—was the most dangerous city in the world, with a
olent death rate of over one thousand people each
month. There were so many different groups at each
other's throats that you almost needed a score card to
tell who was fighting whom. To begin with, there must
have been a dozen militias, each like a particularly
fierce street gang warring with the others to hold its turf.
Then there were the Palestinians and Syrians and the
Christians and Muslims and Lebanese and Jews and . . .
Lord only knew who else.

A particularly hellish list of ingredients. Add gunpowder, mix and stir, and—bombing and shelling and
strafing and shooting each other. Sometimes the Israelis
set up roadblocks manned by Arab-speaking Jews to
check for Palestinians, which they then hauled off and
executed. The PLO wanted out desperately.

Parts of the city resembled Berlin following Allied attacks on it during World War II. Shops that somehow remained in operation were multilayered with sandbags.
Stray cats stalked equal-sized rats among mounds of
garbage piled twenty feet high; normal city services had
almost ceased functioning. Rotting garbage on street
corners fouled neighborhoods with a stench that re-
volted the stomach and hung over the city like a noxious
green cloud of gas. Beirut might have been called a dys-
functional city.

U.S. Marines moved into this armpit of the world,
occupied the international airport, and, along with
French Foreign Legionnaires, secured a safe corridor
through the city down which PLO fighters might pass
to the docks, where a fleet of international ships evacuated them. Another sniper, Lance Corporal Jeff Graham, and I were assigned to this corridor to conduct ob-

servation and provide precision fire, if necessary, from the top of what must have been a grain elevator near the docks.

From our towering observation post, we commanded an unobstructed view the length of the evacuees' approach route, a rather narrow street between aged buildings, some of which were nothing now but scorched, bullet-riddled frames. Marines and Legionnaires lined the street as far as we could see into the tattered heart of the city.

The PLO came down the corridor in noisy groups, either walking or crammed into the backs of pickup trucks. A motley-looking bunch wearing filthy Arab garb or equally filthy Western attire. After passing through the checkpoints, they arrived at the docks firing their weapons into the air, shouting and hooting in triumph as though they were the victors rather than losers slinking out of Beirut with their tails between their legs.

Then they would lay down their weapons and cram onto the next ship, which soon chugged out of the harbor to deliver them to Syria or Libya or some other who-the-hell-knows place.

As Jeff and I watched, alert for any overt hostilities, a truck full of Palestinians pulled up to the docks. Naturally, the passengers began their typical shoot-weapons-in-the-air ritual as they offloaded. I was on the spotting scope and Graham had the scope on the bolt gun. These guys were spraying the sky good. I always feared we would get hit by stray falling rounds.

"Goofy bastards," I muttered sourly.

A PLO fighter with an AK-47 jumped off the rear of the truck with his finger on the trigger. The jolt of his landing accidentally discharged his weapon. Graham and I recoiled in fascinated horror as the bullet smashed into the chin of the guy above him, still on the truck. It exited through the top of his skull, spewing out a crimson geyser of blood and brains.

His body plunged to the street, kicking and "doing the chicken," as people shot through the brain sometimes will. Utter chaos reigned around the truck and the dead man, but it didn't last long. The PLO was in a hurry to get out of Dodge and away from the Israelis. His comrades simply left the body lying where it fell. He lay there several days, getting ripe under the near-equatorial sun, before some of our Marines bagged him and hauled him off somewhere in a six-by to be with Allah. I sometimes wondered if he might not have ended up in one of the garbage dumps on a street corner.

The evacuations were almost completed when a long procession of vehicles rolled down the corridor toward the docks, in the middle of which traveled a sleek black car. Obviously it carried someone important. PLO security teams rode trucks both in front and rear and engaged in none of the old shoot-in-the-air bullshit.

It was my watch on the rifle. I was peering through the scope, accustomed from my high vantage point to being the spectator to surreal sights playing themselves out below day after day. I followed the black car with my crosshairs until it stopped at the docks. Armed men quickly surrounded it, facing outward in a threatening manner. A little runt of a man in a gray-green military tunic and a red-and-white checkered head rag got out and strutted around as though waiting for someone to rush up and kiss his ass. I failed to recognize him.

I looked at Graham. "They've brought somebody through," I said.

"Let me see."

I rolled off the rifle and we changed positions. Graham pored over the scene for a moment, then seemed to get excited.

"Get on the spotting scope," he snapped.

I did. Jeff identified the cocky little dignitary. "Chairman Yasser Arafat. Call the wind for me."

We had already set up a range card. I stared disbelievingly at Jeff for a split second.

"What's the wind doing?" he repeated.

"You have zero wind, range 550."

I held my breath. Jesus. Was he really going to do it?

He suddenly relaxed. The rifle barrel lowered. He turned his head toward me. Neither of us said a word, but both of us understood. We could have killed Yasser Arafat that day. But, of course, being Marines and disciplined Marines at that, we didn't. Later, I sometimes thought, pondering that day, that we might have saved a lot of lives and the world a lot of trouble had Jeff gone ahead and squeezed the trigger.

CHAPTER TWENTY-FOUR

U.S. Marine
Lance Corporal Carey Fabian
Beirut, 1983

The 2nd Marine Division, to which I was attached as a sniper, was sailing to Lebanon when it was diverted to Grenada for that little affair of weeding out a nest of commies. After we finished restoring calm and democracy to the island, we resumed our float to Beirut. Less than two weeks before, the BLT command center had been blown up by a suicide bomber, killing 241 American servicemen. That changed the equation in the beleaguered city.

I had been in Beirut as a sniper in 1981. Things had indeed changed considerably since then. A cartoon appearing in the Marine Amphibious Unit newspaper showed a map of the American presence in 1981 compared to 1983. In 1981, Marines had occupied much of the city. In November 1983, Marines were at the international airport and everything else was *them* surrounding *us*.

I discovered a kind of siege mentality when I arrived. Marines hunkered down in their holes and bunkers at the airfield and simply waited for—no one knew exactly what. We got shot at on a daily basis while rules of engagement imposed upon us by higher headquarters remained as wacky as when I had been here previously. No firing at them unless they *first* fired at us.

It seemed everyone in Beirut carried a firearm. It also seemed that at least 90 percent of the people we watched cavorting about were just waiting for the right moment to kill one of us. Yet, we couldn't do anything unless they actually fired a shot. After a while, like everyone else, I began feeling that I had been committed to some kind of macabre insane asylum.

Echo Company occupied the perimeter of the Mideast Airlines building at Beirut International. Golf Company was dug in across from Hooterville. Fox tied into Golf Company's flanks and burrowed into bunkers on the south facing the direction of the ocean. Corporal Jeff Graham and I were senior snipers of the STA [Surveillance and Target Acquisition] platoon. As such, we acted more or less as joint NCOs in charge. We assigned sniper teams to each of the battalion's three companies.

It was difficult from day to day to figure out who out there beyond the wire was with us and who was against us—*if* indeed *anyone* was with us. Along about dusk each evening, groups of armed militia gathered underneath streetlights at various points outside the wire to smoke and joke and scope out Marine defenses for action later that night. We knew what they were up to, but still all we could do was watch them. Whenever they disappeared, we could almost set our watches a half hour to forty-five minutes ahead and expect to receive incoming fire.

The division artillery battery kept getting shot at every night. It had set up opposite an old PLO field hospital that had been abandoned when the Palestinians evacuated and was now in ruins. Scrub brush grew as thick as dog fur around the hospital until the terrain dropped straight off beyond in a thirty-foot cliff. Behind the cliff rose the rusted corrugated roof of some kind of factory.

People went to work at the factory in the morning and got off in the late afternoon, just like blue-collar workers anywhere in the rest of the world. It was only at night after the factory shut down that the artillerymen took fire from the vicinity of the hospital building. I was determined to put a stop to it.

I gathered binoculars, spotting scope, scoped rifle, water, and chow and climbed to the top of one of the airport buildings to place the hospital and factory under observation. A sniper was also a scout and an observer. I soon noticed that all the men who arrived for work at the factory in the morning were not leaving again in the evening. Eight guys might come to work, but only six leave. It was a pattern that played itself out after nightfall with snipers shooting at Marine artillery.

I took a patrol through the wire to check out my theory. Sure enough, there was a worn trail leading from the factory, up the cliff, around the abandoned PLO hospital, and into shrubbery just outside the perimeter wire of the airport. There were even large sections of cardboard spread on the ground so the shooters wouldn't have to lie on the cold sand while they waited to take a shot or two.

STA platoon had what were called 1 Alpha seismic intrusion detection devices. These were tiny electronic gadgets that informed a controller of movement within a certain listening radius. I rigged a couple of them in the bushes to warn us when the factory workers arrived for their nocturnal after-hours employment.

The artillery battery was ready a night or so later when the snipers opened fire from the hospital vicinity and the gadgets tattled on them. Imagine their surprise and shock when an HE [high-explosive] artillery round dropped right into their pockets and immolated them in a big white-fire boom. Marines received no more gunfire from that location.

Still, as soon as you knocked out one batch, another popped up. Spillover fire accounted for some of the rounds striking the airport. At least a dozen different factions and militia groups were out there in those destroyed streets, battling each other. We sometimes watched fierce firefights raging outside the Marine perimeter. It was inevitable that at least some of it spilled over onto the airport.

Most of it, however, was deliberate, with the intent to kill Marines.

Some group—it made no difference which—set up an 82mm mortar on the flat roof of a building overlooking Echo Company's position and began firing high explosives periodically onto the airfield. One Marine was wounded when shrapnel sliced off his finger and buried into his inner thigh, barely missing his femoral artery.

It took us three or four days to locate it. When we did, one of my shooters armed with an Iver Johnson .50-caliber rifle smashed the lip around the roof that hid the big gun, showering the crew with concrete and putting the weapon out of action. You didn't actually have to hit a man with the .50-cal to do him in. Concrete blown out of a hole in the wall did the job just as well.

Dueling like that continued day after day. Mortar fire,

122mm Katyusha rockets, sometimes artillery shells, regularly pasted the airport. Pickup trucks on the streets outside the wire drove recklessly about loaded with armed men and rockets. As soon as it got dark, they disappeared and rockets were launched at Marines. Loudspeakers were scattered all over the airport. Sirens went off during a shelling and a mechanical voice magnified through the loudspeaker intoned, *"Condition One! Condition One!"*

Corporal Graham took charge of half the STA platoon while I oversaw the other half. Corporal Louis Butler and I established a kind of sniper command post in a large steel sea-land shipping container that had been half-buried in the ground, then sandbagged. We even slept there.

One evening I hugged the deck of the container while we got thoroughly lambasted with incoming mortar. Some of the rounds exploded so near they actually jarred me off the floor. The artillery battery rang me on the field phone. I crawled over and answered it.

"How close are the rounds?" a voice asked.

"Close. Come down here and find out. I'm not going to stick my head out to give you a precise measurement."

It was the night of 6 December. Two of my snipers—Corporal Biddle and Corporal Sherman—were out with Sergeant Manuel Cox and his squad on an OP [observation post] that Golf Company had occupied forward of its lines in a two-story mortar-and-brick building near the wire. Two factions were battling it out on the outside of the perimeter. Spillover fire peppered the building in such quantity that at least some of it had to be intentional.

Two Marines normally manned the OP on the roof while the others waited below in relief. Expecting an attack, however, all the Marines, including Biddle and Sherman, were on the roof to reinforce the position. An 82mm round landed directly in the middle of them.

Someone field rang my bunker. Louie Butler answered it. There was presently no shelling in our area.

"Corporal Fabian, it's for you."

It was another corporal I knew and had befriended in the communications section.

"Did you know the OP was hit?" he asked.

I hadn't heard about it yet. His voice broke.

"Shannon and Sammy got killed," he said.

I went numb and dropped the handset. Biddle and Sherman had been with me in Grenada, even before. We were friends. We were tight.

Louie Butler shot a look at me. He knew by the shocked expression on my face that something had happened. I finally found my voice.

"Shannon and Sammy were killed out on the OP."

Silence as heavy as soured molasses oozed into the bunker.

"Take a couple of minutes," I said.

I needed them as well. I walked out of the bunker and stood in the dark. All was quiet now. Less than three weeks until Christmas. Christmas would never be the same again for the families of my dead snipers, my dead friends and comrades.

I walked back inside and looked at Louie. "Are you all right?" I asked.

He said, "Are *you* all right?"

I nodded. I said, "Let's get on with it."

CHAPTER TWENTY-FIVE

U.S. Army Sergeant Eric L. Haney, Delta Force

U.S. Army Sergeant Andres Benevides, Delta Force Beirut, 1983

During the 1970's and 1980's, the men of the U.S. Army's counterterrorist 1st Special Forces Operational Detachment—Delta (Delta Force) were frequent flyers into Beirut. It was the beginning of worldwide extremist Islamic terrorism. Hijackings of airplanes and occasionally a tourist ship often either started in Lebanon or ended up there. Political kidnapping victims were also held in the Beirut slums. Toward the latter half of 1983, U.S. Marines occupied Beirut International Airport and virtually nothing else as the United States under the auspices of the United Nations attempted to bring peace to a savage land torn by fratricidal warfare.

Throughout the occupation, Marines found themselves targeted by Amal and other factions fighting each other in the streets of the beleaguered city. Snipers regularly shot at Marines and sometimes engaged them with mortars and rockets. Although the Marines had excellent countersnipers of their own, a problem arose when the shooters began using crowds of teenagers and kids as cover. Marine snipers were unable to return fire and put an end to the harassment because of their military-issued ammunition—solid, hard-jacketed, 173-grain rounds made for long-range accuracy and penetration.

As a U.S. Forces commander explained to Delta Force snipers Eric Haney and Andres Benevides when they arrived in Beirut to help unravel the complication: "We can't shoot back when they use crowds. Our snipers tell me that even though they can probably pick off each shooter, it's almost a certainty that the round will go completely through him and hit at least one other person. That other person could be a child, and that's a price we're not willing to pay."

So far during the recent guerrilla tactics, several Marines had been wounded, though none had been killed.

"We were told you men had an answer," the Marine commander concluded.

Delta Force had experimented with and built a lightweight sniper bullet for use against terrorists in crowds or crowded situations, such as during aircraft or ship hijackings. While the high-velocity bullet was accurate and deadly, it spent most of its energy upon impact and therefore remained inside the body of a human target. Its main drawback was its limited 400-meter maximum range. Marine snipers at the airport were shooting at targets as far as 1,000 meters out, which meant the Delta shooters would have to go outside the wire at the airport and nest into a position that provided range and view of the Hooterville slums from which the shooting originated.

As a first step in conquering the problem of the crowd shooters, Haney and Benevides spent a day glassing areas frequented by enemy snipers, getting the lay of the land while they identified potential hides and made a detailed range-card sketch. Finally, satisfied with what they had learned, the two wiry men from Fort Bragg moved out under cover of darkness with their rifles, side arms, radio, and small packs containing supplies for a four-day standoff. That meant food, water, a few comfort items, and bottles and plastic bags for use in storing liquid and solid wastes while they were encamped in their hide. Once they were in position, they would not move out again for at least four days, not even to relieve themselves. A sniper above all else required patience.

They made their nest in a large pile of rubble and garbage at the site of what appeared to be the remains of a bombed-out building. From there, the ground ahead sloped gradually upward through scattered empty buildings and piles of junk to some abandoned greenhouses where the shooters commonly appeared.

When daylight came hot and bright, the two professionals completed their preparations by calculating distances and angles to various potential target sites. They designated and numbered the sites beginning with "Position One" for easy identification and reference. Ranges varied from 250 to 350 meters.

They settled in, watchful but patient. They had been told the enemy snipers usually came out in the later afternoon. Each man took a rotation tour on the spotting scope, limited to a half hour each time to minimize eyestrain.

The first day passed uneventfully. A donkey nosed about in the dry brush and weeds in search of graze, and some small boys came near to chase lizards. People went about their daily lives, such as they were in a chaotic environment, unaware that they were being watched through high-powered lenses. When night chased dark shadows into Hooterville, broken only here and there by dim pinpricks of light, muted conversations and other sounds drifted up from this sad little finger of Beirut to the two untiring Americans hiding in the rubble.

Day two was almost a repeat of the first: lazy, hot, quiet. That night Haney and Benevides received an unexpected treat: They took turns on the scope watching a movie on a TV seen through a distant window—*The Searchers*, starring John Wayne.

Day three duplicated the previous days—until about 1735 hours, not long before sunset. Four or five teenage boys ventured from the mouth of a narrow alley abutted on the right by a high concrete wall. More and more appeared until about twenty of them, bolstering their boldness in numbers, were leaping about, jeering and pointing at Marine positions inside the airport perimeter. Noticeably, they kept glancing back at someone behind the concrete wall who seemed to be orchestrating the event.

Soon enough, when the gathering was large enough, two Lebanese men armed with AK-47 rifles stepped into sight. The teenagers treated the newcomers like heroes, slapping them on their backs and shaking hands and laughing. Everyone was having a great party. They had learned all too well that Marines at the air base would not shoot into a crowd.

What they didn't know, however, was that the equation this afternoon had changed. They were being watched through powerful scopes mounted on M24 sniper rifles.

"Action at [Position] Four," Haney said quietly.

"I see 'em."

Haney adjusted his sights for a range of 320 meters, the distance precalculated for that particular target position. He seated the bolt on his rifle, fully chambering the round. Benevides was doing the same thing. The order of targets had also been predetermined. Haney centered his crosshairs on his man's upper lip. Each sniper carried out his duties calmly, dispassionately, professionally. Another day at the office. Emotion—at least in the process of the mission—could not be allowed.

"Call it when your target is out, Andres, and you have a shot," Haney said softly.

The man in Haney's sights lifted his AK and pointed it at the air base. Benevides was ready, his target also crosshaired. He intoned, "Snipers . . . ready . . . *fire!*"

The two rifles cracked at the same instant. Both targets dropped as though a giant invisible hammer had whacked them to the ground. A faint pink halo of blood and atomized flesh hung momentarily in the air.

"Dead," Haney announced. He chambered a fresh cartridge.

"Dead," Benevides repeated.

The teenagers scattered like dead leaves in a whirlwind. A couple of the bolder ones dared to drag away the bodies. Then the alley was quiet again. It was over.

"We didn't have much to say the rest of the afternoon," Haney later wrote. "But I could read Andres's mood, and I am sure he could read mine. We had accomplished our mission, but it was nothing we could take pride in. I felt soiled and slightly guilty—as if I had stolen something and nobody knew it but me. When the action is hot and you know you're saving innocent lives with your shooting prowess, there is a certain elation to sniping. But this one didn't feel that way. It had been a necessary act, but an unpalatable one. And the only thing that remained was a vague, nasty taste in the back of my throat that refused to go away."

CHAPTER TWENTY-SIX

U.S. Marine Sergeant Brian Barber
Quantico, Virginia, 1990

At the U.S. Marine Sniper Instructor School at Quantico, Virginia, where I was an instructor for a number of years, shooting in training is conducted at ranges from 200 yards out to 1,000 yards, the length of *ten* football fields. Targets are man-sized silhouettes, most of which present the narrow side view to make the shooting more challenging. At the beginning of the course, the targets are stationary. Then Marines working the butts start walking the targets across at a normal sentry pace. Finally, the speed is sometimes increased to a sprint.

A shooter is concerned with two mechanical elements when looking through his rifle scope: the crosshairs and the mil-dot scale. The crosshairs, of course, are the sights. The mil-dot scale consists of a series of measured tics arranged both vertically and horizontally in the center of the telescopic sight where the crosshairs intersect. It assists the shooter in determining range and in adjusting for weather [primarily wind] influence and target speed.

The old way of engaging a target required the use of "Kentucky windage." The shooter held high or held low for range and led a moving target according to his best estimate of its speed. The mil-dot systems on most newer scopes, starting with the Unertl 10X fixed telescopic sight, brings science into the equation and makes the sniper much more accurate and therefore more deadly. The one shot—one kill of the Vietnam war was not exactly that. Each kill, to be precise, required 1.3 to 1.7 rounds. Theoretically, at least, the mil-dot system reduces that statistic to more nearly one kill for every shot.

To use the mil-dot system, you first need to know the height or width of a particular object or target—say, a stop sign that is three feet wide or a man who is approximately six feet tall. Snipers carry range data books which contain predetermined charts to help with scope settings. Measuring the target on the mil-dots using the known height or width factor provides a range, a known distance, which the sniper then uses in a simple formula to adjust and calibrate his scope (size of target in yards times 1,000, divided by size of target in mils equals distance in yards to target). The result of these calculations is then dialed on the scope for point of aim/point of impact application. The Unertl has a quarter-minute-of-angle increments, which means one click on the adjustment knob lifts or lowers the expected impact of the bullet one quarter of an inch at 100 yards. Four clicks on the knob therefore raise or lower the bullet one inch.

You apply the same principle for windage, although it isn't quite as scientific. The shooter's judgment and experience come into play here. His range data book lists conversion charts for wind speeds and their effects to help him make expedient adjustments in the field. Flags on the range are used to determine approximate wind velocity and direction. Quite obviously, flags will probably not be available under real world shooting conditions. Therefore, improvised methods will have to be used.

The "clock" method is one. You drop a small handful of dust or sand or a few strands of grass and watch them flutter to earth, pointing with your arm at where they land. The angle of your arm can then be calculated to determine wind speed and direction. Again, the sniper's range data book assists him in dialing wind into the scope. One click on the knob moves the impact of the bullet either right or left a predetermined amount depending upon bullet weight and powder load.

There are various other methods for determining wind velocity and direction as well: the tops of grass or the leaves on trees blowing in a breeze; the ripple of water; clothes left out to dry on a line; the feel of wind against your cheek; heat mirages . . . all such methods, however, are merely estimates. Winds may be blowing at different speeds and in different directions between the rifle and the target, especially at longer distances. Experience with shooting under varying conditions and at different times of the day and night is the only way to learn to cope with wind.

What these adjustments for range and wind do is provide a known variable for each shot. All other conditions being equal, with the scope correctly set, the bullet is going to hit a still target exactly in the center of the crosshairs. No longer is there the "Kentucky windage" need to hold over or hold under according to estimated ranges or to compensate for wind as you squeeze the trigger.

A sniper with such a system should be able to kill another man every time he shoots. Theoretically.

CHAPTER TWENTY-SEVEN

American snipers played a role in Operation Just Cause, the successful U.S. effort in 1989 to unseat Panamanian dictator Manuel Antonio Noriega and bring him to justice in the United States on charges of money laundering and drug trafficking with Colombian cocaine lords. Planning for the invasion under the code name Operation Blue Spoon began more than a year previously, on a contingency basis, because of increasing tension between the United States and Noriega.

As commander of the Panamanian Defense Forces (PDF), Noriega had been the de facto ruler of Panama since 1981. He was indicted in absentia by a U.S. federal court in February 1988 on a number of drug-related charges. He merely laughed. On 7 May 1989, he showed contempt for his own country's democratic institutions by dismissing the country's freely elected president and nullifying the subsequent election to maintain himself in power. In December, Panama's National People's Assembly, most members of whom were handpicked Noriega appointees, named him "maximum leader" and officially installed him as head of the government. That same meeting declared that a state of war existed between Panama and the United States.

The crisis that precipitated Operation Just Cause occurred the next evening, 16 December 1989, when Panamanian troops in Panama City shot and killed U.S. Marine Lieutenant Robert Paz, who had gotten lost driving with other officers to a local restaurant. A U.S. Navy lieutenant and his wife, who witnessed the shooting, were arrested, beaten, and brutalized.

According to treaties signed in 1979, the United States had the right to defend the Panama Canal against outside threats. President George Bush ordered that Operation Blue Spoon be converted into action as Operation Just Cause. He designated three goals: the quick neutralization or removal of military resistance; the capture of Manuel Noriega; and the installation of a stable democratically elected government. General Colin Powell, chairman of the Joints Chiefs of Staff, and his director of operations, General Thomas Kelley, prepared to accomplish these goals by applying such overwhelming force so swiftly and at so many locations simultaneously that Noriega and his followers would be removed and his 23,000-man PDF and "Dignity Battalions" neutralized without causing grave damage to Panama or danger to its largely friendly population or the 50,000 U.S. military dependents and other U.S. personnel employed in operating the Panama Canal.

Twenty-seven targets were scheduled to be hit at H-hour, 0100 hours, 20 December 1989, an enterprise that ultimately required over 27,000 American troops. It would be the largest airborne operation since World War II. Special Operations forces would pave the way. Army

Rangers would parachute onto military airfields to seize them; Green Berets would form blocking forces; Delta Force would rescue an imprisoned American citizen, Kurt Frederick Muse, from the Modelo Prison and then seek Noriega in Panama City. U.S. Navy SEALs were assigned to put out of action the sixty-five-foot PDF patrol boat *Presidente Porras,* which Noriega might use in an escape attempt, and to disable Noriega's personal Learjet at the Paitilla Airfield.

Snipers would be used to suppress enemy snipers and positions when there was a clear civilian population in the area of operations and collateral damage was a concern; to secure key positions; and to screen flanks, thereby freeing infantry to clear buildings and conduct patrols. And they would be used during MOUT (military operations in urban terrain) to perform an effective economy-of-force role.

The campaign was generally well conceived and meticulously choreographed. Command and control, communications, intelligence, and operations were all coordinated down to the smallest details. All objectives were attained, including the capture of Manuel Noriega. He sought refuge at the Vatican embassy in Panama City but finally surrendered to American forces on 3 January 1990. He was convicted of charges against him and is still incarcerated in a federal prison in the United States.

CHAPTER TWENTY-EIGHT

U.S. Army
Lieutenant James H. Johnson III
Panama, 1989

As Scout Platoon leader, 2d Battalion, 504th Parachute Infantry Regiment, 82d Airborne, I knew there was some serious planning going on a few days prior to the battalion assuming DRF-2 [Division Ready Force 2]. On Monday morning, 18 December, we started the day with PT as usual. At 0900 hours I was notified that we were alerted. Alerts at Fort Bragg, North Carolina, were common occurrences for drills and training. I had no reason to assume this one was any different than previous ones.

Immediately we began drawing sensitive items and weapons as per SOP [standard operating procedure]. My platoon stored all our deployment bags and field gear in our CP [command post] during mission cycle, so we had it all there. We pulled the gear out at our formation area where squad leaders went through one last layout and inspection.

The battalion sniper squad attached to the Scout Platoon consisted of three sniper teams of two men per team, with Sergeant Darren McAllister the senior sniper team leader. These men were the most highly trained infantry soldiers within the battalion, having gone through Special Operations sniper school at Fort Benning, Georgia. They used the M24 weapons system. The M24 was a return to bolt-action sniper rifles by the U.S. Army. As with the U.S. Marine M40A1, the M24 used the Remington 700 action with the receiver adapted to take the 7.62mm NATO round. The sights were 10x42 Leupold Ultra M3 scopes, plus detachable emergency iron sights. Snipers had a specific mission separate in the battalion, for which they required ghillie suits, drag bags, spotting scopes, and other items specific to a sniper mission.

We took all the gear we might need for any contingency down to the PHA [personnel holding area] at nearby Pope Air Base. The platoon itself was ready to move to the PHA when I went down to battalion for an N-plus-2 briefing. Our strength was one officer and 24 enlisted men, plus the six snipers.

The battalion S-3 along with the battalion commander, Lieutenant Colonel Harry B. Axson, came to the conference room and said we were being briefed on this EDRA [emergency deployment readiness exercise] to occur on DZ Sicily right at Bragg. Just as I thought. More training.

However, both officers were holding maps of Panama in their hands. It occurred to me that we weren't getting jerked around this time, that we were going real world.

The men of the platoon drew a basic load of 5.56mm for their M16s, 180 rounds per man. The snipers drew something totally different. Normally when they fired at Fort Bragg they got M118 special ball ammunition.

However, when we got the supply pallets at the PHA, their ammo was 7.62 match grade, 150 rounds per sniper. It was, said Sergeant McAllister, a real world combat load.

We also received as issue: three or four smoke grenades per fire team, a mix of colors for marking purposes; two Claymore mines per squad; four M203 grenade launchers; six AN/PRC-77 radios; and eight AN/PRC-126s. No pistols or SAWs [squad automatic weapons] were issued.

Colonel Axson drove all the leaders back to Bragg to watch a VCR aerial film of the battalion's objective areas. By this time we had been informed of the nature of the overall mission, Operation Just Cause. The United States was preparing to invade Panama.

My platoon's objective area after the battalion parachuted into Torrijas-Tocumen International Airport, which the Rangers would secure in advance northeast of Panama City, extended from Albrook Air Station up the coast all the way to Panama Viejo [Old Panama]. The area around Panama Viejo, I saw on the aerials, had a lot of trees, which masked some of the slum areas. Our mission was to occupy two OPs [observation posts] which basically covered the major routes and bridges coming into Panama City. The sniper teams would accompany the platoon as counter snipers.

On the evening of 19 December, after an all-nighter and most of the day at the PHA, the platoon moved with all the other chalks over to Green Ramp for loading onto C-130 aircraft. We did a loose rig by donning the parachutes and reserves but keeping the ALICE packs and weapons free to store under the seats or behind the seats. It was still night out and it started to drizzle and snow. I cross loaded planes, half the platoon on one aircraft, the other half on another, so that if anything happened to any one plane I wouldn't lose the entire element.

It was weirdly quiet as we loaded—none of the usual clowning around and goofing off. Absolute quiet. Even the safeties weren't in their normal behavior mode; they were actually trying to help people, helping guys rig out, and not yelling at them.

It was still snowing and raining when we took off. Most of the guys slumped down in the canvas seats and slept on the flight south. I slept fitfully. I was watching the time to see when we were getting close to TOT [time over target]. We got a twenty-minute warning and that got everybody awake. Colonel Axson stood up with some words of encouragement.

"The Rangers," he said, "are working toward their objectives. Enemy fire on the DZ is light. Everybody have a good jump. I'll see you on the DZ."

Doors opened. Green lights came on. I exited the aircraft at 0212 hours. The first thing I saw after my chute opened were the glow lights below on the ground from the heavy equipment drops. There wasn't much moonlight, only 20 to 30 percent illumination, and there were a few red tracer rounds going off way off to the north. Someone on the ground was shouting up through a bullhorn that we were dropping among friendlies—the Rangers— and that we should not be shooting.

I started to get the shapes of dark areas. I realized I was too far east of the DZ at the airport and over the trees or rough areas. I never hit the ground. Instead, my toes were almost touching as I sort of hung suspended in a big bush.

I pulled the canopy release assemblies, got my weapon out of its weapons case, dropped my ALICE pack, and got a radio check with some personnel that were already up on the net. I didn't hear any firing. Only some sounds in the general area where people were trying to move equipment.

I started walking to the west and crossed over two heavy drop platforms that were still there. The first person I ran into was Sergeant First Class William Lucas, who was the battalion S-3 [Operations] NCO. He used to be my platoon sergeant in the scout platoon. He had been a Marine Corps sniper in Vietnam and was now carrying an M21 sniper rifle. [The M21 was the upgraded redesignation of the 7.62mm M14 that had been the American military's main battle rifle at the beginning of the Vietnam War. Lucas had scored 38 kills as a sniper in Vietnam, and would make a further kill in Panama.]

We linked up with two other people from the battalion. I still didn't hear any shots fired or any activity. Just before I reached the airfield I linked up with my platoon sergeant, Sergeant First Class Angel Serrano. When we came out on the airfield we saw some elements from the Ranger battalion that were de-rigging one of the platforms that had hit the airfield.

The battalion assembly points were farther up. I had designated them for the platoon on the southern tip of the airfield. So I moved down there with SFC Serrano and linked up with one of my sniper teams, and then slowly the platoon came in. The last element came in at 0556 hours. The reason it took them longer was because they were dropped way to the southeast in some really wet, marshy areas.

Choppers arrived and on my lift were 23 people going into LZ Lion. Part of my platoon would be on Lion while the other element proceeded to LZ Bobcat. We flew basically along the coastline. The LZ looked almost exactly as it had on the video I saw at Fort Bragg. I was looking closely trying to identify where the ZPU-4 [Soviet-manufactured heavy machine gun] was because that was the major threat in the area.

On that first lift of four choppers going to Lion, there was no problem because they all landed on the beach and no one hit the mudflats. We jumped off the aircraft and started running to the embankment for cover. It was 0705 hours and the sun was up. We heard a few sporadic shots.

All ten choppers of the second lift came into Lion. That was when the problem occurred with the mud. It was too large a lift for that size of LZ. Charlie Company and one of the other companies got personnel stuck in the mud. None of the companies had a rope, so we gave up one of ours for them to throw out to drag people out. My headquarters element attempted to assist, to provide security. I told my other two squads to move out and man their OPs. They were in position at OP-2, the western point, at 0742 hours, and at OP-1 on the north at 0749 hours. We quickly established communications with our scout elements at Bobcat and found they were also in position.

We expected a lot of action at the Panama Viejo barracks, the direction in which all the companies were oriented. I expected the companies and the snipers to be under fire or making fire on the barracks to clear them. Instead, there wasn't much action.

A lot of civilians gathered around OP-2. They were coming up and telling us that there were PDF here or PDF there. OP-2 received fire first, from three personnel in a building just to the north of the OP. My men returned fire. One person ran from the building and tried to get to a car, at which time we fired an M203 round and that silenced the firing. There was one wounded enemy personnel in that incident.

A civilian ambulance showed up. We took the wounded guy's weapon and let him be taken away in the civilian ambulance.

We received reports of vehicles moving with armed personnel in small Nissan trucks and vans. They moved toward the bridge, took a look around, then circled back through some portion of the city and came back and looked again. Under the rules of engagement, we couldn't fire on them unless they fired on us. That was slightly frustrating.

At 0924, OP-1 received sporadic fire. My men stopped one blue Volkswagen and apprehended four men with AK-47s and turned them over to Charlie Company.

Meanwhile, OP-2 apprehended four policemen who tried to run the roadblock. While these four were being detained and questioned and tagged, a blue Toyota with four more came in firing as they came. The bottom line was there were two enemy KIA [killed in action], two enemy WIA [wounded in action], and one friendly WIA from Bravo Company. We captured three 9mm pistols, one 9mm Uzi, one FMLN rifle, seven AK-47s, and one RPG.

All these drive-bys or indiscriminate firings were made much more difficult for us to handle due to the fact that there were about a hundred people standing on the street corner watching.

We continued to man the OP's throughout the night of 20 December. The next day was pretty much the same as the day before, except there was much less activity. We knew there were some enemy snipers in different positions around Panama Viejo. At this point, our snipers were being used primarily to recon, as opposed to being told that if they saw somebody walking around with a weapon, drop him. They were, however, a significant recon asset because of their vision devices.

We repositioned the snipers to rooms up on the top parts of buildings so they could fire down the two major avenues if there was some sort of drive-by activity like the day before. We were concerned about all the people within the Panamanian army who were quality-trained snipers. Since we hadn't caught them in the Panama Viejo barracks, we were concerned that they were still out there and that our guys might really start taking some losses.

At 0800 hours, 22 December, our snipers were in position on the major runs pointing to the east. Reports from there and Charlie Company indicated activity on the other side of a small water inlet. Charlie Company saw two figures sneaking around in ghillie suits. That was to our west.

I immediately shifted all my sniper teams over to orient on the west, using snipers as countersnipers. Two of the snipers said they saw movement of possibly two individuals among some buildings and marshes down by the inlet. This was all within about a range of one hundred meters or less. I popped over to get a feel for what was going on.

One of my sniper teams again saw movement but could not specifically identify targets. They waited. When they did identify targets, they fired. They had no confirmed kills. We waited and saw some more movement. They fired some more but still could not confirm kills.

Since there were no conclusive results, I called in a fire mission of battalion 81mm mortars. They fired seven rounds—a fire-for-effect mission. We suppressed whatever the enemy was trying to do. Two days later we reconned the area. Civilians told us ambulances came in and picked up ten bodies. That may not be totally accurate. We swept the area and found one bush hat, not of U.S. make, and one other piece of army-colored green clothing, but no blood marks or traces. It was basically inconclusive about the effects of the morning's work.

By 23 December, things were really starting to calm down and we got out into the community. The afternoon of 24 December was the first day we started moving through Panama Viejo. A squad moved in front of a rifle company with the psyops [psychological operations] loudspeaker vehicle, moving through and telling people not to worry. We were checking for snipers and PDF and wishing people a Merry Christmas. I would say that by the end of Christmas Eve my platoon had taken the first step, mentally, in the transition from combat operations to stability operations.

CHAPTER TWENTY-NINE

U.S. Marine
Lance Corporal Earl Schooley
Panama, 1989

Rumors about war had circulated among U.S. troops in the Canal Zone since I arrived in October 1989 as a sniper with the STA [Surveillance and Target Acquisition] Platoon, 3d Battalion, 6th Marines. Panama's dictator Manuel Noriega had been indicted or was about to be indicted in the United States for drug trafficking. All that remained was for somebody to come down and arrest him. I didn't have to *go* to war; I was already there.

In between conflicts, a sniper was little more than a glorified grunt. STA was assigned as part of a rotating contingent to guard ammunition dumps. The platoon moved into Quonset huts at Rodman Naval Air Station located on the western end of the Panama Canal at Panama City and Balboa Harbor. We stood watch and listened to the rumors.

On 16 December, Noriega's PDF [Panamanian Defense Forces] murdered off-duty Marine Lieutenant

Robert Paz. On 19 December, at 1810 hours, shortly before dark, word came down for STA to stand by for further orders. Shortly thereafter we were officially alerted, told to grab our combat gear and report to Building No. 2. Something was coming down. There was a different buzz in the air.

If you were a grunt in the Corps, you were only told what you needed to know and nothing more. You seldom saw The Big Picture. Therefore my observer, Sergeant Gama, and I were in the dark about what was happening as night settled around the roof of the building on which we had established an observation post.

Fourth of July seemed to break out shortly after midnight. We still didn't know what the hell was going on. Distant antiaircraft fire burped lazy balls of tracer light high into the night skies. Nearer, just on the other side of the canal, mortar rounds flash-banged on the U.S. bases of Amador and Albrook. Even nearer, on our side of the canal, a brief fierce firefight erupted at the Pan American Bridge when U.S. Marines LAI [light armored infantry] captured DNTT Station No. 2, a rather isolated military outpost for PDF soldiers. One Marine, we soon learned, was killed: Sergeant Isaacs. He was first man through the door at the station and took a bullet in the left side. The impact spun him about. Then he got hit in the jugular and bled to death.

The LAI captured three PDF prisoners and killed a fourth man. The body still lay inside at 1300 hours that afternoon of 20 December when Gama and I were attached to the armored infantry as snipers and linked up with an LAI company at the station. There was the dead man sprawled grotesquely where he had fallen, along with a dead pig carcass buzzed by greenhead flies hanging in a back room. I supposed it was intended to be dinner for Noriega's soldiers. The guy getting bloated on the floor wouldn't need any dinner.

The Marine LAI drove eight-wheeled light armored vehicles [LAVs], which were lighter, faster versions of the Bradley. Each was equipped with a 25mm cannon and M60 machine guns. These weapons had splintered hell out of the PDF outpost, jabbing big holes in the walls through and through and chewing up the interior.

The company was preparing to move out when Gama and I joined it. We had to split up because of space limitations in the LAVs. Gama mounted the commander's machine while I crawled into the first sergeant's vehicle with four other combat-laden Marines. The convoy roared through the streets of Panama City like a column of giant armored insects while a helicopter flew shotgun overhead. It was a bright day with lots of sunshine.

The streets and roads were clear of civilian vehicular traffic. Crowds of Panamanian pedestrians lined some of the streets waving at us as we thundered through. Everyone seemed to be in a festive mood. Work had shut down for the day, except for that work requiring weapons and soldiers.

A few shots banged from a row of houses: some idiot shooting at the helicopter. He caused no damage and was therefore ignored. The first sergeant informed me that our destination was the PDF station at La Chorrera, our mission to neutralize it. American troops in an operation known as Just Cause had air-landed or parachuted all over the Canal Zone last night in a blitzkrieg to depose and capture Noriega and return democracy to the country.

The convoy exited the four-lane highway at speed and continued down narrow La Chorrera streets lined in little pastel-colored plaster houses. Not knowing how much resistance we might encounter, the vehicles "buttoned up," closing all hatches, as we approached the target. Everyone in my vehicle seemed pretty edgy. I *felt* edgy. This was my first combat experience.

The PDF compound consisted of four white-washed plaster buildings surrounded by a high concrete wall and a wide steel-barred gate. Shrubbery and a few palm trees grew among the buildings. The structure nearest the gate appeared to be a small office building. Beyond and to its left stood a two-story monstrosity that was undoubtedly a barracks for soldiers. The third building was a small duplicate of the office building at the gate. The fourth, long and low, was a dispensary or medical building of some sort. It sat off to the right by itself. Nothing or no one stirred within the compound. It almost seemed abandoned.

A Spanish-speaking Marine demanded through a loudspeaker mounted on one of the LAVs that the garrison surrender. No response. The demands were repeated. This time, when there was still no feedback, a pair of armored vehicles rumbled forward and smashed through the steel gate. Several other LAVs darted forward, scuttling onto the compound with 25mm guns blazing. Ordnance splintered the sides of buildings, exploding with bright flashes of light and deafening cracks. Acrid smoke immediately cloaked the station, out of which stabbed muzzle flashes as PDF occupiers mounted a resistance.

"Entry teams!" came an order, followed by "Open hatches. Cover the entry teams."

That was my cue. The first sergeant's tractor, along with the CO's, remained outside the walls to cover and to serve as command posts. I vaulted out of the vehicle and to the pavement where I hunkered down behind the

LAV, supporting the heavy barrel of my M40A1 rifle across its top. To my right, Sergeant Gama assumed a similar position behind the commander's vehicle. My heart pounded like something from *Alien* about to bust out of my chest cavity.

Entry teams swiftly cleared the medical building because it was rather separated from the others. Grenades banged and automatic small arms chattered from inside. Men yelled. I saw nothing but smoke and battle haze, through which flitted the ephemeral figures of Marines.

I focused on the two-story barracks since it was the largest structure and the living quarters for the station's soldiers. We logically expected the most resistance from it. Thin tendrils of smoke seeped out of a hole about a foot in diameter that a 25mm had blown through the outside wall. The lenses of my scope provided a clear if limited view of the interior.

I saw a low partition wall that seemed to separate a room, perhaps dividing the space into bedding cubicles. A bare head popped from around the end of the partition, its owner peering out at us through the blown opening in the wall. The gunner from the commander's LAV spotted the same guy and started yelling.

"There's a person! There's a person there!"

The range was no more than fifty yards. I had never shot targets that near. We zeroed in our weapons on the firing range at a minimum of 100 yards. All practice after that was done in increments of 100 out to a thousand yards and beyond. In hindsight, I was thinking that perhaps we should also fire close-quarter drills as well, the way law enforcement snipers did. Still, I reassured myself, a shot at fifty should hold approximately the same sight pattern as at one hundred.

All this ruminating occurred in the space of the instant it took me to plant my crosshairs just above the top edge of the wall where the head was. The target presented only the top portion of a face. At this short distance, his forehead filled my scope. Dark eyes stared at me through the battle haze. He seemed to be looking directly at me, waiting.

I gently stroked the trigger. The smooth recoil of the heavy rifle into my shoulder failed to interrupt my sight picture. Skin flipped up from the head. The target instantly disappeared.

"Did you hit him?" the first sergeant asked.

"Yeah."

I jacked another round into the chamber. In the excitement of the moment, it wasn't like I had popped a real human being, this first man I had ever shot. I didn't think of it that way. It was my job. I experienced satisfaction in doing my job the right way, the Marine way.

Later, when we had some downtime back at Rodman, Gama went over to Fox Company, [which] had cleared the barracks, and asked if there had been a dead guy inside.

"The whole top of his head was blown off," a corporal said.

CHAPTER THIRTY

U.S. Army
Sergeant First Class William Lucas
Panama, 1989

In the early hours of 20 December 1989, at the start of Operation Just Cause, Sergeant First Class William Lucas, then 43 years old and operations NCO for his battalion, parachuted into Panama with elements of the 82d Airborne Division. Lucas had served in the U.S. Marine Corps in Vietnam (1966–68), where, as a sniper, he logged 38 enemy kills in I Corps in the vicinity of Chu Lai. He had switched services after Vietnam, reenlisting in the U.S. Army. Once again, in a different war more than two decades later, he was functioning as a sniper.

A few days after the invasion, the United States seized an arms cache hidden by General Manuel Noriega's Panamanian Defense Forces (PDF). Among the recovered weapons were a number of modern U.S.-manufactured Army M24 sniper rifles. However, some of the rifles went undiscovered. The 82d Airborne Division and other U.S. troops continued to receive harassing sniper fire in Panama City and its suburbs.

One enemy sniper burrowed into a hide somewhere in the downtown streets of the capital. He had wounded at least one U.S. soldier and would have killed others but for his poor shooting. Sergeant Lucas and an observer were assigned to root him out, or, in Army vernacular, "find him, fix him, and fuck him over." They took up a position in a room on the fifteenth floor of the elegant Marriott Hotel. It only cost a little more to go first class.

The two countersnipers systemically scanned the area of Calle 52 y Ricardo Arias Boulevard with binoculars and a spotting scope. It was in this neighborhood that the shooter had been working. Military action was winding down. Streets were starting to fill up again with pedestrians, although not yet with the customary clot of vehicular traffic. Lucas had to be especially careful not to mistakenly target the wrong man.

Reports of the enemy sniper's activity placed him somewhere within a block of high-rise apartments about 750 meters away. It was upon these apartments that the two Army marksmen concentrated as noon produced a bright sun and sharp shadows. They sat in easy chairs back from the window in the darkened room, watching and waiting. Lucas's M21 rifle, essentially an M14 battle rifle upgraded and equipped with a telescopic sight, rested across his knees when he wasn't actually peering through the scope.

A sniper pitted against a countersniper is rarely permitted more than one mistake. The enemy shooter made his by silhouetting himself in the open window beyond the upstairs balcony off one of the high-rise apartments. Lucas's spotter caught the movement. Both Americans focused their opticals on the window. Insect screens had been removed. It was dark inside. A breeze caught the end of a curtain and tugged it out the opening to flap gently.

The PDF sniper appeared at the window as he scanned Ricardo Arias Boulevard below, apparently seeking a fresh target among the patrolling U.S. troops. He was, Lucas observed, a thin, knife-faced man dressed in a black pullover. He lifted a scoped rifle, making his intentions clear for the first time.

"He's setting up for a shot," Lucas's spotter said.

Lucas nodded and sighted in, crosshairs thinning at a juncture of the target's chest where the heart was located. The wily Vietnam vet, who had had much experience at this sort of thing in the jungles of Vietnam over twenty years ago, adjusted for bullet drop at the range. He had sighted in his rifle at 100 yards. The drop would not be severe, however, because of the downward slope of the shot's pathway.

He took up trigger slack. His breathing slowed, then stopped.

The target stepped back from the window and disappeared.

Lucas waited, his eye glued to the adjustable ranging telescope.

A shadow on the window stirred. The spotter caught the glint of sunlight on a rifle barrel through his binoculars.

"He's back."

Lucas exhaled half a breath, held, and took up trigger slack. The rifle barked in the confines of the room, echoing. The spotter remained at his binoculars.

"He's down. I saw him fall."

There was no further movement in the room. After a

while, a woman who appeared to be a cleaning lady opened the outer door. Lucas and his spotter watched her through the windows as she walked across the apartment toward the balcony. She paused on the balcony and looked through the open window. Her hands flew to cover her open mouth and she hurried away as though chased by devils.

"I'd say we nailed the guy," Lucas said.

CHAPTER THIRTY-ONE

U.S. Marine
Staff Sergeant Neil Kennedy Morris
Camp Pendleton, California, 1987

Whenever you see a sniper in uniform, chances are that you will never know he's a sniper unless you are personally acquainted with him or he chooses to tell you—which is very unlikely. Snipers don't wear badges or flashy things on their uniforms. That's the way it should be. Snipers don't need that kind of recognition. It's our job and our duty to work behind the scenes. However, it was due to this dearth of public recognition that a rather unusual custom evolved. It was 1987, and I was senior scout sniper instructor for the 1st Marine Division at Camp Pendleton, California.

Prior to that year, it had become rather a tradition for sniper students graduating from Camp Pendleton to brand an *SS* rune on their arms or chest as a mark of pride. The initials stood for *Scout Sniper*. Graduates would take a coat hanger or similar material, shape it into the *SS* form, have a few beers, heat the branding iron red-hot, and start slapping the mark on each other. Some brands were as small as an inch or two; others left god-awful big welts.

As senior instructor, I grew concerned with the possibility of Marines seriously injuring themselves or of the *SS* being misinterpreted and associated with Hitler and the Nazis. A box of M-118 special ball ammunition arriving at the school in 1986 gave me an idea on how to replace the branding with something more innocuous.

For lack of a better, more suitable term, that box of ammo turned out to be shit. There was at least one dud or misfire out of every twenty rounds. Growing tired of filling out paperwork to turn back defective ammunition, instructors began pulling the projectiles from the cases, pouring out the powder, and collecting the bullets. I ended up with a basket full of powderless rifle cartridges and projectiles.

One night before a graduation in 1987, myself and a couple of other instructors, Sergeants Lawrence and Conway, were in the office batting around the problem of the *SS* branding.

"We got this big pile of bullets here," I suggested. "Let's drill holes through them, put them on dog chains, and hand them out at graduation. That way they'll have a token of accomplishment without branding themselves."

The bullet soon became known as a "hog's tooth." Although there is some history of British snipers having to go out and kill a hog as part of their graduation ritual, that was not the source of the term. The term came about due to the fact that there was a myriad of division schools at Pendleton, sniper training being only one of them. The leadership and students of the other classes called sniper students "pigs" because we were always running around with camouflage on our faces, half-shaven, and eyes bloodshot from stress and lack of sleep.

We turned "pig" around and made it a symbol of distinction. Marine sniper students were "pigs" until they graduated from training, after which they were known as "hogs"; in keeping with the motif, instructors were called "boars." The acronyms PIG and HOG evolved out of that, created on the spot when I was called on the carpet at Quantico because of an article on snipers published by the *New York Times*. Headquarters Marine Corps had a fit about Marine snipers being compared to swine. As the old saying goes, shit rolls downhill.

I stood before Colonel Willis, commanding officer of WTBN, Quantico, and answered his questions about the terms, thinking fast.

"Pig," I said. "P-I-G: professional instructed gunman. Hog. H-O-G: hired-on gunman [later, hunter of gunmen]."

Colonel Willis kind of grinned. He knew I was bullshitting, but it satisfied him and it satisfied the Marine Corps. The practice of handing out a bullet on a chain, a hog's tooth, caught on and became a tradition.

It wasn't long before the idea spread. Other sniper schools in both the Marine Corps and the Army were soon handing out hog's teeth. Snipers don't wear badges or flashy things on their uniforms, but if you happen to see a Marine or soldier with a bullet hanging on a chain around his neck, chances are he's a trained sniper.

CHAPTER THIRTY-TWO

Iraq's Saddam Hussein invaded neighboring Iran in 1980 in a dispute over oil and shipping, an excuse Hussein used to maraud Kuwait a decade later. After Iran's regular army suffered heavy losses, the country's leaders turned to lightly armed infantry units called Pasdoran and a paramilitary organization called Basij. A particularly brutal war raged between the two countries for the next eight years, made all the more savage by the use of poison gas.

Iran's Pasdaran and Basij favored religious zeal over training and reintroduced into the world a level of raw fanaticism with which the United States had rarely dealt. Even the kamikaze pilots and human-wave attacks of World War II paled in comparison. The first shock to the world occurred in November 1981 when Iran hurled a barbarous attack against the Iraqis near the town of Bostan. Hundreds of youths, many no more than 12 years old, began the assault by running through a mine-field and deliberately blowing themselves to pieces in the name of Allah in order to clear a path for Basij and Pasdaran waves. The Iraqis, no amateurs themselves when it came to brutality, were overwhelmed by the fanaticism and retreated.

Kuwait and many other Arab nations, along with the United States and NATO countries, sided with Iraq against Iran and the Ayatollah Khomeini out of fear of Iran's Islamic fanaticism. In fact, America was already confronting Muslim zeal in Lebanon. In 1983, Americans personally suffered grave losses at the hands of Muslim zealots when a suicide bomber blew up the U.S. Marine headquarters in Beirut, killing 241.

That incident reinforced the notion among progressive military thinkers that America must refashion its armed forces in order to deal with new kinds of actions involving terrorism and nontraditional warfare. Restructuring began with the 1986 Goldwater-Nichols Defense Reorganization Act which, among other innovations, created the U.S. Special Operations Command (USSOCOM). For the first time, all U.S. Special Operations warfare units from all branches of the military would be coordinated under a single command to combat terrorism and sabotage and conduct covert and clandestine missions. An amendment to the act spelled out USSOCOM's mission requirements: direct action, strategic reconnaissance, unconventional warfare, foreign internal defense, counterterrorism, civil affairs, psychological operations, humanitarian assistance, and "other activities as specified by the President or Secretary of Defense."

Snipers from all military branches were to become an integral part of Special Operations. However, as these snipers discovered in their deployments to the Persian Gulf when Iran began attacking Kuwaiti oil tankers in

July 1987 (the so-called tanker wars), being a marksman was not so much a specialty as it was an extra duty in the overall picture of special warfare.

U.S. Navy warships escorting Kuwait tankers in the gulf soon sailed into harm's way. On 14 April 1988, an Iranian minefield blew up the USS *Samuel B. Roberts*, almost ripping the frigate in half. Three days later, U.S. Joint Task Force Middle East responded with Operation Praying Mantis. During a two-day period, the Navy, Marine Corps, Army, and Air Force demolished two oil platforms used by Iran to coordinate attacks on shipping, sank or destroyed three Iranian warships, and neutralized at least six Iranian speedboats.

Marine snipers were utilized on U.S. warships in defense against expected small-boat swarm attacks by the Iranians and to provide precision fire on offensive operations.

CHAPTER THIRTY-THREE

U.S. Marine Corporal Frank Galli
Persian Gulf, 1988

Marines and squids queued up in double rows nearly the entire length of the USS *Trenton*'s two-spot helicopter flight deck, standing in line for ice cream. As far as you could see, the Persian Gulf—or *Arabian Gulf* as it was being called, as not to favor either side in the stalemated Iran-Iraq War, was like a pond weighted into submission by air heated to 130 degrees. Ice cream helped a little with that. At least it made you feel better about it.

I was only a few men back from the head of the line. Had I been taller than five-two, hell, I might even have been able to *see* ice cream over the shoulders and heads of the sweaty brown-T-shirted guys in front of me. I could almost *taste* that ice cream when—wouldn't you know it?—the ship's alert horn suddenly went off, shrilling its two-noted blares with startling presence.

Battle stations! Battle stations!

"Oh, shit!"

The ice cream lines disintegrated. Men grabbed gear

and weapons and scrambled to man their stations for combat, expecting armed dhows and speedboats in a swarm attack. Iranians could be as crazy as insects swarming around a bug zapper, all of them willing to sacrifice their lives and sacred honor and all that for Allah and the Ayatollah. If a Muslim died in battle, it was said, he ascended immediately into heaven, where Allah trotted out fifty-six or seventy-one or some such number of virgins and gave them to the revered martyr as his reward.

I suppose if a virgin died and went to heaven, *her* reward was to serve the Ayatollah's heroes as a forever member of an eternal harem. It sounded to me like she got cheated.

Battle stations turned out to be another false alarm. A boat filled with Navy SEALs coming in to get some ice cream had been mistakenly identified. A SEAL could smell ice cream from five miles across the water. Break out a single bar and there they were. Christ! Now we had to get back in line and start all over again.

Was this what snipers did when there was no other work for them?

I had completed sniper school at Stone Bay, Camp Lejeune, in December 1986. Somehow in those innocent days, the image of "sniper" held a romantic connotation different than the reality of actually being a sniper. I was only nineteen when I went through training. The picture we sniper trainees held in our minds as we crawled through stalks and into hides, shooting, shooting, *shooting,* was of marksmen like Carlos Hathcock and Chuck Mawhinney, U.S. Marine Corps legends from Vietnam. That construct evaporated in the heat of being assigned to sea as a member of a 105-Marine air-ground task force.

"Versatility," preached Staff Sergeant Taylor, NCOIC

of the six-man sniper contingent assigned to the Persian Gulf Marine Amphibious Group (MAG). "First, you are Marines."

The 1st Battalion, 2d Marines, became the first Special Operations–capable unit in the Marine Corps under the recently established U.S. Special Operations Command (USSOCOM). In January 1988, the MAG deployed to the Persian Gulf aboard the amphibious transport dock USS *Trenton* (LPD-14), a 570-foot warship carrying landing craft and capable of recovering a boat as big as a Landing Craft Air Cushion (LCAC). Helicopters, including the CH-46 Sea Knight and CH-53 Sea Stallion, operated from her two-spot flight deck. The mission of the MAG and the other ships and units in the Gulf was to protect neutral shipping and stop Iran's seeding the waters with mines. The U.S. and Iran had had several violent clashes with each other during the past year in the so-called tanker wars.

The sniper team had deployed to Southwest Asia with one new Iver-Johnson single-shot .50-caliber sniper rifle and our standard 7.62 M40A1 rifles for long-distance shooting against possible small craft swarm attacks. So far, all we had done was stand four-hour night watches on the *Trenton*, using night-vision devices to keep a lookout for intruders. Every so often a dhow or speedboat came too close, at which time Major Kelly, commander of the on-ship Marines, ordered us to fire a few rounds across their bows as a warning. It had worked so far. It didn't seem these guys wanted their virgins badly enough to attack into the fire.

The rest of the time we either patrolled the waters in Zodiacs looking for mines or we practiced fast roping from helicopters onto the decks of ships in the task force. That was in case we had to assault oil platforms the Iranians used as bases from which to seed the Gulf with mines. We could unload a stick in less than eighteen seconds.

"Patience," Sergeant Taylor counseled. "You all may see some action yet."

Corporal Beausoile grinned. "Patience, hell. Let's go kill something."

The prospect of action appeared to draw nearer on 14 April when the USS *Samuel B. Roberts* (FFG-58) wandered into a minefield while transiting to Bahrain after an escort mission. The frigate nudged a mine when she tried to back out. The explosion blew a twenty-foot hole in the hull and cracked her keel.

Trenton escorted the crippled craft to harbor in Dubai. Word came down that President Reagan had authorized a retaliatory strike against Iranian forces in an operation code-named Praying Mantis. Excitement sparked like electricity from bow to stern aboard the *Trenton*. Snipers were bound to play a part in the operation.

Offshore oil platforms dotted the slate-blue gulf, rising four and five stories out of the water like huge multilegged steel crabs, or like structures invented for *Star Wars* or *Star Trek*. Some of the modules—generally the hotels, or living quarters—were painted white. Otherwise, the fixed decks were rusted steel jumbled into huge blights on the ocean, supporting entire communities and littered with drilling and production equipment, gas turbines, generators, pumps, compressors, flare stacks, revolving cranes with their arms sticking up, survival craft, helicopter landing pads, offices . . . SEAL or Marine Zodiacs or helicopters went out all the time scouting them.

On the evening of 17 April, while the *Trenton* was still under way returning from Dubai, Major Kelly and the air wing commander, whom we knew only as

Colonel Bull, summoned Marines to the galley. The air crackled with tension as they announced the launching of Praying Mantis with a dawn assault against a platform in the Sasson oil fields.

According to the operations order, Marines would fast rope onto the platform from CH-46 Sea Knights to clear it of hostiles and secure it for engineers to land and blow it up. At least eighteen heavily armed Ayatollah Revolutionary Guard manned the platform. They may or may not resist.

"If they do," Major Kelly said, looking around at Marines crammed into the shiny steel galley, "take them out."

Snipers in the Marine Corps were, first of all, *Marines*. We didn't lay around when there was no one to snipe and practice our shooting. I was issued an MP5 submachine gun and a Beretta 9mm pistol, hardly equipment for a sniper, and assigned to fly in with the first of three birds in the assault element. I was trained primarily to kill at long distances, one target at a time. The MP5 was a CQB [close-quarter battle] weapon used for killing at very near ranges. Like Sergeant Taylor always said, a sniper had to be versatile.

The assault element assembled shortly after dawn on 18 April. It consisted of three Sea Knights each loaded with a stick of ten heavily armed troops, two Cobra gunships for direct air support, a Huey to act as command and control, and a small fleet of SEAL Zodiacs, beach raiding craft and rigid hull inflatable. I was seventh man in the fast rope stick of the first helicopter.

Choppers sprang off the ship like a flight of angry bees, accompanied by *music*. It seemed everyone had suddenly acquired [the AC/DC] *Back in Black* album. It played from everywhere. It blared through the ship's PA system. Ground crews had boom boxes and radios turned up full blast. Corporal Hagnann commented that it was like a scene from *Apocalypse Now:* "How I love the smell of napalm in the morning"—that kind of stuff. Music inspired, got the juices to pumping. I had always thought troops ought to go into battle with a suitable soundtrack—and now we were.

I leaned forward and looked out and down through the lowered tail ramp as the *Trenton* receded against the sea and the notes of *Back in Black* faded. The sea was as smooth and hard looking as a pond in bright sunlight. The airmada formed in the sky, then poured on the coal. The rope master's solemn demeanor as he looked out the open ass-end of the bird jolted me with the realization that this was the *real thing* and not another training mission on an *Apocalypse Now* movie with soundtrack. I mentally checked my equipment to keep my mind occupied. In addition to my two weapons and a sheath knife, I wore a Kevlar helmet, sand goggles, flak vest, battle harness to which were attached a gas mask, flash-bang grenades, nine spare magazines of ammo, and a light butt pack filled with "just-in-case" stuff. I had dummy-corded the Beretta from its holster to my harness, but I carried the stubby MP5 slung over one shoulder and ready for use.

Now and then I glimpsed the other birds in formation to the rear. They were staggered out across the sky. A sleek black Cobra streaked by.

Then there was no more time to contemplate things. Action began as the airmada swept down to just above the sea and went clipping above the smooth water at a heart-pounding pace.

"Here we go!" exclaimed Sergeant Taylor, who would exit on the rope right behind me.

I was so focused that I barely heard him above the throbbing of my heart. I became aware of a .50-cal machine gun pounding nearby and of explosions and the ripsawing of 20mm chain guns from the Cobras attacking in advance of the troop insertions. I later learned one of the Cobras went down from antiaircraft fire, but for the moment none of that concerned me. I concentrated on the open door, waiting for the coiled rope lying on the floor to be tossed out and for the command to *Go! Go! Go!*

Suddenly the oil platform popped into sight. The Sea Knight air-skidded to a hover, its nose almost straight in the air. The rope master sat on the edge of the open tailgate with his legs dangling, looking almost straight down. He tossed the thick cotton rope. I watched it uncoiling in the air, its end hitting the platform.

"Go! Go! Go!" came through the commo receivers built into our helmets.

Then it was assholes to belly buttons. I grabbed for the rope and was out on it, my feet almost touching the helmet of the man below. Dangling, sliding down it like on a fireman's pole. Spinning. Sergeant Taylor was hard above me, coming fast.

I hit the deck facing in the direction of the bird's nose, peripherally aware of a white barracks to my right upon which appeared a face portrait of Ayatollah Khomeini. There was junk everywhere: crates, barrels, rusted mazes of pipes. I bound out of Sergeant Taylor's way before he landed on me and reduced my five-two frame to an even five feet.

The entire stick hit the steel deck one man after the other within a few seconds. It fanned out, ready for combat, while the Sea Knight that had delivered us sprang back into the air, clawing for altitude.

A Cobra slid past like a swift shadow to get between us and gunfire flickering from a barracks window. It roared return fire from its chain gun, chewing into the barracks and sparking on the steel like strings of giant firecrackers. The noise was deafening. My ears rang even before a pair of TOW missiles contrailed through the window. The resulting explosion shook the platform, almost knocking me off my feet.

Black smoke boiled from the barracks. Flames licked tongues out the windows through the smoke. The Cobra zipped back into the air, leaving the cleanup to the Marine ground element while it darted elsewhere to deliver death and destruction.

Seven individual platforms all linked together by catwalks made up the enormous complex. They resembled New York City office buildings, only rattier-looking and not as tall. My stick of ten Marines went to work on our platform while leathernecks from the other assault choppers worked over theirs. I heard automatic weapons barking from somewhere, sharp and banging in the clear morning air.

We broke into groups of two or three to conduct clearing operations. I teamed up with Sergeant Vann and a guy from Recon Force. So far we had received no direct hostile fire, other than that from the barracks before the Cobra set it to blazing.

"Spread out! Cover each other!" Sergeant Vann barked through his throat mike.

"They're running!" someone called out. "They're jumping into the water."

We went through our area fast and furiously, clearing. Working from top decks toward the bottom of the platform. Rooms, conex boxes, building modules. Pipes running everywhere.

First, toss a flash-bang grenade into the room. It shattered glass and rattled teeth. Then dart in like raiders, weapons ready and fingers on triggers.

There were no Iranians. They were too busy scrambling to the lower reaches and desperately jumping into the drink where SEALs in boats waited to police them up. They abandoned everything as they fled—AK assault rifles, rocket-propelled grenades, four two-barreled ZU-23 heavy machine guns . . . A Russian 12.7mm pointed outward to sea against potential attackers. Its operators must have been eating breakfast when they saw us coming. They dropped their food and ran.

Sporadic firing banged here and there from the other platforms of the complex, but I never determined what the shooting was about. My stick encountered virtually no resistance. I didn't even *see* the enemy.

The white barracks the Cobra set afire was burning pretty good. Paint that made up Khomeini's face on the outside wall curled and peeled from the heat. Flames began eating their way out of the barracks onto the rest of the structure. Fearing the entire complex might go up prematurely while Marines were still on it, commanders began recalling us while engineers quickly laid their charges. CH-46s snatched us off the burning time bomb.

Although the Praying Mantis task force destroyed two oil platforms, sank or captured several warships and boats, and took a number of prisoners, I don't think any Iranians collected their virgins. The long-stalled Iran-Iraq War finally petered out toward the end of the year.

And that was what snipers did when there was no other work to be had.

CHAPTER THIRTY-FOUR

It takes time to mold the ordinary American boy into a hardened killer. Military commanders of snipers and sniper training understand the specific skills, physical abilities, and craft qualities that a good sniper must possess.

"The sniper is the big game hunter of the battlefield," said Captain Jim Land, who arrived in Vietnam in 1966 to build a sniper school on Hill 55 that became the prototype for those that followed. "He has all those skills regularly studied, admired, and accepted by people who would apply them to hunting deer, elk, or perhaps bear. Certainly the sniper, like the big game hunter, must know and understand the habits of the quarry which he hunts. He must possess the field craft to be able to successfully position himself for a killing shot. . . . sniper must be self-reliant and possess the keen skills of a still hunter or poacher. . . ."

"Of course, superior marksmanship was an absolute requirement that we never waived," said Lieutenant

General Ormond R. Simpson, who commanded the 1st Marine division in Vietnam. "Given this talent or ability, a good sniper needed to have infinite patience, even nature and temperament, ability to get along with his team members, willingness to remain in his position for often long periods of time regardless of wind or rain, the skill to move quietly and escape detection. . . ."

"You have to be strong enough to endure lying in the weeds day after day," added a sniper instructor, "letting the bugs crawl all over you and bite you, letting the sun cook you and rain boil you, shitting and pissing in your pants. Lying there because you know that Charlie's coming and you're gonna kill him."

Such qualities are a given in any man who would be a hunter of men. Quite another matter both imprecise and inexact, however, are the mental conditioning and psychological aspects of what it takes emotionally and mentally for a man to coolly take aim and calculatedly blast another human being into eternity. Captain Land understood psychological aspects that had rarely been touched on previously. What did it take, he asked himself, to be a sniper and not be destroyed by it then and afterward? A man could possess all the necessary skills and *still* not have what it takes. Land and others like him understood the "killer factor."

"When you look through that scope," he wrote, "the first thing you see are the eyes. There is a lot of difference between shooting at a shadow, shooting at an outline, and shooting at a pair of eyes. Many men can't do it at that point."

"It is not pleasant," concurred Victor Ricketts, a World War I British sniper with the Gloucestershire Regiment, in his unpublished memoir, "to have a fellow human in one's sights with such clarity as to be almost able to see the colour of his eyes and to have the knowledge that in a matter of seconds another life will meet an untimely death."

Both the Army and the Marine Corps now acknowledge the psychological factor of killing and attempt to address it in training. What kind of man *does* the profession require and how must he cope with what he does?

"The sniper must not be susceptible to emotions such as anxiety and remorse," was how a U.S. Army training circular bluntly put it.

Editions of a U.S. Marine Corps Fleet Marine Force manual (FMFM) elaborated somewhat: "An infantry Marine in the heat of battle kills the enemy emotionally and reflexively, lest he be killed himself. A sniper, however, must kill calmly and deliberately, shooting carefully selected targets. . . . Candidates whose motivation towards sniper training rests mainly in the desire for prestige which may accrue to them in performing a unique function may not be capable of cold rationality which the sniper's job requires. A proper mental condition cannot be taught or instilled by training."

Snipers, former snipers, and sniper instructors often discuss the sniper's psychological dynamics.

"As for the psychological aspects," said Major R. O. "Dick" Culver, who joined Land and a handful of other former snipers after the Vietnam War to establish the U.S. Marine Corps Scout Sniper Instructor School at Quantico, "the sniper must feel that he can kill when the time comes. He has to have no compunction against killing, but must also have compassion. He has to have a conscience, not necessarily a tremendously religious person, but one who kills wantonly is worthless. You don't want a man who will kill for the sake of killing."

"In the dynamics of the course," said Lieutenant

Colonel Randy Smith, later the commander of the Quantico Marine sniper school, "a Marine comes to realize what he's going to do. The thing I'm trying to get across . . . is, sniping is so much more personal. The enemy is not just a gray uniform running across the road. He's a guy you watch lighting a cigarette, crossing his legs. You may sit there and watch him for an hour before you take him out. . . . You may even have a profile of him: He smokes with his left hand, he's got blue eyes. . . . At a thousand yards, a sniper is actually going to see the face and body of the person he's going to shoot. . . ."

"Psychologically," said Marine Corps sniper Chuck Mawhinney, who killed 103 enemy soldiers in Vietnam, "the sniper candidate has to search his mind and determine that he can make killing shots. We've all been brought up to believe 'Thou shalt not kill,' so we have to put that in context and deal with it. I did this in my mind in the format of 'Thou shalt not kill; thou shalt not kill me or my comrades, either.' You have to have the mind-set. You have to pre-think your shots well in advance and be mentally prepared to eliminate some mother's son. You have to have the ability to self-justify what you do so it doesn't eat you up later on. Some take shots to save lives, some take shots because they hate the enemy, some because it's their job. But for whatever reason, you have to be able to justify what you do out there. . . ."

Nonsnipers in the military sometimes refer to snipers as Murder, Incorporated. Many shooters even promote the image. For example, a sign at the entrance to the 1st Marine Division sniper school on Hill 55 during the Vietnam War proclaimed "War Our Business, Death Our Only Product." Snipers composed a verse during the 1991 Iraqi *Desert Storm* war, sung to the tune of "Winter Wonderland":

As my M40 fires,
His life will expire.
A shot to the head,
My target is dead.
Walking in Sniper Wonderland. . . .

This is all typical of the black humor snipers employ to help distance themselves emotionally from the dark demands of their job. Every sniper, whether he openly admits it or not, is in some way altered forever by the job and the eyes he sees through his scope and instant before he squeezes the trigger.

CHAPTER THIRTY-FIVE

U.S. Marine Corporal Robert M. (Full Name Withheld) Vietnam, 1966

Corporal Robert M. was one of the first students to complete training after Captain Jim Land established his school for snipers on Hill 55 for the 1st Marine Division, Republic of Vietnam. He proved particularly adept at hunting and in very short order accumulated a kill count of seven Vietcong. He seemed to have no problem justifying to himself the systematic slaughter of enemy soldiers.

Enemy elements freely prowled the villages and rice paddies in a valley not far from Hill 55. Like ghosts, however, they vanished into the jungles and surrounding hills whenever Marine forces swept through in attempts to make them stand and fight.

"Why don't we set up some snipers in the hills as a blocking force?" Land suggested. "Ol' Nguyen Schwartz knows where the grunts are all the time, but he may not be able to detect our sniper teams."

Under cover of darkness, several two-man sniper teams moved into the hills opposite where Marine companies would sweep the next day and burrowed into strategic hides. Sure enough, just as Captain Land predicted, VC fleeing from advancing Marines blundered into the accurate sights of the snipers. Corporal Robert M. killed eleven men in the course of that bloody day.

A couple of days later Robert M. unaccountably missed formation when Captain Land called an equipment inspection. Land sent a man to find him. The Marine returned quickly.

"Skipper, you had better come take a look."

Sergeant Carlos Hathcock was the school's NCOIC; he hurried to Robert M.'s tent. It was in total darkness and appeared empty. After a quick look around, Hathcock found the missing sniper huddled on the ground at the back of the tent with a poncho pulled over his head. He crouched there, motionless. Hathcock shook him and called his name. There was no response.

Corporal Robert M., who had been such an outstanding sniper student and who had done so well with eleven kills at the valley "turkey shoot," had gone catatonic. A division psychologist back at Chu Lai later explained what happened.

"Corporal M. never told you this," he said, "but he was only in-country for a short time when one of his buddies stepped on a mine that killed him and the platoon's lieutenant. Robert couldn't do a thing about it since all the line troopers see most of the time are shadows, moving bushes, and muzzle flashes. Corporal M. wanted to see his enemy die. He joined the snipers to get even."

He got even all right, big-time, with eighteen personal deaths. He got even for his buddy. He got even for his lieutenant. He got even for himself. He got even until his mind simply snapped from all the bloodletting.

Corporal M. seemed to recover from the trauma after a few weeks of treatment. He would not return to the snipers, however. He was about to be released to return to his old line outfit as a regular grunt when two Reuters correspondents interviewed him for a feature article. He made it okay through the interview up to the point where one of the journalists cleared his throat and unexpectedly asked, "What is it like to take another human being's life?"

The Marine's body stiffened. His eyes darted wildly about the room, as though looking for a place to hide. Finding nowhere to run physically, he retreated inwardly. He suddenly relaxed. His eyes turned dull and still, as though whatever life force existed to animate them drained away in the space of a single heartbeat.

Corporal Robert M., ex-sniper who knew eighteen times what it was like to kill one accurate sniper's shot at a time, did not want to remember ever again those eyes he had peered into through his rifle scope.

"Corporal? Corporal?"

No response.

CHAPTER THIRTY-SIX

U.S. Marine John R.
(Full Name Withheld)
Somalia, 1993

Killing only one man, snipers say, especially your first, is normally worse than several kills. The more killing you do, the more they blend together and the easier it is to forget them as individuals. The memories are therefore less troublesome.

U.S. Marine John R., a fresh graduate of sniper school, had heard it all. He did not know how he would react should the time come for him to drop the cap on another human being. Killing another up close and personal while looking at him through the scope turned out to be a lot more traumatic than he bargained for. He had yet to pull the trigger on a live target when he was sent to Somalia in 1993 as part of a contingent of U.S. Army troops and Special Forces, Navy SEALs, and Marines to conduct operations in support of United Nations humanitarian and peacekeeping efforts.

John was assigned as a sniper to help protect the port

where supplies were being offloaded from relief freighters. Mogadishu "skinnies," as American GIs referred to the local guerrillas, often took potshots at troops under UN command.

Trucks loading and offloading jammed at the entrance to the port under the searing African sun. John set up a position on top of a building that overlooked the area. At one minute before noon, he spotted an armed man darting among the trucks: a skinny black character with baggy cargo pants, loose shirt, and sandals. He disappeared from sight, then reappeared a few minutes later climbing up the back of a truck loaded with sacks of grain.

As the alerted Marine watched, waiting for some overtly hostile gesture, the skinny raised the rifle to his shoulders and aimed over the grain at a squad of soldiers in the vicinity of the docks. There was no time to waste, no time for introspection or qualms. John centered his crosshairs on the man's chest. Instinctively, smoothly, in the manner he had been trained on nonliving targets at Quantico, he squeezed the trigger.

For John, the world instantly morphed into a movie run in slow motion. The rifle shot from his M40A1 cracked above the heads of the masses of people swarming the docks. They either scattered like fowl or flung themselves to the ground.

The target's shirt went *poof!* in the center of his chest where the bullet slapped him. He looked surprised. His eyes lifted toward the sky and he gave a last gasp for air with his mouth open. The rifle dropped from his hands. He spun a little to one side, as though getting ready to jump off the truck and run. Then he slumped forward over the sacks of grain.

There was no blood that John could see from his distant perch. It was that simple. John continued watching through his scope, thinking, *He's going to get back up.*

He didn't. John racked the bolt of his rifle, almost ripping it out the back. Sweat stuck his eyes.

He's going to get back up.

He would never get up again. John later learned the dead man had been forty years old and that he had a wife and several children.

"That wasn't really something I needed to know."

John and his wife talked about it when he rotated back home. She wept. Years later, the experience continued to trigger difficult emotions.

"I do think about it. . . . I have to relive it every time I retell it. I mean, I'm not shaking or anything, but I'm back there. I'm thinking about it. There's always . . . Sometimes you just wish it would go away or whatever."

CHAPTER THIRTY-SEVEN

U.S. Marine Corporal Gary Reiter
Vietnam, 1967

Call it shoot on demand. I was out on patrol with a platoon in Quang Tri Province early enough in the morning that thin wisps of fog still oozed out of the river course that we were following. The platoon leader, a second lieutenant, called a halt low on the crest of a hill line that overlooked the brown thread of the river. On the other side of the stream was a deserted little ville. Down next to the bank squatted a gook washing his clothes. The lieutenant passed the word for sniper up. He pointed.

"Drop him," he said.

I got into a kneeling stance with my scoped Winchester, lay my crosshairs against the poor bastard's chest while he was wringing out his skivvies and laid a round in on him.

I fucked it up. I was zeroed in for 600 yards and the range couldn't have been more than 200. The bullet *thuck*ed into the muddy bank just over the target's head.

Startled into needing to wash out *another* pair of shorts, he jumped up and ran into a grove of trees. The lieutenant gave me a perplexed look: *What kind of fucking sniper are you?*

"He's standing in there just behind a tree," I observed. Charlie was still confused about what had happened.

"Take him."

I shot through the tree branches. A little puff of blood and dust popped from his shirt when the high-powered projectile thumped him and the guy's body literally exploded from the trees. All right! *That* was a good shot. The lieutenant looked at me. "Yes!"

At almost the same moment I fired, a group of five NVA, with more likely pushing up from behind them, marched around a bend in the trail and appeared out of the brush. They wore pith helmets and backpacks and carried weapons. Like a bunch of Boy Scouts on a field outing. They had no idea of what had happened. I doubted they even heard the shots.

I swung the barrel of my rifle toward them, selected a target, and dropped the second man in the formation. They heard *that* shot. All hell broke loose. The lieutenant pulled us back from the river after a brief exchange of shots and we departed the AO.

That was a shoot on demand. I was accustomed to it, working the way we snipers did first with one outfit and then another.

I extended in-country for an additional six-month tour of duty. After going home for an all-too-short thirty-day leave, I returned to the war refreshed and ready for action. Ex-biker David Schemel, whom we called Von Zipper, was assigned as my teammate to work with a platoon in Thua Thien Province. A gunnery sergeant was acting platoon leader. He directed a route around the base of a large jungled hill and down into a valley. Nightfall was beginning to seep into the valley like spilled ink. Word came back down the column: "Snipers up."

Von Zipper and I made our way to the head of the formation and knelt next to the gunny. He pointed into the darkening skyline to our front where I detected two human silhouettes about 600 yards away.

"Take 'em out," he said. A shoot on demand.

I centered my crosshairs hard against the figure on the right. At this distance, in the failing light, he was little more than a shadow against the lighter sky. I took up trigger slack.

Just before the trigger broke, he disappeared from my scope, bending over suddenly for some reason and disappearing. That saved his life.

I immediately switched concentration to the second man, aiming for his head. He remained standing. The rifle cracked, the sound reverberating in waves down the valley. He dropped hard and stayed down.

That initiated a brief, fierce firefight, each side shooting at the other through the gathering darkness. Muzzle flashes winked like enraged fireflies. The gunnery sergeant was on the radio reporting the contact and requesting artillery assistance. He suddenly went ape shit, running up and down the firing line shouting hysterically: *"Cease fire! Cease fire!"*

As soon as the area dropped into a deathly stillness, I was shocked to learn that we had fired on another platoon of U.S. Marines. I had shot and killed a fellow American with a bullet through the skull. He never knew what hit him. Like me, Corporal Donald Robard [not his real name] was a sniper with the 4th Marines. I had never met him, but I knew his partner. His partner had been the first target I selected; he would have been dead instead had he not knelt in the bushes before I could get off a shot.

Jesus Christ. That was a tough one to take. I was dragged off to Dong Ha under house arrest and thrown into a holding area, a small pit in the ground containing a candle, an apple box from Wenatchee, Washington, and a few C-rats. The investigation took five days. The gunnery sergeant admitted he had issued the order to fire and I was cleared. He was reduced in rank and fined two months' pay.

My personal cost was much higher and it was to be lifelong.

CHAPTER THIRTY-EIGHT

U.S. Marine Corporal Greg Kraljev
Vietnam, 1969

It was so odd as to be almost surreal, going to war so cavalierly the way we did. About twenty-five of us from my recon sniper class went to Vietnam together on Continental Airlines, complete with attractive stewardesses, in-flight meals, and the little canned speech when the airplane landed at Da Nang: "Welcome to beautiful Vietnam, Marines. We hope you enjoy your stay here—and we'll see you again on your way home."

All of us? I wondered.

It was April 1969 and not yet as tropical hot as it became later on. The first thing that struck me was the odor when I stepped out of the air-conditioned aircraft. It slapped me in the face—the mixed stench of diesel fuel and burning charcoal and raw human shit from the nearby Vietnamese villages and rice paddies. The Vietnamese fertilized their crops with night soil.

Another Marine at the transit facility opened a conversation about the different outfits and places in the AO [area of operations] to which we might be assigned. Replacements sometimes had to wait around Da Nang for several days before they received orders.

"The one place you don't want to go," the Marine warned, "is the 5th Marines up at An Hoa. It's hot up there."

He wasn't referring to the weather. He had been at the travel facility for a day or so, long enough to acquire some insight.

"Real hot," he emphasized. "Gooks as thick as fleas on a dog."

Ten of the twenty-five from my sniper class were assigned to the 5th Marines. Sure enough, I was among them. We were trucked in a convoy some twenty or thirty miles across the Arizona Territory to the An Hoa combat base. The base was located only four miles from the Laotian border in a large valley surrounded by a horseshoe of mountains. A busy branch of the Ho Chi Minh Trail ran past just inside Laos. That kept the area "real hot." The base got rocketed only a few minutes after I arrived.

Just because new meat came in trained as snipers didn't mean they automatically went directly to the sniper platoons. There had to be an opening first, a vacant slot. My best friend and fellow sniper Jim Seely and I went to Delta Company as common grunts, but we were only there for a week or two before we got tapped. We turned in our grunt gear and were issued sniper equipment. That meant scoped M14s initially, since we would function as spotters for more experienced snipers until we got our feet on the ground.

The sniper platoon consisted of three squads. A squad was detailed out to each battalion of the regiment. I was assigned as spotter to Steve Suttles in Hotel Company,

2nd Battalion, while Seely went with John Tate in Bravo Company of the same battalion. My real education as a sniper began. Suttles was an excellent mentor and an even better sniper. He ended up with something like 60 or 70 confirmed kills.

On my first morning with Hotel, on my first patrol, the point element got hit in an ambush from a tree line. I was out in the middle of an open rice field toward the rear of the column when the firefight commenced. I figured since I was a sniper I probably should be up front where the action was. I started running across the field toward the front, a lanky six-foot-five idiot with a nose that had earned me the nickname The Beak. Funny noises zipped all around me, buzzing and snapping. Rocket-propelled grenades snaked smoke through the air. Every gook within range must have trained in on me. I was too green to know what I was doing.

The commander looked up from where he lay belly down in the muck as I raged past. He jumped up and grabbed me by the front of my combat harness and threw me to the ground.

"What are you trying to do, boy? Get your ass shot off?"

Welcome to Vietnam. Only 364 more days to go. No way was I going to make it home alive.

Steve settled into the business of getting me home alive while he trained me as a proper sniper spotter. We made a very successful team. Our MO, modus operandi, was a simple one. Most of the time we hooked up with a patrol going out, then dropped off from it somewhere in the grass or in a tree line to wait for some gook to skulk by within our kill zone.

After about a month of spotting for Steve, I was issued my own stick, a Model 70, and started hunting as a sniper leader. Jim Seely became my spotter; he adjusted to that position more comfortably than he did dropping the hammer himself.

Although a man adapted quickly to the blood and gore of combat—I knew men who became *addicted* to it—there was still a period of indecisiveness when emotion played a part in killing. Compassion for the enemy was not necessarily a good quality to possess in a war zone.

On my second mission behind the scope when I had yet to make my first kill, Seely and I and a radioman named Chambers went out with a platoon and dropped off in high grass. The platoon was hardly out of sight before I spotted a young Vietnamese in black pajamas walking across the large diked rice paddies that lay in front of our hide. He was about 700 yards out.

I laid the scope on him and brought him close. I watched him for about twenty minutes as he continued to stroll across the clearing. Arizona Territory was a free-fire zone, which meant anything you saw out there not wearing Marine green was legitimate game, whether armed or not. Still I held off and got to know that guy out there as a human being during that short period of time I watched through the intimacy of my telescopic sight. He was a small, weird-looking kid with black hair sticking out from his head like porcupine quills. I would have guessed his age at no more than thirteen or fourteen. He certainly looked no older.

Of course, I had heard all the horror stories about young boys, and even girls, of 6 or 7 years old walking up to Marines with grins on their faces and dropping a grenade into their laps. I had not yet learned the lesson that there was no such thing as a noncombatant in Vietnam.

I continued to watch the kid. Seely lay next to me in the grass, watching through the spotting scope, not saying anything. Chambers sprawled next to his radio. His job was to call in support should we step into something over our heads.

"He's too young," I finally decided.

Seely emitted a sigh of relief. We were not baby killers, no matter what war protestors were saying about us back in the States.

As luck had it, the Marine combat base got hit that same night. As soon as the attack was repelled, Chambers radioed in that there were KIAs lying outside the wire. His platoon leader ordered him to go out and do a body check. It was three in the morning following a fierce firefight. A stupid order.

Chambers dutifully clambered out of his fighting hole. Not all the gooks had withdrawn. A single rifle shot spat from the distant darkness. The AK-47 round penetrated Chambers's chest and exited his lower back. It took him two painful hours to die.

The gooks who shot him took off around the outside perimeter and ran into one of our observation posts. Marines in the OP cut them down in their tracks, killing all six, undoubtedly including the one who shot Chambers. I went out after daylight to take a look at the bodies. There on the ground in the midst of the carnage, all twisted and distorted and riddled with gunfire, lay the weird-looking kid with the porcupine hair whom I had had the opportunity to kill the day before and didn't.

I would never know if this kid was the one who shot Chambers. Nonetheless, I felt responsible for the radioman's death. I always thought there may have been a chance I could have saved Chambers if I had taken the shot when presented the choice.

It was a defining moment in my pilgrimage as a sniper. The incident filled me with such guilt and rage that it turned me into a robo-sniper for the rest of my tour. I never faced emotional conflict again about whether or not I should shoot.

CHAPTER THIRTY-NINE

The female warrior has played some role throughout history in various societies. Legends of Amazons, mythical stalwart women who rained death and destruction upon their enemies, have arisen at different periods and in different cultures. They may, in fact, have actually existed in North Africa. However, where women have participated in combat, they are more likely to have been guerrillas than Amazons.

Women guerrillas fought in wars in Vietnam, South Africa, Argentina, Cyprus, Iran, Northern Ireland, Lebanon, Israel, El Salvador, and Nicaragua, to name a few in modern times. Their most common type of involvement was as individual fighters rather than as organized groups. Women fought openly as females or disguised as men. Deborah Samson, for example, served as a male during the American Revolution. Frances Day took the name "Frank Mayne" to fight in the U.S. Civil War, while Jennie Hodges fought under the alias "Albert Cashier."

Documented instances of girl snipers, however, are quite rare, likely because females within combat arms themselves have been relatively rare. The most celebrated examples of female snipers sprang from the Russian Front of World War II.

Because of enormous losses of men suffered by Soviet forces during the first months of 1941 when Germany invaded Russia, women were brought into the war in large numbers. More than 70 percent of the estimated 800,000 Russian women inducted into the army fought at the front. They served on the various battle fronts as nurses, doctors, aircrew, gunners, paratroopers, tank crews, infantry soldiers, frontline laundresses—and snipers.

Some female snipers racked up respectable body counts against the German invaders. One female training instructor claimed 122 kills. Sniper Maria Ivanova Morozova became one of the Soviet Union's most highly decorated soldiers, male or female, while serving with the Soviet 62d Rifle Battalion. The most celebrated lady sniper of all times, Ludmilla Pavlichenko, amassed no fewer than 309 kills against German soldiers while fighting with the Red Army on the Dnieper Front. She made a tour of the United States in 1943 to help build up war support. She, a female sniper, became the first Soviet citizen to be received at the White House.

Other countries, to a much lesser degree, have deployed women as snipers. The Turkish army used them at Gallipoli against an Allied landing and siege. Emilienne Moreau saw combat in the front ranks of the French army during World War II, engaging two enemy snipers with her long-range marksmanship and killing them. Officially, 3,000 women served in the South Vietnamese Women's Army in 1966. A number of them from the Min Top region, such as Ding Le Tunn, Dho

Minde, and Hui Po Yung, were noted for their superior marksmanship skills against Vietcong guerrillas and the North Vietnamese Army. In return, the NVA sent out females to snipe American soldiers.

In 1999, an article that appeared in the Russian newspaper *Sevodnya* reported that Russian troops fighting in Dagestan after it was invaded by Chechen-based Muslim militants encountered three female mercenary snipers, two of whom they killed. The third was caught attempting to escape by holding a baby and pretending to be a mother.

Increasingly, nations of the modern world are beginning to experiment with opening combat ranks to admit women.

Although Israel drafts both sexes, women are not permitted to join combat units. However, women *are* instructors at the Israeli Defense Force (IDF) Sniper School at the Mitkan Adam Army Base.

On 31 December 2002, the Muslim nation of Bangladesh accepted twenty women to become commissioned officers in its 100,000-strong army. Some of the women outperformed their male counterparts in marksmanship and are now eligible to become snipers.

In 2001, Senior Airman Jennifer Donaldson of the Illinois Air National Guard made history by becoming the first American military woman to be trained as a sniper by the National Guard Sniper School at Camp Robinson, Arkansas. Her training, however, was not in the conventional sniper role. She was to be used only in a defensive posture to guard airfields and military installations.

So far, public policy and federal law prevent American women from serving in frontline combat units. That policy may change in the near future under pressure from feminist organizations. Many senior women officers and NCOs are determined not to be denied the right to serve in any assignment they are qualified to fill, whatever the risk, including that of sniper.

"I have the same training as men," argued a female major. "I get the same pay. I signed the same oath. I should take the same risks."

Resistance to the notion of women in combat is strong and visceral among rank-and-file U.S. male soldiers, who feel that something must be terribly wrong, even immoral, with a society that will send women, especially mothers, into combat. More than half of the 212,000 women in the U.S. military are mothers. We should be ashamed and embarrassed, *Military* magazine editorialized, by scenes of small children holding tightly to the legs of their combat-uniformed mothers as they prepared to depart for the Iraqi war.

As for female snipers . . .

"Sure, why not?" sarcastically retorted a grizzled former Marine sniper and drill instructor who preferred to be identified only as Gooch. "Makes the hide a lot cozier. If it gets real cold, the sharing of body heat would be great. . . . And all of the rape and sexual harassment charges that will be floating around will improve the good order and discipline in the grunt units. Also, the lowering of standards which will no doubt happen can make it easier for all men and women to get in elite units so that our armed forces are a reflection of the sheep that we protect. . . .

"I trained women recruits in small arms at Parris Island for about three years. Sure, they were easier to teach, if you didn't accidentally touch one wrong or have one fall in love with her coach. . . . They cried when it got cold and wet, they could barely handle the rifle 'cause of its length, had a hard time grasping an M9 pistol because of its grip size, and some couldn't press the double-action trigger with one trigger finger. Half of them couldn't see out of a fighting hole and had to have help getting out of said fighting hole. . . .

"War is a terrible thing. No one should have to go. Leave the women out. Sure, the Russians had women snipers. They also had 10- and 12-year-old boys. Their country was being overrun and everything had to be thrown at the Nazis. If we ever get down to the same point . . . we would have to do the same thing."

CHAPTER FORTY

By September 1991, as a result of a fierce civil war that had raged for the past three years in the West African nation of Somalia, the country had been left with no semblance of government, civil society, or essential services. Food supplies dwindled, remaining vegetables and fruits were infested with worms and insects, water services were poisoned and contaminated, the army and police force had disbanded, hospitals and schools shut down, and government ministries and the People's Assembly ceased operation. On top of everything else, a two-year-long drought devastated agriculture. The country slid into anarchy as fighting erupted between the various factions and clans, each attempting to gain and hold power.

Diplomatic efforts by the French colony of Djibouti, the League of Arab States, the Organization of African Unity, the Organization of the Islamic Conference, and the United Nations were unsuccessful in negotiating an end to the fighting. By mid-October 1993, 350,00 to

500,000 Somalis had died, 700,000 were displaced and completely dependent upon outside assistance, and more than a half-million were refugees in bordering countries. Relief officials estimated that a quarter of Somalia children under age 5 had already died. Over 40 percent of the population of the city of Baidoa had died, and the rest were expiring at the rate of hundreds a day.

Warlord bandits, gunmen and general lawlessness disrupted humanitarian efforts. Supply convoys were ambushed. Stockpiles were plundered at gunpoint. Relief officials were murdered. The cauldron of anarchy brewed most violently in the capital at Mogadishu, where Ali Mahdi Mohamed of the Abgal clan held the northern part of the city, while the former commander of the Somalia army, General Mohamed Farrah Aidid of the Habr Gidr clan, took control of southern Mogadishu. The two factions fought incessantly and turned Mogadishu into another Beirut.

Vast quantities of arms and ammunition previously supplied by the Soviets and the United States to the former Somali armed forces were readily available. All civil servants and public school and university students had been required by previous administrations to undergo military training. The Somali citizens were therefore well armed and trained to handle weapons.

It was into this chaos that the United Nations had sent military forces on 18 August 1992 to protect food supplies and establish a secure environment. American troops were subsequently sent to Somalia, arriving the night of 9 December to occupy the Mogadishu airport. Their arrival raised expectations among the Somalis that an end to their terror and starvation was in sight.

However, lack of direction and a clear mission order left military forces in an open-ended situation where the parameters of proper action were flexible and situational. Within two days of the arrival of U.S. Marines and the French Foreign Legion in Mogadishu, two Somalis were killed at a French checkpoint when a loaded truck attempted to run the roadblock. On 13 December, U.S. Marines making a food run were engaged by three "technicals" in a firefight. A "technical" was a small pickup truck carrying guerrillas and their weapons. The guerrillas were all killed.

Clan gunmen, aware that their power was slipping away, stepped up sniper attacks and ambushes against American forces. Guerrillas in Mogadishu killed U.S. Marine PFC Domingo Arroyo after a fierce firefight with what Marine Colonel Michael W. Hagee called "a substantial number of Somali gunmen." Hagee announced that he would increase his search for arms and guerrillas. In one week Marines confiscated sixteen truckloads of arms and ammunition, including 265 rifles and 55 machine guns.

As tension ratcheted up in the highly charged atmosphere of Somalia, death lurked around every corner and became a constant companion.

A battalion command sergeant major summed up the situation: "We're here to give help to a people half of whom want us desperately to get the hell out, and the other half want us desperately to get the hell out after we give them all our money and kill the other half."

"This is the worst kind of warfare," added Lieutenant Colonel Jim Sikes, commander of the 2d Battalion, 87th Infantry, "because it is insidious. You are surrounded by the enemy. You are surrounded by friendlies. You are surrounded by the innocent and the guilty."

CHAPTER FORTY-ONE

U.S. Marine Sergeant Michael Carr
Somalia, 1994

In June 1994, I was on the roof of the White House, the main building in the American embassy compound, with my elbows propped on sandbags as I gripped binoculars and scanned the field spread out toward the Medina area in Mogadishu. The sonic snapping of several rifle bullets over the heads of Sergeant McFarland and myself seemed to get progressively and uncomfortably closer with each round.

Another spiteful *crack!* McFarland, a fellow sniper with 1st Platoon, FAST Company, glanced at me. I looked back. *Are they shooting at us?*

He shrugged his shoulders and continued scanning the wide field for some sign of the shooter.

Crack!

Someone *was* trying to nail us. The passage of the bullet between our heads buzzed as it split the air, scorching it. I cranked the handle of the TA-312 field phone. The boss would want to know about this.

"It's just spillover fire," he tried to reassure me.

Spillover, my ass. Some Somali was targeting us. Yet, we always had to ask ourselves the question of whether shots were aimed at us or whether they were spillover from clan fighting in the nearby streets. Heavy fighting in Mogadishu raged more or less constantly from about 1100 hours to about 1600 hours. That seemed to be the normal fighting day. Aidid's gunmen and the other clan fighters slept in most mornings, then went out to do some shooting before going back home in time for sunset prayers.

It was frustrating, standing by like that and doing nothing while some Somali whacked out from chewing too much narcotic *khat* sneaked up and winged a few shots at the compound. According to the rules of engagement, we had to wait until we actually *saw* gunmen using their weapons against *us* before we fired back. It was always much simpler, considering the history of this place, to look at all fire as "spillover" unless it actually struck someone. If we confronted it, we had to do something. Better to pretend it didn't happen.

I had read about snipers in Vietnam and Desert Storm. Their mission seemed relatively simple and straightforward compared to that of a sniper in Somalia. If they spotted an enemy carrying a weapon, the guy was paid for. Not so here.

Crack!

"Keep your head down," Sergeant McFarland dryly commented. "Wouldn't want to get hit by spillover."

Somalis had already killed 45 Americans over the past year during the UN-sponsored "relief and aid" mission to the war-torn little nation. Eight months ago, on 3 October 1993, two Blackhawk helicopters were shot down over Mogadishu, eighteen Americans were killed and dozens more wounded in the most intense firefight fought by Americans since the Vietnam War.

What was intended to be a quick in-and-out mission that day to snatch two top lieutenants of renegade warlord Mohamed Farrah Aidid turned into a massive ambush. For a long and terrible night, [the] U.S. Army's Task Force Ranger and subsequent rescue forces were pinned down inside a hostile city in arms, locked in a desperate struggle to kill or be killed. Hundreds, perhaps even thousands, of Somali guerrilla fighters were mowed down in the streets and inside buildings.

That battle was the turning point in Operation Restore Hope. Hope turned to hopelessness. America's last combat elements withdrew from the Mogadishu airport on 25 March 1994. Immediately after the exodus, mobs knocked Mogadishu's port to the ground, looted warehouses, and seized weapons in full view of 19,000 Third World troops remaining in Somalia on the UN mission. Looters descended upon the airport even before the last Marines loaded onto giant C-5A aircraft, helicopters, or amphibious assault vehicles to return to their ships and bases. Only a handful of Marines, myself among them, remained behind to guard the American embassy compound until the diplomats could also be evacuated.

On 24 May 1994, Aidid, who had been in exile, returned triumphantly to Mogadishu. Since then he had worked to consolidate his hold over the city and push out rival clans. Automatic-weapons fire rattled throughout the city at all hours of the day and night. Sometimes from the roof of the White House we watched as clans clashed on Dead Cow Road or Afgoye Road. At some point we expected them to attack the embassy. Ol' Aidid might get out of bed on the wrong side some morning and give orders to human wave the compound.

When that happened, the other snipers in the platoon and I would break out our M40A1s and, along with four designated marksmen armed with scoped M14s, start eliminating clansmen. It was a weird time in a war that wasn't a war—all those hostiles armed to the teeth scuttling about like violent cockroaches waiting, *waiting,* to start killing Americans again.

There was a sort of low lip around the flat roof of the White House, behind which we had built a sandbagged weapons emplacement. I had stood on the roof and drawn a field sketch of the area for defensive purposes. Below, a high wall encircled the few buildings and houses of the U.S. compound, beyond which lay the open field transfixed by Market Street, then Afgoye Road farther out. Afgoye Road was about 500 yards away to my left, gauntleted by walled mud huts and the all-but-abandoned Medina Hospital. Dead Cow Road passed by in front of us at a lesser distance. Snipers were tuned to think in ranges to possible targets.

Now, after the unseen rifleman quit firing our way, a pair of "technicals" rolled up Afgoye and stopped. The battered little Toyotas were jammed with clansmen who poured out of the pickup with their weapons. As McFarland and I watched, they quickly broke into fire teams and began maneuvering parallel to the compound, advancing from left to right in a fire-and-maneuver pattern by leapfrogging from one pile of rock or debris to the next. After a while they loaded up again and left.

"Are you going to call that in?" I asked the Marine watch stander on the roof with Sergeant McFarland and me.

"What was it all about? Besides, they're gone now."

"They just conducted a rehearsal," I explained. "Fire and maneuver, assigned sectors of fire, and then a debriefing. They were rehearsing an attack on the compound."

"I'll call it in."

Marines were always on duty guarding the compound while a second section stood by for escort duty, manning Humvees bristling with machine guns and MK19 automatic 40mm grenade launchers. The city remained so dangerous that even travel on the periphery had to be accomplished with a heavily armed three-vehicle convoy. That was how the American ambassador and his DCM [deputy chief of mission] were escorted about on duties outside the compound.

Snipers and designated marksmen took turns on watch at the White House, waiting to be used. We did six hours on, twelve hours off, as tensions in Mogadishu continued. One night Lance Corporal Langmeyer saw muzzle flashes winking at him and engaged them with his own rifle. The shooting stopped.

Corporal Barwell on convoy duty saw a Somali in one of the buildings lift a rifle to his shoulder and aim it at the passing vehicles. Barwell responded with two quick shots. Some guys showed up at the embassy a week later trying to collect money for a man they claimed Marines in a convoy killed. Right. That was the way it went. They shot us, chopped us into little pieces, and dragged the remaining torsos through the streets. But if we shot back, they came to collect money. It was a screwed-up situation.

My outfit of 52 Marines was the last American military in the battered, hungry capital. We were there specifically to guard the embassy and its personnel. We would leave, too, when the embassy was no longer needed. More than 4,000 U.S. Navy and Marine Corps personnel waited in ships offshore prepared for the evacuation of final U.S. diplomats. Aidid must have been thrilled: He was driving out the last of the Americans who had come on a humanitarian mission to help his starving people. His war and his power were more important to him than his people.

Daily convoys hauled gear from the compound to the airport to be flown out to Kenya. They had to pass near a checkpoint Aidid's men set up on Afgoye Road, about 600 yards away, to extort money from passersby. A battered white pickup truck technical sat at the roadblock with a 106mm recoilless rifle mounted on it one morning as a Marine convoy prepared to depart. Eight Humvees and an armored Suburban were lined up in the courtyard ready to pull out. Captain Bertholf, the platoon commander, climbed to the roof.

"Keep an eye on that vehicle," he warned. "Take them out if they look aggressive or even point that 106 at us or at the compound."

"Roger that, sir."

A mission like that I understood. That 106 could do some major damage. I had my M40A1 and Corporal Middleton, my spotter, had an M14 with a 6X Leupold scope and a spotter scope. Those Somalis would never stand a chance.

An hour passed. Two hours. Nothing happened. The convoy left. The 106 technical pulled out of the area. I told Middleton to secure our rifles in their cases but to leave them on the roof, ready for use. I went down to check on the guard posts. The roof watch stander was to notify me immediately if the 106 returned to Aidid's roadblock.

Only eight Marines were left to hold the fort. The watch stander called down from the roof: "Sergeant, the 106 is back. There's a guy manning it and it's aimed right at the compound."

Middleton and I raced to the roof, hearts pounding with excitement. I peered through the M49 spotter scope.

"I've got him," I murmured. "He's up on the gun and aiming it at the compound."

I quickly uncased my rifle and chambered a round. I took up a firing position using the sandbags for support and brought the scope to my eyes. I settled the crosshairs on the man at the big gun. He swiveled the muzzle of the gun off the compound and into a neutral position. I let out a breath and eased my finger off the trigger. I had been a heartbeat away from killing the kid; he had been a heartbeat away from dying.

He jumped off the pickup and no one so much as got near the gun for the rest of the day. It was almost like they knew what would happen.

As it turned out, we were not forced to engage the Somalis during the final days of the embassy's existence. They made it clear that they would leave us alone. All they cared about was that we left.

The last of our people departed the American compound on 15 September. We lowered the flag. The remaining diplomatic staff went to Nairobi, Kenya. The Marines went to Mombasa, and then back to the United States of America.

CHAPTER FORTY-TWO

U.S. Army Master
Sergeant Gary Gordon

U.S. Army Sergeant
First Class Randy Shughart
Somalia, 1993

"To me, they were Batman and Robin, only much better," said Chief Warrant Officer Mike Durant, pilot of a Blackhawk helicopter downed in the tangle of slums and shanties that was Mogadishu, Somalia, on 3 October 1993. "They just walked up to my aircraft like they were out for a stroll in the park."

The Americans had not expected to become engaged in a lengthy firefight when they launched Task Force Ranger on that Sunday afternoon. Earlier in the day, Somali spies on the payroll of the Central Intelligence Agency reported that warlord Mohammed Aidid's foreign minister, his political adviser, and his propaganda chief were planning to hold a meeting in the Olympic

Hotel in the Wardigley District of Mogadishu. Task Force Ranger's mission was to capture them.

The neighborhood around the hotel was a sprawling rat's maze of walled compounds and alleys populated by at least 50,000 people, most of whom were loyal to Aidid. Guerrillas opened fire on the raiding party shortly after Rangers rappelled down ropes from a hovering UH-60 to link up with a security patrol in an adjacent street. A squad leader was wounded, forcing the patrol to drag its casualties into the temporary cover of a nearby building. Thousands of Aidid's armed supporters filled the streets, turning the district into a battleground.

Early in the fight, rocket-propelled grenades smashed into a low-flying Blackhawk assault helicopter flown by pilot CWO Mike Durant, copilot CWO Ray Frank, and two crew, Sergeant Tommy Field and Staff Sergeant Bill Cleveland. It crashed belly-down in a Villa Somalia neighborhood of rag shacks and tin huts.

A second Blackhawk had also been shot down about a mile away, but an airborne search-and-rescue force reached it immediately and evacuated its crew. The rescue of *Super Six-Four,* Durant's bird, was not going to be that easy. Durant's wing mate, CWO Mike Goffena, flying Blackhawk *Super Six-Two*, spotted hundreds of Somalis spilling through alleyways and footpaths and surrounding the downed chopper, homing in on it like ants to sugar. Rescue from the air was impossible against such intense volumes of small-arms and rocket fire. Emergency ground convoys en route from the American base at the airport would never arrive in time.

RPG smoke trails streaked into the sky, seeking out the swarming helicopters. Goffena and his copilot Jim Yacone heard the fast ticking of bullets piercing the skin of their aircraft whenever they attempted to dart near

Durant's smoking chopper on the ground. At this rate, it was only a matter of time before *Six-Two* suffered a similar fate.

Aboard Goffena's helicopter, in addition to its pilots and two crew chiefs, were three trained snipers from the U.S. Army's elite counter terrorist unit, 1st Special Forces Operational Detachment–Delta. Delta Force. Team Sergeant Gary Gordon, 33, and Weapons Sergeant Randy Shughart, 35, were lean, sinewy, rawhide types with full mustaches that made them look enough alike to be brothers. Gordon might have been an inch or so taller. Sergeant First Class Brad Hallings was the most outgoing of the three and was known as something of a practical jokester in Troop C, Delta. All were serious career soldiers, experts in killing and staying alive.

The crewman manning one of the bird's two door miniguns took a hit and dropped to the deck, saved from falling out by his safety line. Hallings took over for him, laying down on the gun's trigger to hammer away at armed militiamen scurrying about in the city below.

Shughart carried a Remington-framed M24SWS (sniper weapon system), a high-tech rifle scoped for long-range fire. Gordon had a short-barreled CAR-15, better suited for close-in fighting. Both sharpshooters lay on the bird's steel floor for stability as they picked away at African gunslingers rushing to overrun the crash site.

Shughart fired as rapidly as he could operate the bolt and select a fresh target from among the hundreds below. Nearly every shot scored a hit. Bodies crumpled and lay sprawled in odd clumps in alleys and on the tops of buildings. Hallings on the minigun and Gordon with his carbine likewise gave a good accounting of their deadly skills.

No matter how many skinnies the Deltas shot or how many fell to the Blackhawk's integral weapons, Somali warriors filled in like water from an opened floodgate. Gordon requested that he and Shughart be inserted, arguing that they would be far more effective on the ground where they could hold the mobs off *Six-Four* until help arrived. Goffena thought the request crazy.

Nonetheless, the pilot made a low pass over the site to check for survivors, roaring in at no more than thirty feet above shanty rooftops. Rotor wash literally blew thickening crowds back like a whirlwind through autumn leaves, providing easy targets for the Delta snipers.

There were survivors. Goffena saw Mike Durant struggling in the cockpit of the wreckage with a piece of roofing tin that had somehow ended up partly inside with him. Copilot Ray Frank feebly lifted his head, more unconscious than not. Movement from the bird's crew belly indicated that Cleveland and Field might also have survived.

Two "Little Bird" helicopters had joined the force in the air in an attempt to cover the crash site.

"We've got to get some ground folks down there," a Little Bird pilot pleaded over the radio, "or we're not going to be able to keep them off. There are not enough people left on board the downed aircraft to do it."

Lieutenant Colonel Tom Matthews and Lieutenant Colonel Gary Harrell, joint mission commanders, grimly assessed the situation as they circled the battle zone in their command-and-control chopper. As things stood, the four survivors were as good as dead unless help arrived immediately. At the same time, to invest two men, as the Delta Force snipers were insisting, almost certainly risked their loss as well.

"They're your guys," Air Commander Matthews said to Harrell, the ground commander and himself a member of Delta. "What do you want to do?"

"What are the choices?"

"They're the only two guys we have available. We can put them in or not put them in. Nobody else is going to get to that crash site that I can see."

CWO Yacone, copilot of *Six-Two*, kept Gordon and Shughart informed of the situation in much the same terms.

"Things are getting bad now, guys. The rescue convoy is taking intense fire. It doesn't look like they're gonna make it to the crash site."

The two snipers indicated they were ready to go down. Hallings would stay behind to man the minigun.

Colonel Harrell made the decision: If his men had even the slightest chance to succeed, they owed it to the fallen Blackhawk crew. Two men, heavily armed and experts with weapons, just might be able to pull it off and hold back the maddened hordes until more help arrived.

"Put them in."

Six-Two selected an LZ about fifty yards from the crash site in a small debris-cluttered opening behind a tin hut.

"Once you get to them," Yacone suggested to the snipers as Goffena maneuvered the Blackhawk toward the opening, "you can either hunker down and wait for the vehicles, or try to get the wounded to an open area where we can come back in and get you."

Gordon gave him a thumbs-up.

Goffena flared the helicopter suddenly, having come in fast to avoid offering an easy target, and hovered five feet above the ground between the hut and a tin fence.

The two Deltas tumbled out of the helicopter. The uninjured crew chief hurled a smoke grenade in the direction of the crash to point the way through the jumble of shanties and shacks. Hallings's minigun continued to ripsaw out streams of death as *Six-Two* leaped back into the air to resume its coverage of the crashed chopper.

Minutes later, "Batman and Robin" appeared on Durant's side of the wreck, their load-bearing harnesses slung with ammunition and grenades. Neither said much. Businesslike, they simply asked the pilot about his wounds.

"My right leg's broken. And I think my back is broken."

"Uh-huh."

Ray Frank was in even worse shape as he drifted in and out of awareness. The two crew chiefs were alive but unconscious. Gordon and Shughart gently lifted Durant from his seat and carried him quickly to a small open spot triangled inside a tree, a high wall of rusted tin, and a matching tin shanty with only three walls. They left him there with his MP5 submachine gun and a single spare magazine, about 60 rounds total. Then they returned to the chopper, removed the other survivors, and placed them in available cover in a defensive perimeter around the Blackhawk.

They had four seriously wounded men on their hands and could move them no farther than they already had. The helicopter had crashed in the only uninhabited flat spot in the middle of a cluster of huts. The Deltas checked the area for another clearing large enough to land a helicopter but found nothing suitable. They returned to the crash site and prepared to defend it.

From above, *Super Six-Two* watched Somalis streaming through the slums, moving in fast on the crash. They filled all the trails and streets back out to the main road. Durant heard voices on the other side of the tin wall. Skinnies poked heads around corners.

The wounded pilot banged away at them with his MP5, forcing the hostiles to scurry for cover but exhausting his ammunition at the same time.

The Delta men were out of Durant's sight, having taken up positions on the other side of the Blackhawk at the most vulnerable avenue of enemy approach. Precision sniper shots from Shughart's M24 and the double-tapping of Gordon's carbine answered the deep, hollow hammering of AK-47s. Durant noticed that the sun had turned red in the west as it shimmered low on the horizon. They might have a chance if they could hold out until nightfall.

The first Blackhawk down had been designated as Crash Site One. Durant's chopper was Crash Site Two.

"Are there any ground forces moving to site two at this time?" CWO Goffena in *Six-Two* asked over the radio net.

"Negative, not at this time," responded the C & C bird.

"This place is getting extremely hot," Goffena radioed. "We need to get these folks out of there."

Colonel Matthews warned the Blackhawks and Little Birds not to fly so low lest they also be shot down. The Little Birds carried no integral ordnance. Copilots using M16s were plinking from the windows at African gunfighters.

On the ground, Durant heard Gordon cry out in an annoyed voice as though he had been stung by a bee: "Damn! I'm hit."

He died lying on the pale sand on the other side of the chopper from Durant.

In the sky above, an RPG round struck *Super Six-Two* in the belly at almost the same moment Gordon died. It blew off Hallings's leg and knocked Yacone, the copilot, unconscious. Goffena nursed the crippled bird to the nearby port facility and crash-landed it on friendly ground. That left crash site two virtually on its own. Maddened mobs moved in with thunderstorm rolls of rifle fire.

Randy Shughart came striding around the cockpit toward Durant carrying weapons salvaged from the aircraft. He handed Durant the CAR-15 previously used by his friend and partner Gary Gordon.

"Good luck," he said, still businesslike, and moved back around the chopper out of sight.

A fierce fusillade of gunfire erupted from his sector. It lasted for a long two minutes. Over the din, Shughart cried out in anger and pain. Then the firing stopped.

Durant by this time was in a fight for his own life, shooting skinnies who charged in on him until he again ran out of ammunition. He placed his empty weapon across his chest, folded his hands over it, and turned his eyes toward the sky, accepting death. The sun was setting.

There was no more shooting. He assumed all the others must be dead. Excited skinnies swarmed over the wreckage.

"Do you have video over Crash Site Two?" base control asked the C & C chopper.

"Indigenous personnel are moving all over the crash site," came the reply.

"Indigenous?"

"That's affirmative, over."

Though badly injured and helpless, CWO Mike Durant somehow survived capture and captivity. He was the only survivor. He was held eleven days until the CIA arranged his release.

Master Sergeant Gary Gordon and Sergeant First Class Randy Shughart were awarded America's highest wartime medal, the Medal of Honor, for their heroism in attempting to save and rescue fellow soldiers.

CHAPTER FORTY-THREE

The sniper is not superhuman, but he is nonetheless skilled in ways that many misunderstand. Skilled individuals with specialized equipment have influenced the tides of battle throughout history, sometimes to the point of changing it. Long-range riflemen have felled enemy commanders, destroyed equipment, and driven fear into the hearts of their foes. At the same time, the sniper is not a cold-hearted, calculating murderer. Rather, he is a soldier called upon to accomplish missions.

"For the sniper," said Jim Land, former U.S. Marine Corps sniper and a founder of the USMC Scout Sniper Instructor School, "there is no hate of the enemy, only respect of him as a quarry. Psychologically, the only motive that will sustain the sniper is knowing that he is doing a necessary job and having the confidence that he is the best person to do it. On the battlefield, hate will destroy any man—especially a sniper. Killing for revenge will ultimately twist the mind."

Below is a "kill list" of known snipers from various nations. No political or value judgments are made:

NAME	CONFLICT	SERVICE	CONFIRMED KILLS
Simo Hayha	WWII	Finland	500+
Nikolay Yakovlevich	WWII	Russia	496
Suko Kolkka	WWII	Finland	400+
Ilyin Vassili Zaitsev	WWII	Russia	400
Matthias Hetzenauer	WWII	Germany	345
Ludmilla Pavlichenko	WWII	Russia	309
Sepp Allerberger	WWII	Germany	257
Billy Sing	WWII	AIF	150
Adelbert Waldron III	Vietnam	U.S. Army	109
Chuck Mawhinney	Vietnam	U.S. Marines	103
Neville Methven	WWI	South Africa	100+
Eric R. England	Vietnam	U.S. Marines	98
Carlos N. Hathcock, II	Vietnam	U.S. Marines	93
Thomas R. Leonard	Vietnam	U.S. Marines	74
Helmut Wirnsberger	WWII	Germany	64
Joseph T. Ward	Vietnam	U.S. Marines	63
Herbert W. McBride	WWI	U.S. with Canada	60+
George Filyaw	Vietnam	U.S. Marines	56
Gary Reiter	Vietnam	U.S. Marines	50+
Raymond W. Westphal	Vietnam	U.S. Marines	49
James C. Peters	Vietnam	U.S. Marines	43
T.B. Graves	Vietnam	U.S. Marines	43
Lynn Bushnell	Vietnam	U.S. Marines	43
Daniel L. Greene	Vietnam	U.S. Marines	42
Joe York	Vietnam	U.S. Marines	42
K. Tatang	Vietnam	East Timor & North Vietnam	41
Tom Ferran	Vietnam	U.S. Marines	41
James Gularte	Vietnam	U.S. Marines	40

CROSSHAIRS ON THE KILL ZONE

NAME	CONFLICT	SERVICE	CONFIRMED KILLS
R. D. Bundy	Vietnam	U.S. Marines	40
Michael E. Duncan	Vietnam	U.S. Army	40
William Lucas	Vietnam/ Panama	U.S. Marines/ Army	38
John M. Perry	Vietnam	U.S. Marines	37
Dennis Oscier	Vietnam	U.S. Marines	36
Bill E. Nation	Vietnam	U.S. Marines	35
Riel	WWI	Canada	30
Clifford L. Wallace	Vietnam	U.S. Marines	27
Craig McGary	Vietnam	U.S. Navy	26
Jim O'Neill	Vietnam	U.S. Marines	25+
Lloyd Crow	Vietnam	U.S. Marines	23
Jim Lever	Vietnam	U.S. Marines	20+
Bobby J. Lee	Vietnam	U.S. Marines	18
Craig Roberts	Vietnam	U.S. Marines	18+
Ed Kugler	Vietnam	U.S. Marines	17
Joshua Hamblin	Iraq	U.S. Marines	17
Gary J. Brown	Vietnam	U.S. Navy	17
Karl H. Grosshans	Vietnam	U.S. Marines	16
Owen Mulder	Iraq	U.S. Marines	15
Greg Kraljev	Vietnam	U.S. Marines	15
Frank Grieci	Iraq	U.S. Marines	15
Timothy Dunn	Vietnam	U.S. Marines	14
Joseph McElheny	Iraq	U.S. Marines	13
Thomas R. Cohenour	Vietnam	U.S. Army	13
Ron Szpond	Vietnam	U.S. Marines	12
William B. Martin	Vietnam	U.S. Marines	12
Roy Lafon	Vietnam	U.S. Marines	5+
Gabriel J. Gradney	Vietnam	U.S. Marines	4
Tom Rutter	Beirut	U.S. Marines	4
Dan Barker	Vietnam	U.S. Marines	3+
Chuck Kramer	Beirut	U.S. Marines	3+
Alan Bruce Hartung	Vietnam	U.S. Marines	3

NAME	CONFLICT	SERVICE	CONFIRMED KILLS
Dave Dayter	Iraq	U.S. Marines	3
Colin McGee	Vietnam	U. S. Marines	3
Frank Roberts	Beirut	U.S. Marines	2+
Robert Miles	Vietnam	U.S. Army	2
Jonathan Crumley	Beirut	U.S. Marines	2
Eric L. Haney	Beirut	U.S. Army	1
David Baldree	Beirut	U.S. Marines	1
Earl Schooley	Panama	U.S. Marines	1
Andres Benevides	Beirut	U.S. Army	1
Jacob Heal	Iraq	U.S. Marines	1

CHAPTER FORTY-FOUR

U.S. Marine Sergeant Marty Williams
1991–2003

Being a sniper in peacetime is rather like being a race-horse in training for some big race in the future that may never arrive. You may go an entire career and never be needed. Still, you have to be ready. You never know when the word will come: "Sniper up!"

I became a sniper following the first Gulf War in 1991. I had landed with the 5th Marine Expeditionary Brigade in Kuwait at the beginning of the war, as a grunt with 3/5. RCT-5 [Regimental Combat Team 5] conducted a mop-up sweep from Kuwait Beach up through Kuwait to the Al Wafrah oil fields. One of the men in the RCT accidentally shot himself, which was our only casualty. Otherwise, we took a little small-arms and mortar fire, policed up a bunch of Iraqis with their hands reaching for satellites, watched day turn into night from all the oil well fires around Kuwait—and then we went home.

On the way back, the company first sergeant stood

with me one afternoon on the fantail of the LST troop ship USS *Barber County*.

"Williams, you're one of the top guys in the company," he said. "What do you want to do? You want to try out for Recon? You want to go into sniping?"

I thought about it a moment. "Yeah," I said. "I'd kinda like to do both."

He grinned with approval; he was an old Force Recon leatherneck. "Ask and Mother Corps shall provide."

Sniper school was more physical than technical. Thirty students began Class 2-91. It was a good sign if you woke up the next morning and you weren't dropped. A little over 50 percent of us graduated in December 1991 and were distributed into the fleet in STA [Surveillance and Target Acquisition] teams. Life as an individual sniper became a constant movement of training, more training, and training missions, interspersed occasionally with a "real-world" assignment that was generally little more than another training assignment.

For example, in June 1992 snipers were dispatched to the Philippines to oversee the pullout of U.S. forces from U.S. Naval Station Subic Bay as it was being evacuated. Islamic terrorist organizations like Abu Sayyaf and New People's Army were busy all over the islands, bombing things and threatening Americans. Since snipers with our M40A1 rifles and 10X scopes were well equipped with good standoff weapons capable of shooting accurately a thousand yards or more, we were deployed primarily at the American embassy to watch over a Vietnam-style evacuation should it become necessary.

Everything went off without a hitch. Simply another training mission.

After a couple of years like this in the fleet, I was assigned as a sniper instructor to the 1st Division Sniper

School, Camp Pendleton, California. Training other snipers means you also train yourself. Sergeant Todd Parisi was NCOIC at the time. We pushed through six Marine classes between October 1993 and June 1995, in addition to training SWAT team snipers for police departments like Los Angeles, San Diego, and Burbank. In return, federal agents came out to Pendleton and ran Marine sniper instructors through their FBI sniper observer courses.

The big difference between military and law enforcement sniping is that law enforcement sniping occurs at much shorter ranges. Whereas military shooters train for shooting targets out to 1,000 yards and beyond, police normally consider shots of 100 to 300 yards to be the maximum range in an urban environment. While training lawmen at Pendleton, we extended their range—and their confidence. They began shooting accurately out to 600 and 700 yards.

"Holy cow! I'm hitting what I'm aiming at!"

"It makes me feel better," I chided. "If I'm ever a hostage, I want it to be here because you guys are a lot better shooters now."

Concepts of warfare and the strategy and tactics to match are a constantly changing process. Future wars are expected to be faster and shorter, and to occur to a large degree in urban areas. In 1995, after transferring to MEUSOC [Marine Expeditionary Unit, Special Operations Command] of the 1st Marines, I attended the urban sniper course, shooting in cities and built-up areas. Later, I would also instruct the course.

Training continued in combined arms skills. Everyone in the regiment trained in his individual skills and specialties—parachuting, CQB [close quarter battle], reconnaissance, SCUBA . . . Companies trained as units:

helicopter companies, boat raid companies, amtracs . . . We practiced raids and landings, frontal assaults, urban warfare, single involvements such as those a sniper might confront . . .

Interoperability, or interop, followed. MEUSOC had to be capable of accomplishing several different missions: direct action; gas/oil platform takedowns; NEOs [noncombatant evacuation operations]; HADR [humanitarian assistance disaster relief] . . . In interop, elements formed to work together on their missions in FTXs [field training exercises]. For example, the R & S element [reconnaissance and surveillance], which included snipers, linked with the Force Recon Platoon and with Naval Special Warfare SEALs to practice. Part of the sniper interop was conducted in Guam, operating in an urban environment.

Eventually, I ended up back in the Persian Gulf, where it was more of the same: training. Long-range shooting and reconnaissance, surveillance operations, shooting from helicopters. Sniping from the air is not a one shot—one kill proposition, although most of us became good enough to place accurate rounds and serve as a fair suppression weapon.

A "real-world" alert sounded in February 1996 while sniper teams were wrapping up a training session at Udary Range in Kuwait. An Iranian freighter had been setting out in the Gulf for the past several months, under lock and denied permission to port anywhere in the region because of his hazardous cargo. The ship's crew was on the verge of mutiny. A SEAL and Marine Force Recon boarding party was tasked with going aboard the ship to restore order and prevent a catastrophe.

My orders were to take out any individual who made an overt movement with a weapon. Sergeant Danny

Mainville acted as my observer and secondary shooter. We lifted in a UH-1 "Huey" helicopter, flying with the cargo doors open, and circled the distressed freighter, watching for any sign of hostile action as the boarding party approached in fast boats. No one at this point could be sure of the crew's intentions.

The ship was a rusty old tub, obviously in need of upkeep. It floated dead on a sea so still under the equatorial sun that it might also have been dead. Several boats approaching rapidly inscribed white wakes across the Gulf's still face. Having been provided the number of the crew, I counted it as the chopper circled above. Everyone had been ordered to present himself on deck, unarmed, and prepare to be boarded.

I came up one man short on the count. Mainville and I recounted and compared figures.

"There's one man missing," I intercomed to the Huey pilot.

"Are you sure?"

"Yes, sir. There's a man missing— Wait one."

I glimpsed movement on the bridge, a flash of clothing. Scoping the bridge, I picked up a single dark-skinned man leaning over a railing as he peered down at his fellows on the lower deck. My report of the sighting followed a chain through the pilot and MEU commander to the boarding party, which was in direct radio contact with the ship.

I continued to watch the prospective target through my scope, prepared to take action should he try anything. Apparently, the boarding party radioed a stern command, because the lost sheep on the bridge suddenly scrambled from his perch to join his shipmates. It turned out he was a cook who hadn't got the word and didn't know what was going on.

The boarding went off without a hitch. The call for help turned out to be a need for humanitarian assistance rather than a mutiny. I slipped my rifle back into its case.

It was good training.

I became a drill instructor at San Diego pushing boots through basic training for a couple of years before shipping over to the R & S section of SOTG [Special Operations Training Group]. What did we do there? More training. I was an Advanced Marksmanship R & S Instructor, pushing snipers through the SOTG Urban Sniper Course in Okinawa and Guam. Sniper students came from the 5th and 7th Marines and the 3d Marines in Hawaii, as well as from the Army's 1st Special Forces Group and the Navy's Special Warfare SEAL units.

In 2001, because of my training association with Army Special Forces, I was temporarily attached to Army SF on a foreign internal defense mission to train Filipino armed forces snipers in their continuing war with Abu Sayyaf and other radical Islamic groups. That was during a period when three Christian missionaries, two of them an American man and wife, had been kidnapped by Abu Sayyaf and held for ransom. The husband was eventually shot and killed, but the wife was rescued.

Now I'm going to 1st Force Recon. What will I do there? What else? More training for that unknown date when my skills as a sniper will be required.

CHAPTER FORTY-FIVE

The first American troops deployed on "peacekeeping" missions to Bosnia arrived at the airport in Tuzla two weeks before Christmas 1995 where they confronted a threatening mixture of snipers, ethnic hatreds, and millions of mines planted under snow-covered fields. Under the provisions of the Dayton Accords signed in November, the United Nations would oversee an uneasy peace after four years of Europe's bloodiest war in a half-century.

The insanity had begun in April 1992 with attacks by Serb militia against a number of Bosnian cities occupied largely by Muslims and Croats. In Sarajevo, in Grbavica, and in a number of other cities, Bosnia's Serb soldiers seized cities and neighborhoods to allow thousands of Serb civilians to rush in after them to occupy abandoned apartments and houses. The Serbian minority of the former republic of Yugoslavia intended to extend by force its Greater Serbia plan of "Where there are Serbs, there is Serbia."

Nearly two million Muslims and Croat civilian refugees poured out of the mountains and valleys of war-ravaged Bosnia-Herzegovina to the relative safety of Croatia. Behind them, Serb snipers used high-rise buildings as hides from which they picked off literally anyone who moved in the "sniper's alleys" below.

"They [the Serbs] were bombing the city [Sarajevo] for 24 days," a teenager named Nikola Rakocevic later wrote, describing his experiences. "From May 2nd to May 27th, we had to go to the basement every single night. The most harm in Sarajevo was done during this time. . . . May 27th is an unforgettable day for everybody in the country. That day the aggressors killed 90 people and injured 160 more. I am never going to forget that day. People were standing in line to buy bread and maybe some milk for breakfast. My mom was standing in line, too, but then she remembered that she had some bread from the day before. She left the line and turned the corner. This was fortunate because at that exact time a bomb fell and killed many of the people in the line and injured many more. . . ."

The tally of fatalities was estimated to be in the hundreds of thousands, although the exact number may never be known. Fighting went beyond conventional warfare to that of medieval times. "Ethnic cleansing," the eradication of a different culture, was pursued with gunfire, flames, torture, and rape. People in the streets and fields killing each other had been friends and neighbors before chaos took over.

As late as 2003, the Bosnian government charged that Serbs were still holding some 1,000 people in forced labor while another 20,000 were still missing. United Nations officials unearthed "genocidal" charnel grounds where Muslims had been summarily executed and buried in mass graves. While thousands died from falling bombs, thousands of others may have died looking into the eyes of their executioners. Many were left to rot where they fell.

Reporter Greg Campbell described a nighttime attack on supposed terrorists in the small village of Lybeniq:

"In the front yard of a farmhouse lay six or seven bodies. Most were in their underwear or pajamas; they had been sleeping soundly until Serb police stormed their homes and forced them outside, where they were shot and left where they had fallen. . . .

"I counted eight or nine bullet holes in the chest of one man, who lay on his back in the dirt, eyes wide open. Another, an old overweight man in tight brief underwear, had been shot in the back of the head at point blank range. . . . More disturbing was . . . a young pregnant woman who hadn't even made it out of bed, much less out onto the lawn. The bullet that had killed her took her whole face away except for a small rubbery portion of the chin and lower lip. . . ."

By February 1996, 20,000 U.S. soldiers had moved into a country whose people had spent the last four years savaging each other with murder and torture. Most of them were headquartered in Tuzla, with small auxiliary deployments in Croatia and Hungary. Some 40,000 troops from twenty-five other countries also moved in to "keep the peace" under the auspices of the UN.

American forces feared they would become targets of rogue elements from all sides. Patrolling was restricted to the point that some soldiers spent tours in-country without so much as speaking to a native. U.S. Marine, Army, and Navy snipers were deployed primarily in a countersniper or supporting role to protect air bases.

As recently as July 2003, service-rifle shooters from

the U.S. Army Marksmanship Unit were sent to Bosnia to provide advance marksmanship training, sniping, and field-craft techniques to thirty soldiers from the 1st Cavalry Division. The soldiers trained in engaging stationary targets, sniper employment, and marksmanship in the M24 sniper system, which was prototyped and tested by the USAMU Custom Firearms Shop.

CHAPTER FORTY-SIX

U.S. Marine
Master Sergeant Neil Morris
Bosnia, 1995

For the past six days, forty fully equipped and fully armed Marines of the 24th Marine Expeditionary Unit [MEU] had been sleeping on the hangar deck of the amphibious assault ship USS *Kearsarge* as it cut squares in the Adriatic Sea, waiting for word to go in and get downed F16 pilot Captain Scott O'Grady out of Bosnia. Three CH-53E Super Stallion helicopters with crews also remained on alert, prepared to leap into the air within five minutes after news came that O'Grady had been located.

So far, nothing had been heard from him since a missile struck his aircraft and forced him to bail out over hostile territory.

Most of the Marines assigned to the combat search-and-rescue [CSAR] belonged to the weapons company, tasked with providing the landing-zone ground-protection force if a pickup were made. I was senior sniper and sniper instructor attached to Weapons Company. My job in the event we flew was to coordinate sniper actions and actions on the objective with the company commander. Regretfully, that meant I operated over the radio and remained behind on the ship, out of the ballgame: a coach and not a player.

At least four of my snipers with M40A1 rifles and equipment were always on the hangar deck with the CSAR, ready to go. Their mission was to provide long-range accurate cover fire to support the rescue once air searchers located the pilot. Military commanders were discovering a variety of uses for snipers other than the traditional one.

Hopes of O'Grady's recovery began to dwindle rapidly after the fourth or fifth day. Everyone in the world seemed to be looking for him the first few days. Now some units were starting to stand down from the effort. Chances that he had survived so long were getting slimmer and slimmer. The *Kearsarge* pulled back from the coast and toward the middle of the Adriatic.

Captain Scott O'Grady had been one of the pilots involved in Operation Deny Flight, the NATO operation to police the skies over Bosnia under the auspices of a UN resolution. Numerous types of aircraft were deployed from bases within Europe, including those from the 555th Fighter Squadron in Avano, Italy, where O'Grady flew F16 Fighting Falcons.

At 1315 hours on 2 June 1995, Captain O'Grady and his wingman, Captain Bob Wright, took off from Avano in a two-ship formation for the Bihác area of northwestern Bosnia. At 1503 hours, a surface-to-air [SAM] missile struck O'Grady's fighter. Wright saw him eject. He was in the air under silk for twenty-five minutes before the parachute settled into wooded terrain.

The enemy immediately initiated a ground search while NATO searched from the air. Through continuous monitoring of Serb communications, UN personnel knew that the pilot was either successfully evading capture, or that he was dead. U.S. rescuers had received no confirmed contact from him since his ejection.

It was now 8 June. Six days had passed with no contact. The search for O'Grady was gradually drawing down.

At 0206 hours of that predawn, Captain T. O. Hanford was flying O'Grady's E & E [escape and evasion] route, calling for him in the blind on the SAR radio frequency without much hope of eliciting a response. He received several clicks on the mike but dismissed them to radio interference. Suddenly, however, a voice jumped out of the radio, calling Hanford by name.

"Basher 52, this is Basher 11," Hanford quickly responded. "Basher 52, this is Basher 11. Are you up on this freq?"

"This is Basher 52."

Basher 52 was O'Grady's call sign. The signal was weak.

"Say again. Understand this is Basher 52?"

"This is Basher 52. . . . I'm alive!"

"Say again, Basher 52. You are weak and unreadable. This is Basher 11."

"This is Basher 52. . . ."

"Basher 52, what squadron were you in at Kunsan?" Hanford asked by way of authentication, although by now he recognized O'Grady's voice.

"Juvats! Juvats! I'm alive!" Most fighter pilots had handles. Juvats was Hanford's. Only another U.S. pilot in the same unit would know that.

"Copy that. You're alive! Basher 52, sit tight and come back up at fifteen past the hour."

Hanford relayed the news to the Flight Command Center. He had made positive radio contact with Zulu, O'Grady's handle. The command center responded that Hanford should advise Zulu with one word: Manana. It was by now two hours before sunrise in the Balkans. Since a daylight extraction attempt would be hazardous to both rescuers and rescued, a pickup would have to wait until the following night.

"I want to get picked up *tonight,*" O'Grady insisted.

Go figure.

Out in the Adriatic, the *Kearsarge* and its CSAR force were alerted of the decision to launch a rescue attempt immediately. The pressure was suddenly incredible as the *Kearsarge* reversed course and steamed full speed back toward the coastline. From the communications center, still chafing at being left behind, I monitored the action as the CH-53s lifted off the flight deck and highballed it toward land. My snipers along with Force Recon Marines flew in the third chopper, ready to either cover a position to suppress enemy fire or to provide a ring of steel and lead for the rescue.

A rescue behind enemy lines is an extremely complicated process requiring minute-by-minute coordination. Radio waves literally crackled with excitement and tension. I listened, spellbound, as the mission quickly unfolded. The skies over Bosnia, beginning to lighten with the approach of dawn, filled with a variety of warplanes all concentrated toward a single goal.

The CH-53 containing snipers and Recon Force provided close escort and protection for the two Super Stallions that would actually set down in enemy country to snatch the pilot out of harm's way. Also included in the escort and security armada were two AH-1W Super Cobra helicopter gunships, a brace of AV-8 Harrier jets, and several A-10 Thunderbolts and FA-18 Hornets armed with a variety of guided and unguided weapons.

Flying higher in combat air patrols were F15 and F16 Falcons, their objective to intercept and destroy any enemy aircraft that might pose a threat to operations. Other aircraft—F-111 Aardvarks, EA-6B Prowlers, A6 Intruders—were tasked with the suppression of enemy air defenses by using electronic countermeasures to jam radar and missile guidance centers or to direct hits against SAM sites.

A Boeing E3 Airborne Early Warning and Control aircraft oversaw the entire mission, maintained control of the elements involved, and used its own search radar capability and data-linking facilities to maintain lines of communications between the rescue force and the Combined Air Operations Center in Vicenza, Italy.

Zulu's location on the ground had already been confirmed through RDF [radio directional finding] and through O'Grady's own reports. Inbound helicopters authenticated Zulu's identity a second time, as required by SOP, before committing themselves. They asked him what he was called in high school when he got drunk, a question so intimate that only O'Grady and a few close friends could answer it. O'Grady got it right.

The downed pilot popped smoke when he had the helicopters in sight. He remained hidden in forest next to a small green field until the two rescue Super Stallions flared over the field and sat down. One of them jammed a fence post into its belly as it landed but sustained no disabling damage to either itself or its crew. From higher up, overlooking the rescue, snipers in the third CH-53 kept a sharp lookout for enemy threats as O'Grady scurried out of hiding and was ushered aboard one of the birds.

Both rescue choppers sprang into the air and turned balls-to-the-wall for the coast and "feet wet." The entire on-ground operation took less than ten minutes.

No mission was over, however, until all forces returned safely to base. Shortly after the pickup, an escort Cobra broke a warning over the air, directing it toward the Super Stallions.

"Impacts underneath you . . . . SAMs in the air! SAMs in the air!"

Everyone in the communications net held his breath until assurance came that the SAMs had missed their targets. A few minutes after that, a machine gun on the ground opened up and sprayed bullets through the tail section of one of the Stallions. Cobras banked into a combat sortie and tore up the countryside with rockets. There was no further hostile fire.

Captain O'Grady landed on the *Kearsarge* at 0729 hours. The CH-53 with my snipers aboard was one of the last out of the air. If something had gone wrong out there—an actual firefight or if one of the choppers were shot down—snipers and Force Recon would have been dropped on the ground to fight and help clean up the mess. Sometimes a successful mission meant you didn't have to be used.

CHAPTER FORTY-SEVEN

U.S. Army Sergeant Andrew Measels

U.S. Army Specialist Damian Mackie
Bosnia, 2003

The peace plan for Bosnia known as the Dayton Accords, the child of U.S. envoy Richard Holbrooke, was negotiated in Dayton, Ohio, in November 1995. The plan created a deceptively simple arrangement by which all three sides in the civil war—Bosnia, the Serbs, and the Croats—would stop fighting and work toward achieving a durable cease-fire to allow Bosnia to rebuild. American "peacekeeping" troops under the UN mandate were inserted into the equation for a one-year commitment—and were still there nearly a decade later.

In April 2003, Sergeant Andrew Measels and Specialist Damian Mackie, of the U.S. Army's 3rd Battalion, 325th Infantry Regiment, prepared to go to work on the outskirts of Tuzla, Bosnia-Herzegovina. They were trained snipers armed with a thick-barreled, bolt-action M24 sniper rifle, a harpoonlike .50-caliber single-shot rifle, and a variety of optical instruments for viewing potential threats from the city and countryside that stretched out from the main U.S. base and airfield in Bosnia.

For the past ten years, the primary menace to peace-keepers in the war-torn land has come from snipers. During the war itself, nearly all the cities from Sarajevo to Tuzla had a "sniper's alley" where one dared not walk the streets for fear of being picked off by one group or another. Snipers still ply their terror against NATO forces and each other, although not as regularly as before.

In 1992, U.S. Marine sniper instructor Sergeant Neil Morris trained two Canadian warrant officers in his Advanced Sniper Course. The warrants and their men were the first snipers to put boots on the ground in the Balkans to clear out the sniper's alley in Sarajevo. Since then the Canadians often telephoned Sergeant Morris from Eastern Europe to seek his advice on matters of insertion, extraction, countersniper fire, and urban camouflage and movement. Morris made several flights to the region. On one of these, he used snipers to assist in the extraction by helicopter of a battalion of Bangladeshi soldiers caught in a cross fire between Croatians and Serbs.

Morris wrote a letter to the commandant of the Marine Corps requesting permission to take a full company of snipers to the Balkans, promising that if allowed to do so he would clean up Sarajevo's sniper's alley within a week. Although the request was denied, a large number of American snipers from various branches of the military has rotated in and out of eastern Europe since 1992, their job to plant fear in the hearts of enemy snipers.

Sergeant Measels and Specialist Mackie were among

the most recent snipers assigned to keep peace in Bosnia. They were, more precisely, *countersnipers,* whose job it was to locate and eliminate riflemen who sought targets on the U.S. base.

The two men went to work by perching inside a sandbagged bunker high atop a coal-fired heating plant. On this particular late April afternoon, the sun was dying in red throes against the quaint hillside as they settled in for their shift. From their high vantage point, they scanned the surrounding terrain for the merest hint of approaching danger while life went on more or less at a normal pace around them. A lady came out to feed her chickens, as she did every day. A farmer shouted at his cattle. Children carrying backpacks laughed merrily as they headed home for dinner. What the countersnipers looked for was the first slight indication that routine was being broken.

"It's a lot of pressure on my snipers," explained platoon leader Lieutenant Greg Beaudoin. "They must make a call to shoot or not shoot, all within a split second, with no guidance from their superiors."

Eleven of the eighteen men in Lieutenant Beaudoin's platoon were trained snipers, experts at stalking, camouflage, target detection, and range estimation. They worked in two-man teams of one shooter and one spotter in three elevated locations around the airfield on the outskirts of Tuzla, protecting it and the U.S. base by posing as a strong deterrent to enemy attack or harassment. Any potshot at the base invited instant and lethal "target reduction."

In one of the most serious recent incidents, Serb snipers opened fire on U.S. Marines manning a roadblock checkpoint in the village of Zegra. None of the Marines was hit in the encounter, but Marine countersnipers killed one enemy sniper and wounded two others.

A few days later snipers fired on 82d Airborne soldiers near U.S. sector headquarters in Urosevac. Two men were captured.

"The biggest challenge facing U.S. forces," said Task Force Falcon commander Army Brigadier General John Craddock, "is a rogue element that doesn't know about the military technical agreement or refuses to abide by the cease-fire agreement."

Everything high atop the coal plant designated as OP-1 (Observation Point 1), however, remained normal and routine as Mackie and Measels watched dusk fall over the Bosnia countryside. The sandbagged bunker was roofed and floored. A shoe box-size opening cut in the wall afforded them observation of their area. The tools of their trade were arranged in convenient spots around the post: rifles, a radio, a high-powered viewing scope, a laser range finder, a box of MREs (meals, ready to eat).

"Generally, it's the same thing day in and day out," Measels commented. "You see the lady with the chickens. She goes out, feeds the chickens. Then there's the Muslim lady who lives down the hill. She walks down the hill, gathers water from the drainage ditch, then she walks up the hill with two pails of water."

Everything has been quiet for the past few weeks. Any change in the locals' routines would be immediately noted.

"If something's going to happen, they're going to know before we're going to know," Measels reasoned. "By watching their routine, if there is anything different, we can react to that difference."

"Kind of like the suspicious man next door," Mackie added. "We're always staring at things that have always been there, just seeing if there are any changes. It's the little things that usually show up."

Darkness descended on the rural landscape as the snipers kept watch. House lights blinked on, a car negotiated a tight lane with its headlights leading the way. Measels peered out the little makeshift window, always alert. Mackie attached the big night-vision scope to the M24. The vigil continued.

"The most feared soldier on the battlefield is a trained sniper," said Specialist Jason Shepherd, who manned OP-2. "It might take him weeks to get that one shot. But when he gets it, he'll get it and it will be right on."

CHAPTER FORTY-EIGHT

Afghanistan, 2002

"They have killed in the hundreds," said a White House official, speaking of U.S. Special Forces troops operating against Taliban and al Qaeda members in Afghanistan during the first phase of the War on Terror in 2001–2002. "There have been no deaths on our side. They're not leaving a footprint. When these guys do sleep, they sleep on the ground. They don't have a fixed base camp."

Due to the open terrain, snipers using the Army's M24 sniper system and the Marine M40 system, along with the powerful .50-caliber Barrett sniper rifle, were liberally sown among ground troops. One night Army Green Berets and accompanying snipers raided a convoy of fuel truck drivers delivering gasoline to Taliban soldiers. The truck drivers had stopped alongside a mountain road for a few hours' sleep when heavily armed Americans with night-vision goggles surprised them, bound them, and escorted them away. A pair of Apache helicopters then swarmed in with missiles and blew up the trucks.

Such Taliban convoys often ran between Kandahār and the nearby city of Lashkar Gah. U.S. Marine Corps sniper Corporal Curtis Arndt, 15th Marine Expeditionary Unit, participated in raids against them.

Arndt, a native of Washington state, had been assigned to Camp Rhino south of Kandahār before the city fell to U.S. troops in December 2001. Prior to deployment in Afghanistan, he had provided security cover as a sniper for medical personnel in East Timor in Southeast Asia and had guarded and patrolled an America rescue helicopter air base in Jacobabad, Pakistan. Duty at Rhino, he discovered, could be both tedious and unnerving at the same time. Small four-man scout sniper teams pulled recon missions and established listening posts as security for the American base.

"There was no one there, just rocks and sand," Arndt said. "Extremely desolate. It was dead quiet. You could hear silence. I had never heard silence before."

Arndt and his partner teamed up one afternoon with a larger Marine element to ambush a Taliban supply convoy. The two snipers set up in a clot of rocks on a high point overlooking the kill zone while other Marines stretched concertina wire across the road. It was Arndt's turn as spotter. Two-man Marine sniper teams commonly alternated between shooter and spotter.

Soon, just before darkness began to fall, the convoy of a half-dozen trucks loaded with troops and supplies appeared on the road's horizon in a fast cloud of dust. It swept around a rocky point and barreled headlong toward the blockade. It was too late to turn around by the time the lead driver saw the concertina. He slammed his foot into the gas feed and roared toward it, the other trucks accelerating in order to keep up.

The truck was not going to stop. Arndt watched

through binoculars, calmly identifying targets for his partner on the sniper rifle.

The point truck hit the accordion concertina at full speed and snagged to a halt, like a fish caught in a net. The sniper operating at Arndt's side shot the driver and the passenger; Marine ambushers accounted for killing five passengers still in the truck.

Trailing trucks were spaced out at enough intervals that they were able to switch about and haul back toward Kandahār. U.S. helicopters attacked like hornets, destroying the remaining trucks and leaving an estimated fifty Taliban lying on the road.

Troops from several other nations served alongside American forces during the short, fierce combat to depose the Taliban rule that had supported terrorist attacks against the West. About 900 Canadian soldiers and supporting snipers fought with coalition forces. In March 2002, during the first day of Operation Anaconda, a three-man team of Canadian snipers matched with counterpart U.S. Army Special Forces snipers was credited with rescuing a company of U.S. 101st Airborne Division pinned down in the Shah-i-Kot Valley.

Two three-man Canadian sniper teams from the 3d Princess Patricia's Canadian Light Infantry Battle Group had deployed in support of Anaconda with 2d Battalion, 3d Brigade, of the 101st Airborne (Air Mobile) and the 1st Battalion, 2d Brigade of the 10th Mountain Division. According to the Canadian Department of National Defence, Canadian snipers took out at long range some twenty al-Qaeda fighters in machine-gun nests and mortar positions, thereby accumulating the highest number of confirmed kills in the battle.

"These sniper teams suppressed enemy mortar and heavy machine gun positions with deadly accuracy," noted Vice-Admiral Greg Maddison, deputy chief of the Defence Staff. "As the American battalion was moving down the ridge and dealing with the Taliban and al-Qaeda fighters that they were encountering, the snipers were there to provide defensive capability. As they were moving forward, they would encounter various positions in which mortars were being fired at them and at the Americans and they were able to take out some of those positions and protect the Americans as they were continuing toward their final objective. Their skills are believed to have saved many Allied lives."

"Ed," a corporal from Newfoundland, and his spotter partner (snipers operating in Afghanistan, both Canadian and American, have asked that their real names not be used) encountered a machine-gun nest on their first night in combat. They had laboriously worked their way up to higher ground on the flank of U.S. forces moving up the valley. As the machine gun spat bullets into the Americans below, Ed and his partner quickly set up their McMillan Tac .50-caliber sniper rifle system; the corporal compared firing the weapon to "someone slashing you on the back of your hockey helmet with a hockey stick."

Using the .50, Ed took out the machine gunner at a range of 1,700 meters. After that, he and his spotter began pinpointing other enemy gunners and systematically eliminating them as well.

"Our spider senses were tingling," he said. With every deadly shot, he thought, *That's one less bullet that's gonna be coming at us—one less person we have to think about.*

Although intermittent fire continued throughout the night, sniper action kept it to a minimum. The enemy, it seemed, was afraid to stick his head out of cover long enough to aim and fire. Night-vision goggles allowed the snipers to spot movement easily under the Afghan stars.

At first break of day, an enemy sniper began winging shots to halt the Allied advance. Ed finally located him hiding behind a piece of corrugated steel in a grove of scraggly trees. He eased the barrel of the .50 between two rocks and fired a single shot. The heavy bullet pierced the metal, literally exploding it, killing the man behind it instantly.

Corporal Ed, Master Corporal "Warren," and Master Corporal "Alex," a 30-year-old from Halifax, Nova Scotia, moved on into the fray with a U.S. scout platoon of three Army Special Forces snipers, working with a company of the 101st Airborne's "Rakkasaw" brigade. Troops of the Screaming Eagles made easy targets for heavy machine guns and automatic weapons positioned on the 10,000-foot ridge known as Whale's Back that towered over the west side of the Shah-i-Kot Valley. Fire from an opposing eastern ridge interlocked with that from Whale's Back to inflict heavy casualties on the 101st, pinning down the company in the intense cross fire.

The three Canadian and three American snipers maneuvered out of the valley of slaughter and climbed to higher ground that offered a view of the Whale and its defenders. Master Corporal Alex, armed with the McMillan .50-cal, operated as shooter for the Canadians, while Sergeant "Joe" with his Remington 700 M24 system took that position for the Americans. The four other members of the little sniper patrol carried Canadian 5.56mm C-7A1s, M4 carbines, and M16s with attached M203 40mm grenade launchers.

For more than an hour the little band fought it out with the dug-in Taliban and al-Qaeda fighters at distances ranging from ten meters to 1,500 meters. "As soon as we got rid of one guy, another would come up, and another one," Corporal Alex said.

The snipers had cached their packs before climbing out of the steeply walled valley, taking only what ammo they could carry in their pockets and on their battle harnesses. Under fire, they soon ran low on ammo. They also needed additional optics to seek out the entrenched enemy. Corporal Ed sprinted down the hill, into the valley, and partly up the opposite ridge to get more ammunition and equipment. During the entire run, bullets slapped the ground and ricocheted off boulders all around him.

On his way back, al-Qaeda fighters opened up on him from a dry streambed. He didn't bother to slow down. He returned fire on the run with his 40mm grenade launcher, killing some enemy and sending the remainder packing.

Enemy fighters attempted to maneuver around the patrol's flanks and trap it from behind. One gunman approached to within ten steps, unnoticed until he popped from hiding to spray the area with his AK-47. In his excitement, he missed every shot. An American spotter promptly disposed of him.

Rocket-propelled grenades and small-arms muzzle flashes lit up a nearby woodline as another enemy attempted to flush out the snipers.

"We were taking fire from a tree line and we couldn't see where he was and I wasn't going to waste a shot there," Alex explained.

A Canadian and a Special Forces grenadier flanked off to one side and pumped rounds into the trees, forcing the sniper to expose himself. Alex promptly eliminated the threat.

When all else failed, the Taliban tried mortar fire.

"They were bracketing us," Master Corporal Warren said. "We'd move and they'd adjust fire. Eventually they either ran out of rounds or they just gave up."

Lethal activity by the six snipers took pressure off the pinned-down 101st, which promptly reconsolidated and moved forward into its assigned blocking positions. The combined snipers of two friendly nations had undoubtedly saved a number of Allied lives and put Operation Anaconda back on track.

"The six of us suppressed fire and neutralized the enemy" was how Corporal Alex succinctly put it.

During the following days of the battle, Corporal Ed set a new record for combat sniper marksmanship by fatally killing the driver of an enemy resupply truck with the .50-caliber McMillan at a range of 2,400 meters. The record had previously been held by Marine Gunnery Sergeant Carlos Hathcock, who used a Browning .50-caliber heavy machine gun equipped with a scope to shoot a "mule" off a bicycle at 2,250 meters near Duc Pho, South Vietnam, in January 1967.

Curiously enough, when the United States proposed to honor the Canadian snipers by awarding them Bronze Stars for their bravery, the Canadian government balked. It wasn't as though America hadn't honored previous Canadian soldiers. As recently as the Gulf War, Operation Desert Storm, two Canadian CF-18 pilots received Bronze Stars. But that was before the current era of political correctness.

Dr. David Bercuson, director of the Centre for Military & Strategic Studies at the University of Calgary, said the hesitation was due to official squeamishness.

"Canadians don't kill—they don't even use the word *kill*," he said. "I think the military is not sure that the

government is prepared to accept the fact, let alone celebrate the fact . . . that Canadian soldiers do sometimes
end up killing people."

American snipers who worked with the Canadian
snipers were incensed over the Canadian government's
objection to recognizing the heroism of its own brave
soldiers.

CHAPTER FORTY-NINE

Iraq's Saddam Hussein publicly threatened Kuwait and the United Arab Emirates in July 1990 over a dispute in which he accused OPEC nations of shoving a "poisoned dagger" into Iraq's back by setting oil production quotas and driving down the price of oil. On 2 August 1990, Iraq invaded Kuwait, which it considered a renegade province. A coalition of nations, many of them Arab states, joined the United States to oppose Iraqi aggression. Operations Desert Shield and Desert Storm began.

Coalition forces attained complete air supremacy within two weeks after shooting erupted on 16 January 1991. They relentlessly pounded the Iraqi army for thirty days, knocking out all air defenses and weakening Saddam's ground forces by 50 percent. The so-called 100-Hour War kicked off on 23 February. Ground forces liberated Kuwait almost immediately, losing only four tanks while destroying over 1,000 Iraqi tanks. Once the stated objective of liberating Kuwait was achieved, UN forces called for a cease-fire.

The "cease-fire" endured for over a dozen years, broken repeatedly by Iraqis firing missiles at U.S. aircraft patrolling the no-fly zone and by Iraqi attacks on the separatist Kurds in the north. At one point before the Gulf War, Saddam Hussein had used poison gas in annihilating Kurdish villages, as he had also used chemicals in his war with Iran in the 1980's.

Iraq had started a nuclear program in the 1960's when it procured a light-water research reactor from the Soviet Union. It purchased a second from France a few years later. Feeling itself threatened, Israel bombed and destroyed the French reactor, forcing Iraq to go underground to pursue its nuclear research in secrecy.

Beginning after the 1991 war, UN weapons inspectors amassed mountains of data documenting the Iraqi drive for nuclear weapons. In retaliation, Saddam Hussein kicked weapons inspectors out of his country in 1998. The United States and its coalition allies responded by launching Operation Desert Fox, an aerial bombing campaign aimed at destroying Iraq's capability to produce weapons of mass destruction. Although inspectors were readmitted in late 2002, they were threatened and hampered at every turn.

The United States targeted Iraq a second time in 2003, citing an international threat of weapons of mass destruction, biological and chemical warfare munitions, and Iraq's support of Islamic terrorism of the type that resulted in the 9/11 crashing of airliners into New York's World Trade Center and into the Pentagon. Operation Iraqi Freedom began with massive aerial attacks against Baghdad on 20 March 2003.

Jubilant Iraqis celebrated the collapse of Saddam Hussein's murderous regime on 9 April by beheading a toppled statue of their longtime ruler in downtown

Baghdad and embracing American troops as liberators.

As they have in all wars and conflicts since the American Revolution, snipers played a part in both Iraqi wars, although to a lesser extent in the 1991 "100-Hour War" than in the 2003 race to Baghdad.

CHAPTER FIFTY

U.S. Marine
Corporal Timothy A. Parkhurst
Iraq, 1991

During what became known in Operation Desert Storm as the "100-Hour War" against Saddam Hussein, the U.S. Army's 3rd Infantry Division along with armored and cav outfits punched their way north toward Baghdad, kicking ass and taking names and pictures and letting Saddam know his days in the desert were numbered. The 5th MEB [Marine Expeditionary Brigade], my outfit, followed to conduct clean-up and mop-up. The 3/5 [Third Battalion, 5th Marines], to which I was attached as a STA [surveillance and target acquisition] sniper, swept westward from the Saudi Arabia port of Al-Mish'áb to cut north into Kuwait's Al-Wafra National Forest. It wasn't a forest at all—not a tree in sight big enough to cast much of a shadow. Mostly it was an irrigated agricultural area. Pockets of Iraqis who remained in the region were simply waiting to be mopped up and policed up.

Regimental Landing Team-5 [RLT-5] moved through the "forest" on-line, sweeping up remnants of Iraqi resistance. Lima Company 3/1 took machine-gun fire from a thick mud-walled building to its front. Grunts sprawled bellies-down on the hot afternoon sun and poured out a fierce cone of fire, the apex of which converged on the building. However, the walls were so thick that nothing seemed to have much effect. The battalion commander called a temporary cease-fire and summoned a tank to come up from the rear and take out the obstacle.

Silence descended on the battlefield. A front of Marines five miles wide came to a standstill and waited for a few ragheads in a mud house to be neutralized. My sniper team leader, Corporal James Adams, and I decided to take a look to see what we could do. We scooted over from the company we were supporting and climbed to the roof of a flat-topped house to observe for the possibility of reaching out and tapping someone.

Peering through scopes and binoculars across a 500-yard expanse of sandy geography, we saw a square mud-brown structure with a thick door and a single window next to it. The window was a vertical slit only about three or four inches wide and the height of the doorway. Shadows passed back and forth in the room beyond as the defenders moved about. There was no glass in the window; the machine gun had to be set up right behind it. A tight shot, but what the hell. . . .

I called down to the battalion commander, Lieutenant Colonel Selvidge, "Sir, all right if we take a shot?"

He got on the horn with somebody higher up before responding, "Yeah, go ahead. Do what you got to do."

Adams took the shot while I observed. The round whacked into the wall about an inch to the side of the slit window. I called corrections. Adams jacked another round into the chamber of his M40. He was sighting in for a second attempt when Colonel Selvidge shouted up for us to cease fire.

The occupants were already departing the AO. Someone on the extreme flank of 3/1 where he could see the back of the building watched as the Iraqi gunners darted out, piled onto a Toyota pickup truck, and took off in a cloud of dust. We were informed a short time later that a helicopter gunship pursued and took them out with a rocket.

The regiment saddled up and resumed forward movement.

After nightfall, Adams and I and the other two shooters of the sniper squad teamed up with Sergeant Pribble and his squad to conduct an eight-man reconnaissance patrol out ahead of the regiment. Our final objective was to set up a forward blocking position to pick off enemy soldiers when the regiment began moving again at dawn.

We were punched a short distance into no-man's-land riding in the back of a vehicle, then launched out on foot to hump our way through enemy-held territory. We strung out across the desert in Ranger file under a quarter-moon, using wadis and lowlands for cover. Soon someone noticed we were walking through a field of what appeared to be camel dung. We wended our way on through, not wanting to step in any. Sergeant Chandler suddenly emitted a taut hiss.

"This ain't camel shit! It's a minefield!"

An announcement like that froze your guts. All motion ceased instantly. I knelt to gingerly inspect one of the objects, not touching it—a tiny butterfly bomblet of the type dropped in the scores from Allied aircraft. We had bumbled into one of our own minefields, our only salvation having been in not wanting to get camel dung on our boots.

The patrol navigated the rest of the minefield with far more circumspection, finally emerging once again into open desert.

Ahead in the moonlight, next to an irrigated field, lay a grove of date palms and acacia trees. I wryly assumed it was part of the "forest." The patrol took a precautionary knee while Sergeant Pribble glassed the oasis with an NVD [night-vision device]. He passed it around so we could all take a look and add our assessment to his.

The trees showed up swimming in a liquid green light. A small brick building stood almost hidden in the center of the oasis, around which concentrated an indeterminate number of Iraqis. The site appeared to either have been a school or some kind of government building. We couldn't tell whether the soldiers were setting up for a defense or whether they were simply bivouacking on their way back to Iraq.

"There's too many of them for a stand-up fight," Sergeant Pribble concluded.

The rest of us agreed with him. The patrol called in a SITREP, a situation report, on the stronghold and skirted the oasis without the Iraqis even knowing we were about.

As the first slice of dawn parted night from coming day, the patrol split into two teams to take up separate blocking positions in preparation for the regiment's drive toward us. Adams and I, along with two men from Pribble's squad to function as security, selected a tiny mud house from which the Kuwaiti occupants had apparently fled when the Iraqis invaded. It was like most desert houses: thick earthen walls, two diminutive rooms, and a flat roof upon which sat a tank to provide gravity-flow running water to the household. Adams and I climbed onto the roof with sniper rifles while the security men took up positions in the rooms below.

As the sun rose, helicopter gunships began sweeping the desert well ahead of the regimental advance, buzzing back and forth like a swarm of lethal bumblebees. We first noticed them on the horizon. Gradually, flying back and forth in broad strokes, searching for signs of enemy, they came nearer and nearer to our isolated mud hut. Finally, a Huey flew directly over us in an observation pass so low we could almost see the crew chief's face above his door gun. Armed rocket pods bristled on the aircraft's weapons pylons.

The crew chief pointed at Adams and me lying on the roof. Immediately, the helicopter jinked to one side and roared off low and fast as though anticipating being pursued by an RPG rocket. Adams and I watched with apprehension as it linked up with a pair of even deadlier Cobras on the flat horizon. The choppers hung there in the distant air like birds of prey, weapons pointed in our direction.

"Shit!" Adams exclaimed. "They think we're the bad guys. They're going to make a gun run on us."

I got on the radio back to the operations center since we had no direct communications with the aircraft. My hands were shaking. The strain in my voice must have been almost palpable, even through the air.

"Do they know we're out here?" I asked.

"Yeah, yeah," came the reply. "They know you're there."

The Huey and the Cobras headed toward us in a beeline, noses down, hauling.

"Then how come they're heading right for us?"

"Stand by. Let me get back with you."

"We won't be here."

There wouldn't be anything left of us. Adams shouted below for the security detail to take off running perpendicular to the helicopters' approach paths. I was ready to jump off the roof. I felt the blood drain from my face. Shot by the enemy was one thing; destroyed by friendly fire—well, that sucked.

The choppers highballed toward us, growing larger and larger as they swiftly closed the distance. I expected them to start blazing away any second now.

Suddenly a thought flickered to the front of my head. I recalled having packed a folded American flag into my ruck, intending to fly it over Baghdad or something one day. I dived for my pack and fished it out, quickly draping it over my body like a shield.

It fluttered and flapped from rotor wash as, at the last second, the chopper pilots saw it and peeled off and away. The Huey crew chief leaned out over his gun, waving and grinning. Adams exhaled a deep breath and collapsed on his back, sweating profusely. I realized that I had also been holding my last breath as though it were a precious gem.

God bless the Star-Spangled Banner.

CHAPTER FIFTY-ONE

U.S. Marine
Gunnery Sergeant Robert Reidsma
Scout Sniper Instructor School,
Quantico, 2003

The public tends to associate "sniper" with criminal elements. The so-called Beltway Snipers who killed all those people in the Maryland Beltway area a couple of years back didn't do the image much good, what with all the media speculation chatter about whether or not the snipers were trained by the military. That was just so much hyperbole. In all the years since the United States has been training and utilizing snipers, I don't know of a single incidence in which one of them went bad and started shooting innocent folks. I attribute that to how they are selected and trained. As staff noncommissioned officer in charge [NCOIC] of the Scout Sniper Instructor School at Quantico, Virginia, I see prospective snipers when they report for training and I see the best of them graduate and report back to the fleet to be used where they are most needed.

NBC Newsman Jim Vance came to the school to film a piece about snipers. "The sniper," we instructors told him, "is kind of like a guardian angel of the battlefield. Yeah, we're sneaky, we're deceptive, but we do it to keep our people safe out there, to save lives. We overwatch them."

The U.S. Marine Corps has always been different in its emphasis on fundamental marksmanship, unlike so much of the world's infantry, including that of the United States. After machine guns and fully automatic weapons were invented, most armed forces went with the philosophy that if you cranked enough rounds downrange you were bound to hit something. The Marine Corps stand is that if you don't hit the enemy, you don't hurt him, no matter how many rounds you fire.

By a rough estimate, there are about 400 school-trained snipers on duty in the Marine Corps at any one time. There may be that many—or slightly more—also on duty in the Army, Air Force, and Navy. The Marine Corps and Army also train what are called "designated marksmen" and "squad advance marksmen." These people operate in some capacity like snipers, although they are not snipers. They use different weapons systems. They are not trained in reconnaissance and scouting to the level of snipers, and they are not expected to function behind enemy lines.

The DM is usually armed with an M14 fitted with a 10X scope, while the advanced marksman uses a scoped M16A1 or M16A4. Their presence within a unit, and as a member of that unit, gives the commander the option of an asset ready on hand to take out a high-threat target in immediate support of a squad, platoon, or company.

The U.S. Marine Corps operates three different sniper schools. Two of these are at division level: Camp

Pendleton and Camp Lejeune. The primary school is at Quantico. Essentially, all three schools teach the same curriculum in the Scout Sniper Basic Course, which is ten weeks long. In addition to the basic course, Quantico instructs a five-week Scout Sniper Advance Course and a Scout Sniper Platoon Commanders Course of two and a half weeks.

The basic course in all three schools—as well as basic schools in other branches of the military—concentrates upon shooting, scouting, patrol orders, stalking, land navigation, and other general basic skills that will enable a sniper to function effectively on a battlefield.

Quantico's Scout Sniper Advance Course hones these skills and adds to them. It concentrates on urban reconnaissance and surveillance, urban sniper movements and operations, and tactical tracking. It includes a lot of night shooting and short-range work in support of conventional operations in a built-up environment. One of the focal points of the Advance Course is a sniper-versus-sniper scenario during which students are pitted against each other, rather like the famous World War II sniper duel in Stalingrad between the Russian Vassili Zaitsev and the German sniper champion Major Koning.

Finally, the Advance Course trains future instructors in training, coaching, and establishing curriculum.

The Scout Sniper Platoon Commanders Course is not a sniper training curriculum. Rather, it familiarizes young officers with how snipers work in order to provide them a capability and limitations overview of what a sniper does and what he can and cannot do. The idea is that these officers may end up commanding reconnaissance or sniper platoons.

Even if they return to the infantry, however, they take

back with them the knowledge of how the sniper weapon system works and how it can be used as an effective one shot—one kill force multiplier on the battlefield, and of how the sniper truly is the guardian angel that can save the lives of fellow Marines.

CHAPTER FIFTY-TWO

U.S. Marine
Sergeant Joshua Hamblin
Iraq, 2003

As Operation Iraqi Freedom began, my 3rd Battalion, 7th Marines, the 3/7, busted north out of Kuwait and across Iraq with other battalions of the U.S. Marine Corps and Army, moving as fast in Humvees as the terrain, weather, and resistance permitted. My job as a scout sniper was to provide reconnaissance and surveillance and precision fire when required. I was new at it, as far as actual combat went, and had no real idea of how much carnage a pair of snipers could create. I suspected I might find out, however, by the time the war ended.

In the Humvee with me as we raced through the desert and the heat I carried an M16 rifle for suppressive fire and for precision fire, the latest in the Marine line of scoped sniper rifles, the M40A3. I always kept the rifle in its protective case next to me. When we came to roadblocks, seeing them from a great distance across the parched terrain, the force stopped and word went back for "Snipers up!" The sniper's task was to engage Iraqis manning the roadblocks at long range—600 to 700 yards, out of range of enemy AKs—with "precision fire." That meant, essentially, knocking them down like little ducks at a carnival shooting booth.

Rules of engagement stated we ignore anyone who was not armed or who did not attack us. If they were armed, however, no matter if in uniform or not, they were fair game and legal targets. As we pushed north toward Baghdad we encountered relatively few soldiers; we kept hearing that "the Big Battle," which Saddam Hussein called "the Mother of All Battles" in the 1991 Desert Storm, would break out on the outskirts of Baghdad, where the Republican Guard was preparing for us. There were, however, plenty of young men about in the villages and towns of military age with short haircuts. Obviously, these guys had slam-dunked their uniforms in order to blend in with the civilian population. Whether for fair or foul we couldn't determine at the time. We kept going, laying clouds of dust in our wake that you could see from miles to the rear—and miles to the front.

Scout snipers were attached, or "punched out," to various companies of 3/7 to conduct observation and reconnaissance, which often meant we staked out on some high point of ground while the company took a breather. Or we moved out ahead in small foot or motor patrols to watch the population for suspicious activities when the companies called a halt for a few hours to pull maintenance on equipment, grab some sleep, or wait for supplies and reinforcements to catch up. We were moving faster than Rommel the Desert Fox ever thought about doing.

Since there were so few snipers and so many scout

sniper missions, it wasn't uncommon for us to go two days or more without sleep. When we did sleep, it was seldom for more than an hour or two at a time. We were running on pure physical discipline and willpower.

On top of lack of sleep was poor hygiene—no water for bathing or shaving, and *toilet* meant a brief squat over a cat hole you dug in the sand. Anytime we came across a water hole, oasis, or broken water pipe, guys drenched their heads and soaked their clothing. And then we kept moving.

The most miserable part of it all was the MOPP gear, heavy chemical suits to protect against chemical or biological attacks. The bulky two-piece suits—which also came equipped with booties and hoods—covered the wearer from neck to feet; we carried the booties, hoods, and gas masks either in small back or butt packs or on our web gear but had to wear the body suit even when we slept. On top of the suit went Kevlar bulletproof vests and battle harnesses festooned with ammo pouches and other tools of the trade. Underneath all that you were constantly soaked in sweat. It was like wearing your own personal sauna bath. Never before had the American military—or any military, for that matter—fought for such an extended time in MOPP posture.

Word went through the battalion to expect fighting and heavy resistance at Salmon Pak, the site of an al-Qaeda camp equipped with an airliner for training hijackers. U.S. air cover had bombed, rocketed, and strafed the town for days. Instead of encountering opposition, however, our Humvees, APCs, and, later, tanks rolled into a town that had been thoroughly pounded. Iraqi military vehicles, scores of them, sat abandoned on the streets where the young men walking about with short haircuts had abandoned them. Charred buildings and burnt-out hulks of vehicles scarred the townscape. There was no fighting. We kept moving, always heading north toward Baghdad.

Open desert gave way to the Tigris River Valley and its lush vegetation and farms. Summer was fast arriving and it was starting to get *really* hot. Word finally came down that we could shed our MOPP suits. Joyous day. A major turning point in the war. It seemed the weather cooled by several degrees now that we could continue the fight in desert utilities like normal Marines.

From the sound of it as we neared Baghdad, it seemed the Americans might have finally engaged the Republican Guard and Saddam's other elite troops in a last-stand battle at the entrance to the capital. We heard the constant spatter of small-arms fire and the thunderous storm bursts of artillery. There were minefields to negotiate, but 3/7 rolled right into the outskirts and occupied the ar-Rashid Military Complex. There were breaks in the perimeter fence and wire, some of the buildings had been shelled or bombed, and a few mines lay about, but there were no enemy soldiers. They seemed to have packed their camel meat and rice, or whatever they ate, and hauled their miserable carcasses back into the city to meld their short haircuts into the civilian population.

Expecting a possible counterattack, the battalion set up a defense. My partner, Sergeant Owen Mulder, and I were assigned an area of responsibility overlooking a suburban neighborhood of residences and small businesses on the northeast side of the military reservation. After dark, we climbed to the flat roof of a one-story building where we set up an overwatch position that allowed us to observe street approaches from anywhere in that direction. A high lip around the flat roof provided cover and concealment, permitting us to watch and shoot without being easily seen or targeted in return. Ranges for likely engagement appeared to vary from about 400 meters to a maximum of 750 meters.

Mulder had his M40A1 sniper rifle with the standard-issue Unertl 10X scope. I had the M40A3 equipped with an AN/PVS-10 day-and-night scope. The AN/PVS-10 was a third-generation night image intensifier with day-light capabilities, which meant you could use the scope at midnight or at high noon in the desert. I turned it on for night vision. Mulder had a pair of night-vision goggles. Night-vision capability gave American forces a tremendous advantage over troops not similarly equipped.

The two of us settled in to watch. The nearby streets lay in black ink penetrated by our Superman vision. It was a clear night, almost cold, and the canopy of stars seemed close enough to reach out and touch. The lights remained on in Baghdad, casting that city's glow against the sky. I heard in the distance a machine-gun chatter now and then, but all was quiet on our front.

For about two hours.

Aided by night vision, Mulder and I saw a pickup truck with its headlights doused ease out of one of the streets and stop at the curb about 400 meters away. A bunch of armed men jumped from the bed of the truck, obviously thinking themselves concealed by the darkness.

"I got targets," I said to Mulder. My pulse was racing.

"Let's go for it."

The driver of the pickup jumped out and hurried around to the back of the vehicle, where someone still up in the bed handed him something. Maybe ammunition or a grenade. He was dressed in Western-style clothing, like most of the others, but wore a combat belt and harness. I crosshaired him in the sight of my AN/PVS-10, seeing him through it almost as clear as if it were daylight, and squeezed the trigger. He dropped instantly, like a sack of potatoes. Mulder shot one of the others.

The whole thing was crazy. It was insane. Instead of the survivors taking off for cover, they remained in the kill zone to recover the bodies of their dead. It turned into a real shooting gallery. Mulder and I lined up targets as fast as we could and took the shots. The more shots we made, the more targets seemed to appear as the victims' comrades ran madly about retrieving bodies.

The adrenaline rush was indescribable. However, training and discipline took over where runaway excitement wanted to rule. We paced ourselves: Spot a target, sight in, squeeze, watch the shot, work the bolt. Pick another target and keep the pace going. Over and over.

The Iraqis finally got ahead of us. The pickup truck bolted around a corner, its bed full of a grisly cargo of bloody arms, legs, and corpses. Not many of the fighters who jumped out of the pickup got back in it under their own power. Not a body was left behind. Nothing but smears and little puddles of blood and shreds of flesh on the street. A few scraps of clothing.

Quiet once more settled over the kill zone.

The rest of the night passed uneventfully, as the Iraqis had obviously learned a lesson in attempting to move up on the base at night. They would have to maneuver in daylight in order to even up the odds a bit. They did not understand the capability of a well-trained and well-equipped sniper team.

Shortly after sunrise, two individuals in civvies crossed the street into the open about 450 meters away, strolling along like they were alone in a park. One carried an AK-47. Apparently they knew nothing of what had happened earlier at this same intersection.

"You got those guys?" I asked Mulder.

"Got 'em. You taking out the guy with the AK?"

"Affirmative."

I led him slightly in my sights to compensate for his walking speed, and fired. He dropped flat, squirming and kicking reflexively, since the shot wasn't immediately fatal. His partner jumped straight in the air, startled, and took off. *That* guy wasn't waiting around to help his buddy or to drag off the body.

The dead guy—he was dead, he just didn't know it yet—continued to kick and twitch for another thirty seconds. Then he lay still, facedown in the street. Blood leaked out and pooled underneath him. I didn't look at him again.

Ten minutes later the action resumed. A pickup truck nosed cautiously out of a side street and sat there for a few minutes, engine running, while its driver looked things over. It backed out of sight. I looked at Mulder. He shrugged. We watched the streets, waiting.

Fifteen minutes passed. The same truck returned. Same side streets. Same guy driving. Sitting there partly out of hiding as he looked up and down the street a second time. Deciding all was clear, he goosed the truck out into the open. Seven or eight men clung to the inside of the bed. A second truck carrying an equal number of riflemen darted out right behind the first.

"Watch those guys," Mulder said. "They're armed."

Both trucks braked near the dead man in the street. Riders piled out like they were going to tear somebody from limb to limb. But who? These guys were either crazy or drugged up or didn't know what the hell they were doing, jumping out like that in the open with their weapons.

Mulder and I didn't have to say a word to each other.

We went to work. I took the near truck, he took the far. We began shooting people as fast as we could work the bolts and acquire targets. The rapid cracking of the twin rifles reverberated through the streets, echoing, as men dropped like swatted flies, too confused and shocked to try to escape.

One guy, the last man alive, almost managed to get away. He pulled open the driver's door of the nearest pickup, jerked the dead driver out, and flung himself behind the wheel. As the truck raced in reverse toward the nearest side street and safety, Mulder and I zeroed in on it together. Two 175-grain boat-tailed bullets blasted through the cab's thin sheet metal. One killed the driver. The other must have hit something in the gas line or tank. To our considerable surprise, the truck exploded in a ball of flame. I thought scenes like that only occurred in Hollywood movies.

The burning truck continued moving under its own momentum, coasting around the corner of the nearest intersection and out of sight behind buildings, where it cooked and smoked and smoldered for nearly an hour.

Black smoke swirled and eddied over a street littered with corpses. It looked as though a major battle had been fought. But there was only Mulder and me—and we hadn't yet fired a full box of ammunition.

Later in the morning as I watched the street through my scope, a lone Iraqi soldier, an officer, turned the corner and began walking toward the base. He couldn't see the carnage still spread in the street, and the truck was only smoldering while emitting little smoke. He wore a full uniform, a helmet, vest, and carried a side arm. He probably thought his people still occupied the base, for he strode along like he was going to work. I set my scope on him and followed him as he walked along a row of light posts.

An old man dashed from one of the houses. By his gesturing, it was obvious he was telling the soldier to get out of Dodge in a hurry. The soldier didn't seem to understand. He kept walking. The old man tagged after him, waving his arms and jumping up and down with frustration. It was almost like watching a silent movie comedy, like Charlie Chaplin.

I imagined the old man yammering, "Get out of here! They'll kill you!"

And the soldier, frowning, "Who? Who'll kill me? What are you talking about, old man?"

The soldier shrugged a last time, still not understanding, and started to walk away. I squeezed the trigger. It was a perfect shot. I watched the vapor trail of the bullet through the scope as it flew straight to the center of his chest. It impacted with a little puff of dust. His face contorted in pure shock.

He looked down at the bullet hole in his chest before he slumped to the ground, still surprised. He tried to crawl away, reaching out with his clawed hands in a desperate attempt to pull himself out of the kill zone. It was too late for him. He should have listened to the old man. He managed to drag himself only a few feet before he lay still and died.

Civilians in the neighborhood were very interested in the unfolding drama. It was almost like they were spectators at a sporting event. After each deadly episode, they came out in bunches to look around and laugh and chatter and wave toward the base at us. It was almost surreal, all those people lined up looking at the carnage like it was another day at the market. There were at least seventeen bodies scattered about under the sun, plus two deserted pickup trucks, one of which still smoldered. A scene right out of a Rambo movie.

Some fool thought he was going to do something to even the score. A white compact pickup roared suddenly out of a side street and careened down the center of the road in a charge directly at us. In the back of the little truck, holding on to his AK-47 and the sides of the pickup for dear life, rode the strangest apparition: some guy dressed entirely in black and wearing a black ski mask. A fedayee hellbent on committing suicide and going to heaven as a martyr where Allah would bequeath him 71 virgins or whatever.

I could oblige him. He was looking directly at me as I went down on my scope and followed him in the wildly racing pickup. I found my lead angle, aimed high, and took the shot.

It was a dead-slam hit. The fedayee went down in the truck. The driver swapped the truck about and retreated even faster than he came, disappearing around a corner with the dead man jouncing all over the bed.

Eighteen.

As the morning and early afternoon wore on, we noticed pickups and other vehicles making numerous runs into a nearby neighborhood. They went in loads, their cargos tarped to prevent observation, and came out empty. They were obviously making supply runs, stocking a strongpoint with weapons and ammunition. It was time to put a stop to it.

Rules of engagement allowed us to shoot an armed man or a vehicle obviously carrying weapons. A red Toyota sedan had gone in and out of the strongpoint four times before we were sure it hauled munitions. Mulder took out the driver. I fired into the back of the trunk.

The car exploded in a burst of flames, just like the pickup had done earlier. Consumed in fire, it coasted around a corner out of sight. Minutes later, the street into which it disappeared lit up like an accident at a fireworks factory as its trunkload of RPG rockets cooked off in the blaze. Giant bottle rockets zipped about in all directions, crisscrossing in trails of smoke and detonating against buildings, parked cars, and any other obstacle they struck. It sounded like a small war. Mulder and I watched the show, awed. We—just the two of us—were responsible for this?

So far, we had received no return fire. We completely controlled the position. We had good cover, long-range capability, and there was nothing the Iraqis could do about it. We killed them every time they showed themselves to engage us. It was no contest. We were trained Marine snipers and they were overzealous fanatics with minimum marksmanship training. It reminded me of the old joke about an enemy battalion about to attack a hill occupied by Marines. The enemy scouts came running back, crying out, "Don't attack. Don't attack. It's a trick. There are *two* Marines up there."

In the meantime, Marine units on our flanks were becoming engaged as sporadic fighting broke out against units of well-armed Iraqis. Rounds flew everywhere from these actions, often zipping over our heads. RPGs exploded as close as fifty meters away, giving us concern about our becoming "collateral damage" in someone else's fight.

Sergeant Aaron Winterle of the Scout Sniper Platoon, who carried a Barrett .50-caliber special-application scoped rifle, was manning a vehicle checkpoint outside the military cantonment with one of the line companies when an Iraqi suicide vehicle tried to ram the roadblock. The vehicle exploded prematurely, striking Sergeant Winterle in the face with flying shrapnel, breaking his jaw and putting him out of action.

His partner, Lance Corporal Jacob Heal, a new guy to the platoon, jumped on the Barrett when he spotted an Iraqi associated with the suicide attack running back down the road. The young Marine lit him up with the heavy Barrett, shooting him five times and blowing out his chest before the Iraqi hit the ground.

Mulder and I concentrated on the job of keeping our own front secure. Throughout the day we continued to take under fire any armed men or vehicles that passed through our sights. It was a weird scene to shoot the driver of a pickup with a .50-caliber machine gun mounted in the back and watch the vehicle continue moving as though driven by a ghost. Whichever of us first spotted a target called the shot.

"I'll take the driver. You take the passenger."

Our body counts continued to climb throughout the day.

We were on the roof three days and nights, running on nothing but raw adrenaline, before we got four hours' sleep. Watching and shooting. It got to where no Iraqi entered our zone of control without first taking off his white T-shirt and waving it like a flag of truce. No one else wanted to come out and die for Saddam.

Although fatigued, we dared not lose our edge. We switched on and off the glass, an hour on, an hour off watch. By the time we left this position and the ar-Rashīd Military Complex, Mulder had fifteen kills and I had seventeen. Thirty-two total in one spot!

The 3/7 entered Baghdad proper and pushed in toward the city center, our final destination the Olympic Stadium. The Republican Guard had told the population that the Marines would kill and eat them, or some such nonsense, but the people didn't believe it. They came out by the hundreds of thousands and cheered and danced in the streets. By this time most of the Iraqi Army had thrown down its weapons and said, basically, "Okay, you win."

AFTERWORD

Mobile, mechanized armies have made the modern battlefield almost inconceivable to veterans of World War II, Korea, or even Vietnam. Ground armor and fast-moving vehicles, satellite communications, "smart" munitions, sensor technology, air and space power, and rapid logistical support capabilities have made the battlefield fluctuating, flexible, and rarely static. Witness the American dash of power across Iraq in 2003, the fastest march across an invaded nation in the history of the world.

With each new technological advance, many cry out that the infantry is obsolete. They envision future war scenarios of drones, robots, and virtual reality—machine fighting machine. With the infantry goes the sniper. There are already those within and outside the armed forces who look upon the sniper as a useless relic of an age that no longer exists.

They are dead wrong. The sniper will adjust.

For example, through the use of microphones and compasses, BBN Technologies developed a means to track the targeting of a fired bullet back to its hidden source. Sensors could be installed on vehicles, aircraft, light poles, buildings, and even helmets. They worked by the simple concept of picking up the acoustic vibrations from the muzzle blast of a rifle and the supersonic crack of the bullet, then estimating the trajectory, caliber, speed of the bullet, distance of travel, and elevation of the firer to triangulate the shooter's location.

Inventors claimed this innovation meant the sniper could no longer remain safely in hiding while he operated. It meant sniping as a weapon was outdated.

Not quite.

Three inventors from the U.S. Army Research Laboratory designed countertechnology in the form of radio decoys that could be dispersed throughout an operating area to simulate the exact sounds of a rifle firing, thereby cloaking the true sniper and allowing him to work his deadly skills undetected. Change in concepts and employment does not mean abandoning those methods that still have value on the battlefield.

The so-called air-land battle concept of high-tech warfare is not the only form of making war. Warfare takes many forms. It ranges from economic and cultural competitions through low-intensity "cold" conflict using guerrillas and terrorists to all-out "hot" wars involving entire nations, continents, or the globe itself. The unfortunate reality of man on his planet is that the evil and the power-hungry will always strive to subjugate his fellows. But no matter the nature of warfare, no matter how devastating or advanced the weaponry, it will remain the infantry's job to seize and hold ground, to physically pry the enemy from his holes and secure hostile territory.

Nations involved in conflict have realized again and again the need for long-range individual marksmanship. It is as important today as it was when gunpowder was first invented. As technology advances, so does the sniper's trade and tools. It is not difficult to imagine a future marksman picking off key enemy personnel from space "hides" fifty or 100 miles away.

In fact, the sniper profession has truly come into its own only within the past thirty years or so after the Vietnam War. As a result of the sniper's effectiveness in Vietnam, official attitudes began to change when ranking military men saw the sniper as an effective and legitimate weapon. The sniper finally came out of the closet.

"The man, the weapon, and the bullet became the most efficient and cost-effective weapon we have on the battlefield," said Staff Sergeant Ronnie Kuykendall, then a senior Army sniper instructor at Fort Benning, Georgia.

It made little sense, noted Captain Jim Land, who helped found the U.S. Marine sniper schools, to drop a string of 500-pound bombs, barrage an enemy with artillery rounds, or send in infantry spraying bullets at their opponents until one side struck down the other when the same thing could be accomplished by one man with a single bullet. That is an equation unlikely to change, no matter the advances in technology. For as long as there is war and as long as ground troops are required, there will be a need for the sniper's crosshairs on the kill zone.

A PARTIAL SNIPER'S VOCABULARY

accuracy. Refers to the inherent ability of a rifle, a given load, brand of ammunition, or bullet; also the ability of the shooter and his weapon to deliver precision fire.

action. The working mechanism of a rifle.

adjusted aiming point. The aiming point that allows for gravity, wind, target movement, and other forces.

ammunition. Loaded cartridge consisting of a primed (capped) case, propellant, and projectile.

ammunition lot. A quantity of cartridges from the same manufacturer in a single lot, expected to perform in a uniform manner.

assault rifle. Military rifle equipped to provide both semiautomatic or full-automatic fire, such as the Russian or Chinese AK-47 or the U.S. M16.

ball. Refers to the bullet in military nomenclature.

ball ammunition. Standard service ammunition with a solid-core bullet.

ballistic coefficient (BC). Expresses a bullet's length relative to diameter and its aerodynamic shape, thus indicating its ability to overcome air resistance in flight.

ballistics. The science that deals with the motion and flight characteristics of projectiles.

barrel. The part of a firearm through which the projectile travels.

barrel liner. A thin steel tube inserted into a barrel to either change the caliber, restore the gun, or protect a barrel made of softer material.

barrel time. Interval between when the bullet leaves its seat until it leaves the muzzle. Important because it is linked to recoil

barrel wear. Gradual eroding of the rifling immediately ahead of the chamber throat, resulting in accuracy loss.

battle rifle. Any full-size caliber rifle as opposed to an assault rifle, e.g., the M1 Garand or the M14.

bead sight. Small cylindrical top portion on some front sights.

bedding. The fit of the metal parts of the barrel and receiver into the wood stock.

belted case. A "rimless" cartridge with a raised belt around the case just ahead of the extractor groove to provide a positive headspacing surface.

berm. Embankment used on ranges to restrict bullet impact, as a backdrop, or as a diving wall between ranges. Also a similar embankment or bulwark used as cover in battle.

bipod. Two-legged support attached to the fore-end of a rifle.

boat tail. Bullet design of tapered base or truncated conical base, which raises the ballistic coefficient by reducing aerodynamic drag to provide greater stability at subsonic velocities.

bolt action. Firearms in which loading, unloading, and cocking is conducted manually, of two principle types: the turn bolt and the straight-pull bolt.

bore. Barrel interior forward of the chamber.

bore diameter. Internal diameter of a barrel measured from tops of opposing lands.

bore sighting. A method of aligning a barrel on a target by aiming through the bore.

bottleneck case. Cartridge case with a neck diameter smaller than its body diameter.

brass. Slang for cartridge cases.

breech. Chamber end of the barrel.

breech face. The rear end of the barrel, which contacts the rear of the cartridge.

bullet. The projectile of a cartridge.

bullet drop. Describes the bullet's fall in flight.

bull's-eye. The aiming point or center of a range target.

burning rate. Rapidity with which a powder burns relative to other powder.

butt. Rear of shoulder end of stock that rests against shooter's shoulder.

caliber. Size and specific cartridge for which a firearm is chambered.

cap. Obsolete term referring to a cartridge primer. Also, to "cap" an enemy: to shoot him.

carbine. A rifle of short length and light weight.

cartridge. The entire unfired ammunition, including case, bullet, powder, and primer.

case. Hollow brass container housing the propellant of a cartridge, the neck of which grips the bullet and the head of which holds the primer.

cast. The lateral displacement of the centerline of the butt plate from the centerline of the bore. The centerline is cast to the left of the bore for a right-handed shooter, to the right for a left-handed shooter.

cast bullet. Lead-alloy bullet cast from a mold, as distinct from a jacketed or lathe-turned bullet.

centerfire. Cartridge with its primer situated in the center of the case head.

chamber. The opening at the breech end of the barrel that accepts and supports the cartridge.

chamber pressure. Pressure generated by expanding gases inside the chamber when fired.

charge. Amount of powder used in loading a cartridge.

cheekpiece. Raised part of the side of the rifle stock against which the shooter rests his face.

clandestine operation. Mission to accomplish intelligence gathering, counterintelligence, or other activities in secrecy.

clip. Strip of metal to hold cartridges or shells in proper sequence for feeding into the rifle's breech. An M1 Garand uses a clip; an M16 uses a magazine.

cold-bore shot. First shot fired from a clean, unfired weapon.

compensator. Device attached to the muzzle end of a barrel to reduce recoil.

compressed loads. Case filled with powder to the point that the bullet is compressed against it in the load.

concealment. Protected from view of an enemy or observer.

controlled expansion. Characteristics of bullet designed to expand at a controlled rate in a target.

cook-off. A round in the chamber fires from overheating of the chamber after prolonged shooting.

cordite. Early smokeless rifle propellant.

core. Interior of a jacketed bullet, usually of lead.

cover. Protection from hostile fire, such as a fighting hole or sandbagged emplacement—or, in the field, a cave, boulders, etc.

deflection. Change in the path of the bullet due to wind or passing through an object.

drag. Aerodynamic resistance to a bullet's flight.

drift. Lateral movement of a bullet away from the line of bore, caused by its rotation around its own axis in the direction of the rifle twist.

drop. Vertical distance the bullet falls from line of sight to the target.

dry firing. Aiming and firing a weapon without live ammunition, as in training.

dud. A cartridge that misfires.

effective wind. An average of all the varying winds encountered when firing.

ejector. Device which ejects cartridges or fired cases from a firearm.

energy. Kinetic energy or force carried by a bullet.

exterior ballistics. Applied mechanics that relates to the motion of the projectile from the muzzle of a firearm to its target.

extractor. Device that withdraws the fired case of the cartridge from the chamber.

eye relief. Distance that the eye is positioned behind the ocular lens of a telescopic sight.

feet per second. FPS; unit of measure for velocity of a bullet.

firing line. Line parallel to the targets from which shooters fire in training.

fixed sights. Nonadjustable sights.

flyer. A round fired considerably outside a normal grouping on a target.

follow-through. Continued mental and physical application of marksmanship fundamentals after each round has been fired.

foot pounds. Units of measure for energy of a projectile.

frame. The metal part of the gun that contains the action.

freebore. Distance a bullet travels between chamber and bore before its bearing surfaces contact the lands of the rifles, the purpose of which is to delay resistance.

free-floating barrel. A barrel that is completely free of contact with the stock.

full metal jacket. A jacketed bullet with no lead showing at the tip.

gas leak. Black marks around primer showing where gas has escaped.

gas operated. An automatic or semiautomatic firearm that uses propellant gases to unlock the breech bolt and complete the cycle of extraction and ejection.

grain. Measure of weight applied to bullets and powder.

groove. The low point of rifling within a barrel, as opposed to the raised spiral ribs, or "lands."

group. Cluster of bullet holes in the target.

hammer. The part of the firing mechanism that strikes the firing pin, transfer bar, or primer or percussion cap.

hand stop. Device attached to the rifle's fore end designed to prevent supporting hand from sliding forward.

hangfire. Extended delay when a cartridge is fired.

hide. Term used to describe sniper positions.

hold-off. Compensation for bullet trajectory by using a modified point of aim above or below the target, or to compensate for wind or target movement. Also known as "Kentucky windage."

hold-over. The height one must aim above the target to drop the bullet onto the target.

hold-under. Point of aim below the target to compensate for a projectile on its upward axis of trajectory, as when shooting on slopes or other angles.

hollowpoint. Bullet with cavity in the nose, designed for rapid expansion on impact.

hooded sight. A front sight canopied to eliminate light reflections and to protect the sight pillar.

indexing targets. The method a sniper team uses to identify targets within its field of fire.

inherent accuracy. Inherent ability of a specific caliber in comparison to the accuracy of other calibers in the same class.

internal ballistics. Science of ballistics dealing with aspects of the combustion within the gun barrel.

iron sights. Metal sights as opposed to optical sights.

jacket. Covering of a bullet.

"Kentucky windage." Modifying point of aim to compensate for wind or target movement. See **hold-off.**

killing power. A cartridge's ability to kill with a single shot, assuming adequate bullet placement.

lands. The raised spiral ribs between the grooves in the bore of a rifle.

lead. Modified point of aim in front of a moving target

needed to ensure a hit.

length of pull. Distance from the center of the trigger to the center of the butt plate or recoil pad.

line of bore. Imaginary straight line following the axis of the bore.

line of sight. Straight line from the shooter's eye along the sights to the point of aim.

load. To charge a firearm for firing; to place a cartridge in the chamber.

lock. Refers to the total firing mechanism in a firearm.

long gun. Shotgun or rifle.

magazine. Container holding ammunition in readiness for chambering.

magnum. Term commonly used to describe a cartridge that is larger, contains more shot, or produces higher velocity than a standard cartridge of the same caliber.

magnus effect. Net force on a bullet in flight caused by the drag of air around it.

match grade. Ammunition made with special care for superior accuracy.

mil. An angular unit of measurement equal to 1/6400 of a complete revolution, used to estimate distance and size based on the mil relation formula: 1 mil equals 1 meter at 1,000 meters.

minute of angle (MOA). Angular unit of measure used to describe the accuracy potential of rifles, ammunition, bullets, or loads.

misfire. Failure of a cartridge to fire.

mouth. Opening at the neck end of a cartridge case, in which the bullet is seated.

mushroom. The expansion of a bullet as it penetrates its target.

muzzle. End of a gun barrel from which the bullet emerges.

muzzle energy. Kinetic energy or force carried by a bullet as it exits the muzzle.

muzzle velocity. Speed of the projectile as it leaves the muzzle of the weapon.

natural point of aim. Direction that the body/rifle together are oriented in a stable, relaxed firing position.

natural respiratory pause. The pause in breathing after exhaling and before inhaling.

neck. The section of the cartridge case that holds the bullet.

objective lens. The lens at the front of the telescopic sight, facing the target.

ocular lens. The lens at the rear of the telescopic sight, nearest the shooter's eye.

off-hand position. Shooting position in which the shooter stands upright without support.

off-hand rifle. Rifle designed to be held while fired, not rested.

open sight. Rear sight of traditional metal sights.

parallax. Apparent movement of the target in relation to the reticle when the sniper moves his eyes in relation to the ocular lens.

peep sight. Rear sight in the form of an aperture mounted close to the shooter's eye.

point blank. Distance a shooter can shoot without any holdover.

point of aim. Point on target on which sights are optically aligned when firing.

point of impact. The point on which the bullet actually lands.

port. Opening in barrel to allow gas to operate a mechanism or reduce recoil; opening in a receiver to allow loading or ejection.

powder. The propellant.

primer. Small explosive metal cap in the head of a cartridge that ignites the main charge of powder in the cartridge.

probability of hit. Refers to the percentage chance that a given round will hit a target at a given range.

projectile. Bullet in flight.

propellant. Another word for gunpowder or charge.

rail. Metal track in the fore end of a weapon to accept a hand stop or sling.

ramp. Steel base on which some sights are mounted onto a rifle.

rangefinder. Device for optically measuring or estimating the direct distance to a target.

ranging. Technique a shooter uses to compensate for bullet trajectory by adjusting the ballistic cam of an adjustable/ranging telescopic sight.

receiver. Basic unit of a firearm which houses the firing and breech mechanism.

recoil. The rearward thrust of a firearm upon firing.

recoil operated. A firearm in which the force of recoil is used to unlock the breech bolt and complete the cycle of extracting, ejecting, and reloading.

remaining energy. A projectile's energy in foot pounds at a given range.

reticle. Crosshairs, dots, or other marks used in a telescopic sight to determine point-of-aim or range to the target.

rifle cant. Any leaning of the rifle to the left or right from a vertical position during firing.

rifling. Spiral grooves in the bore of a weapon to spin the bullet in providing rotational stability.

round. Another term for cartridge.

scope. A telescopic sight.

scope mounts. Devices for securing a telescopic sight to the rifle.

scout. Individual dispatched ahead of a unit to conduct surveillance and reconnaissance.

sear. That part of a trigger mechanism that holds the hammer or firing pin in the cocked position until the trigger is pulled.

semiautomatic. Describes a firearm that is self-loading.

service rifle. The primary rifle of a military force.

set trigger. Trigger mechanism with two different weights of pull, one normal and one very light.

shank. The cylinder section of a bullet.

shock. Kinetic energy of the bullet transferred to the target.

sight-in. Process of getting a bullet a point of aim at a preselected distance.

sight picture. Visual image when the firearm sights are properly aligned on the point-of-aim.

single action. Requires the manual cocking of the weapon.

sniper specialist. An individual trained in the proper employment of snipers.

sniper team. Two snipers composed of one acting as a shooter, the other as a spotter.

stalking. Sniper's art of moving unseen into a firing position against a target.

stock weld. The contact of the cheek with the stock of the weapon.

surveillance. Systematic observation of areas, places, persons, or things.

target indicators. Any sign that enables an observer to detect the location of a target.

telescopic sights. Optical sights.

terminal ballistics. The branch of ballistics dealing with the effects of projectiles at the target.

terminal velocity. Speed of the bullet upon impact with the target.

throat. Short, tapered section of barrel's bore between the chamber and the start of the rifling.

time of flight. Time a bullet takes to travel from rifle muzzle to target.

trace. Air turbulence created by the shock wave of a bullet passing through the air.

tracer. Ammunition that is visible at night due to its phosphorous compound.

tracking. Engaging a moving target by leading and moving with the target as the trigger is squeezed.

trajectory. The path of the bullet in flight.

trapping. A technique for engaging moving targets in which the aiming point is established ahead of the target. The rifle is held stationary and fired as the target approaches the aiming point.

trigger pull. Force applied to a trigger to release the sear.

turnbolt. A bolt-action rifle.

turrets. The two capped projections on the top and side of a scope that house the adjustment dials.

velocity. Speed of a bullet measured in feet per second.

windage. Adjustment on the telescopic sight or iron sights to compensate for horizontal deflection of the bullet.

X-ring. Center of a target; the bull's-eye.

yaw. Action of a projectile spinning erratically around its own axis.

zero. The range at which the point of aim and the point of impact are one and the same.

Look for Charles W. Sasser
and Craig Roberts's previous
classic snipers chronicle,
ONE SHOT—ONE KILL

"Shocking and brutal....
The reality of sniping
is achieved superbly by
personal accounts....
Each account is remarkable,
detailing vivid memories
of combat action."
—*Marine Corps Gazette*

Not sure what to read next?

Visit Pocket Books online at
www.simonsays.com

Reading suggestions for
you and your reading group
New release news
Author appearances
Online chats with your favorite writers
Special offers
Order books online
And much, much more!